Two Mather Biographies

Two Mather Biographies

Life and Death and *Parentator*

EDITED BY

William J. Scheick

Bethlehem: Lehigh University Press
London and Toronto: Associated University Presses

Associated University Presses
440 Forsgate Drive
Cranbury, NJ 08512

Associated University Presses
25 Sicilian Avenue
London WC1A 2QH, England

Associated University Presses
P.O. Box 488, Port Credit
Mississauga, Ontario
Canada L5G 4M2

The paper used in this publication meets the requirements of the American National Standard for Permanence of Paper for Printed Library Materials Z39.48-1984.

Library of Congress Cataloging-in-Publication Data

Mather, Cotton, 1663–1728.
Two Mather biographies.

Contents: [pt. 1] The life and death of that reverend man of God, Mr. Richard Mather, teacher of the church in Dorchester in New-England — [pt. 2.] Parentator, memoirs of remarkables in the life and death of the ever-memorable Dr. Increase Mather who expired, August 23, 1723.

1. Mather, Richard, 1596–1669. 2. Mather, Increase, 1639–1723. 3. Congregational churches—Massachusetts—Clergy—Biography—Early works to 1800. I. Scheick, William J. II. Mather, Cotton, 1663–1728. Parentator, memoirs of remarkables in the life and death of the ever-memorable Dr. Increase Mather. 1989. III. Title.
BX7259.M32 1989 285.8'092'2 [B] 88-45761
ISBN 0-934223-06-8 (alk. paper)

PRINTED IN THE UNITED STATES OF AMERICA

For

Joseph E. Scheick

haec limina tendere adegit

Contents

Preface

My editions of *The Life and Death* and *Parentator* are based on extant copies of the first printings of these rare works, and they include the authors' errata, when noted. Modern typographical characters have been used; for example, the long *s* has been changed to suit contemporary type. Italics have been deleted except for titles of books, quotations or apparent quotations, and expressions in foreign languages. But the peculiarities of the Mathers' capitalization, punctuation, and spelling (reflecting the nonstandardization of the English language at the time) have been preserved. This procedure gives the reader a sense of the text as it was experienced by the colonial reader and also prevents the obscuring of any possible plays on words intended by the Mathers, especially Cotton. This means that some words (e.g., privilege/priviledge, Parliament/Parlaiment, renowned/renouned) will appear in various forms in the text.

Obvious misprints have been corrected either by the silent deletion of the mistaken successive printing of the same word or by the use of bracketed inserts, which are also inserted in a few places to interpolate small bits of needed information. In order to avoid confusion with my brackets, Cotton Mather's brackets have been converted to parentheses. Note numbers have been added to the texts so that the reader may conveniently find annotations.

The annotations are as complete as I could make them. Unfortunately, much of the world of books so vital to the Mathers has become utterly obscure and in some cases lost to our times. I have provided, with the help of colleagues, translations for all the Greek and Latin passages, except in the instances when the Mathers provide an adequate one immediately after the citation. Unless otherwise noted, I assume responsibility for these translations. I have deleted two very brief, hard-to-decipher Greek passages from article 32 of the *Parentator*, both of which Mather translates; the deletion is indicated by three spaced periods. And I have identified major passages or echoes of passages from Scripture, although the *Parentator* evinces numerous other minor allusions.

Except for these modifications, the texts presented are faithful to the original editions.

No modern edition of these two works exists. *Parentator* has not even appeared in facsimile; *Life and Death* at least has been reproduced in facsimile by Benjamin Franklin V and William K. Bottorff (1966), and by me (1974). Both of these facsimiles, however, were private publications of a few hundred copies and have long been out of print. The editions undertaken in this book are designed to provide a critical evaluation of these two Mather biographies, singly and together, to furnish extensive annotations, and to make these classics of our culture more readily available for study and appreciation.

No one can work with Cotton Mather's books and remain insensitive to Kenneth Silverman's significant contribution, and I wish that the delay in the publication of Michael G. Hall's *The Last Puritan: A Life of Increase Mather* (Wesleyan University Press) had not prevented me from including it in this study. I am indebted to several people for assistance of various kinds: to Professor Robert D. Armstrong (Classics), Professor Ernest N. Kaulbach (English), Professor W. Thomas MacCary (Classics), and most especially Professor Anthony C. Florek (Classics and History) for their help in decoding the Mathers' Greek and Latin allusions; to Kathleen Blow, retired reference librarian, for her painstaking guidance (many years ago) in resource materials for projects like this one; to the editors of *American Literature*, for permission to use, in much revised form, an essay of mine as part of the Introduction; and to Professor Catherine Rainwater (English), for sharing with me the trials and tribulations that seem to be endemic to such undertakings as this study.

Introduction
Anonymity and Signature: Two Mather Biographies

In many respects the intention of New England Puritan biographies is identical to that of their sermons. Both reflect an attempt to convey religious instruction about the conduct of one's life on earth. Both likewise seek to stimulate the reader to the practice of *imitatio Christi*, discussed at length in numerous sermons as well as reflected in the exemplary lives of Puritan biographical subjects.[1] As a result, late seventeenth-century and even early eighteenth-century New England biographies "aimed less at the modern ideal of accurate revelation of a personality than at the graphic portrayal of the virtues of the Puritan saint."[2]

Although this attitude toward biography proved somewhat rigid and to some extent impeded this genre from developing into a fully accomplished art form, it was sufficiently tractable to yield such disparate works as Increase Mather's (1639–1723) understated *The Life and Death of That Reverend Man of God, Mr. Richard Mather* (1670) and Cotton Mather's (1663–1728) outspoken *Parentator* (1724). Although these books were written in different centuries with somewhat different cultural expectations, both share common religious premises, and both manifest the orthodox Puritan view of biographies. However, these two books have not received much attention individually, nor have they ever been compared, even though Increase's book is specifically mentioned in Cotton's work. Although the *Parentator* has on the whole escaped the scorn of critics, some of whom have described Cotton's prodigious *Magnalia Christi Americana* (1702) as "a showcase of pedantry and elephantine wit,"[3] *Life and Death*, one of the earliest examples of colonial New England biography, has always received a favorable reception by modern scholars. One critic, for example, says of Increase's book that "we read the little biography to-day without boredom and, often, with admiration for a simple dignity that comes close to art."[4]

1

A close look at *Life and Death* reveals that this work is indeed artistic. This biography evinces an artistic structural motif derived from the image of the father. On one level, the motif originates from the fact that Increase is Richard's son. Yet for Increase, as Kenneth Murdock has observed, Richard (1596–1669) is "not merely a dear human father but a father of much that to him and his friends was best in New England."[5] Similarly, Robert Middlekauff has remarked that throughout his life Increase felt the moral authority of his father and could not have escaped it had he wished to: "What gave Richard's example its compulsive power was . . . the fact that it measured up to the highest Puritan ideals"; "to the second generation, the founders assumed the proportion of the patriarchs of the Old Testament."[6] So, on another and deeper level, the image of the father in *Life and Death* points beyond a solely natural or secular sense and discloses a more pervasive religious dimension—the relation between spiritual fathers or ministers, such as Richard Mather, and the New England family as a whole.

This underlying framework of the image of the father is further informed by the fundamental theme of *Life and Death*, that Providence progressively unfolds or unveils the continuity of the divine will through succeeding Puritan generations, particularly through certain individuals. In the context of the primary motif of the biography, these individuals are fathers; and in the light of their role as agents of God's will, their example and guidance, reviewed schematically, contribute to a collective voice. This voice transcends the specifically temporal individuality of each father and derives from each one's membership in that spiritual community in which all true Puritan fathers bear witness to immutable essential truths.[7]

Recognition of this theme and the motif related to it provides for a better appreciation of *Life and death*. It sheds light, as well, on Increase's motivation for publishing the biography anonymously, and it also gives insight into the significance of the book's style and technique, which have received favorable, if evasive, comment. The outcome of such an investigation suggests that *Life and Death* is a seventeenth-century New England biography, unified in theme and method, that deserves to be acknowledged as a special Puritan literary achievement.

The structure of *Life and Death* is based on the image of Richard as Increase's natural father and as Dorchester's spiritual father. This image is presented in the opening line of the preface to the biography: "You have here presented to your view, and for your Imitation in the

Lord, the Life of him that was to many of you a Spiritual (as to me a Natural) Father" (p. 37).[8] But in order to appreciate Increase's sense of the significance of this twofold role, Richard Mather's life must be considered in a larger context—the succession of Puritan fathers, beginning in England, and the continuity of God's design for New England as progressively unveiled in the life and works of these fathers. Increase's fidelity to this theme dictates the brevity and elliptical nature of *Life and Death;* for in order to avoid any diffusion of focus, Increase relates only those features of his father's life and character that are relevant to this theme.

Consequently, although Richard Mather always remains at the center of attention in the biography, the opening pages to a significant extent concern Richard's parents, especially his father, Thomas Mather. Richard remarked, for instance, that as a child his painful experiences with a schoolmaster would have led to his "utter undoing, had not the good Providence of God, and the Wisdome and Authority of my Father prevented" (p. 40). In this comment God, in accord with common Puritan custom, is given primary credit; but in equally typical Puritan fashion divine will is manifested through natural agency—in this case, as throughout *Life and Death,* by means of a Puritan father.[9]

In *Life and Death* the word *father* is interchangeable with the terms *minister* and *teacher.*[10] Appropriately, then, after his natural father the next decisive influence on young Richard's life was Mr. Palin, the minister or spiritual father of Leagh. Of Reverend Palin, Richard often said that "the remembrance of that man was Comfortable and Honourable in his thoughts, even in his old Age, though his knowledge of him was in his Childhood" (p. 40).

Eventually, in compliance with providential design, Richard had to prepare for his own vocation as a servant of God in this chain of fathers, so "he was called to leave his Fathers Family" to teach the children of Toxteth (p. 40). In retrospect, Increase sees that this initial stage in Richard's development as a teacher foreshadowed his future career as a famous natural and spiritual father in New England. Increase writes, "The Lord helped him in those his young years to carry it with such Wisdome and Love and Gravity amongst his Scholars as was to admiration, so as that he was by them both loved and feared, beyond what is usual" (p. 41). If *Life and Death* is to be trusted, similar sentiments were felt by the laity of Dorchester during Richard's later years.

While at Toxteth Richard benefited from still other divinely directed paternal influences:

> The means of his Conversion was påly by seeing a strange difference between himself and sundry in that godly Family, where Divine Providence had cast his Lot in Toxteth, viz. the Family of Mr. Edward Aspinwall, who was a Learned and Religious Gentleman. Now he observed that the way and walking of that holy man, was such as himself had not as yet been accustomed unto. . . . Also Mr. Harrison, then a famous Minister at Hyron, Preaching upon Joh. 3. 3 concerning the necessity of Regeneration, and at the same time reading a Book of Mr. Perkins. (P. 41)

After his conversion, Richard's future as a Puritan father, particularly as an instrument of God's will to the "children" of the Dorchester "family," became more apparent. While still at Toxteth, "Being thus become a New Creature, he was the more eminently a Blessing in the Family, and in the Calling which the Lord had disposed of him in: And such notice was taken of him, as that even from places remote Children were sent unto him for Instruction and Education" (p. 42). Later, as spiritual father and teacher of Dorchester, Richard mirrored the outcome of this preparatory experience at Toxteth in his attitude toward his spiritual children, his parishioners: "If . . . I preach Learnedly, then onely the Learned and not the Unlearned can understand and profit by me; but if I preach plainly, then Learned and Unlearned both can understand" (p. 61). Richard's observance agrees with the traditional Puritan notion of the role of sermons in the experience of conversion;[11] but in the context of *Life and Death* this belief further reinforces the theme that God reveals divine will through a succession of spiritual fathers and that Richard Mather indeed received a special calling to contribute to that succession, to become in fact one of the very founding fathers of New England.

The next important stage in Richard Mather's life was his immigration to the New World, and Increase relates in entirety his father's arguments for the Puritans' departure from England. The inclusion of this document might at first strike the reader as a flaw; it runs several pages in length, seems to interrupt the pace, and is not of the same quality as the rest of the biography. On second thought, however, the imagery in Increase's rationale for including these arguments deserves close attention: "Because they are of weight, and because Posterity may thereby see what were the swaying Motives which prevailed with the First-fathers of N.E. to venture upon the unparallell'd Undertaking, even to Transport themselves, their Wives and Little ones, over the rude Waves of the vast Ocean, into a Land which was not sown" (p. 46). The emphasis of this explanation falls not only upon the Puritan view of the promise of New England but also, in terms of the underlying motif of the biography, upon the establishment, by Richard Mather and the other forefathers, of the New England family out of which there will arise in time generations of subsequent natural and spiritual fathers. This focus on the paternal role in the family is, in fact, readily apparent in the document itself. Richard's justifications for emigration include, for instance, the belief that since all families—whether natural, civil, or religious—require fatherly authority, "removing from a Family where is no Government or good order for suppressing of sin and wickedness, to another where is, be necessary for one that is free" (p. 49).[12] Likewise, Richard reasoned that since "Parents and Masters are bound to remove if they were in such Commonwealths, where they might not be suffered to Rule and Govern their own Children and Servants," it follows that "Ministers being free, are bound to remove, if they be in such place where they may not govern their own Flocks" (pp. 51–52). Thus, even this lengthy document actually proves to be an organic part of *Life and Death*, for it sustains the basic motif on which the entire book is structured.

In his mature years, as minister and teacher of Dorchester, where "he did (by the help of Christ) set upon that great Work of Gathering a Church" (p. 55),[13] Richard Mather fulfilled the promise of his novitiate as schoolmaster by accepting God's call and hence becoming a true elder of the New England family: "Being thus again setled in the Lord's work, he therein continued unto his dying day; the Lord making him an Eminent Blessing not onely to Dorchester, but to all the Churches and Plantations round about, for the space of near upon Four and thirty years" (p. 55). Yet, even during the time of his mature ministry and in spite of the fact that he was himself a founding father, Richard Mather still continued to learn from other spiritual fathers in the Puritan community: from Reverend Norton, for example, "then Teacher to the Church in Ipswich, unto whom (under Christ) God gave the tongue of the Learned to speak a word in season, whereby his [Richard's] Soul was Comforted"; and from "Doctor Goodwins *Discourse about Patience*, in which Book he read till the very day of his Death" (pp. 56, 59).

Consistent with his concentration on the image of the father, Increase bypasses specific details of his father's life. He next focuses on Richard's old age, especially on a bedside scene that reveals that even while suffering a fatal illness Increase's father thought about the generation to follow him. Of particular concern to him, as a spiritual father, are the future children of the Puritan household; and so, speaking of the halfway covenant (which we shall consider shortly), he instructs his son Increase, now "Teacher of a Church in Boston": "A speciall thing which I would commend to you, is, Care concerning the Rising Generation in this Country, that they be brought under the Government of Christ in his Church; and that when grown up and qualified, they have Baptism for their Children" (pp. 57–58). Richard desired that the continuity of Puritan generations, as guided by their spiritual fathers, be maintained. This idea is again evident in Increase's frequent references to his father's six natural sons, references that place some of them firmly within the next generation of spiritual fathers (pp. 43, 54): "The Lord was faithful and gracious to him, in respect to his Children. . . . And the Lord cheered the heart of this his Servant in his old Age, by giving him to see most of his Sons imployed in the Ministry many years before their precious Father's decease" (p. 59).

That his sons should carry on, through the practice of *imitatio Christi,* the work of their natural father is further suggested in Richard Mather's last will and testament. Although it is a seventeenth-century convention to include the will of the biographical subject, that of Richard Mather is particularly appropriate in *Life and Death* because it furthers Increase's emphasis on Richard's role as a father to the "children" of New England, "in which Imployment if any thing hath been done which hath been pleasing unto him [God], or any way beneficiall to any Childe of his, it hath not been I that hath done the same, but the grace of God which was with me" (p. 64). Richard's will similarly expresses the hope that his sons are truly of the elect, from whom such fathers are presumably drawn: "I hope God hath already made them partakers, at least sundry of them, of his saving grace in Christ" (p. 65). Richard's hope, moreover, included the possibility that his sons would contribute to the succession of spiritual fathers, a point Increase discloses just prior to presenting his father's will, when he cites from his father's private papers to indicate Richard's desire that "his Sons after him might see by their Fathers Example, what it is to walk before God" (p. 62).

The closing words of the will center on heaven, where (Richard hopefully anticipated) he and his first wife might "see not our selves alone, but those also that have proceeded and come forth out of our own bowels, to have their part and portion in that Eternal Glory" (p. 65). Then, he hoped, his entire natural family would be reunited in Christ's heavenly family. But in terms of Increase's prefatory designation of Richard as both a natural and a spiritual father, the implication of this final passage of the biography extends beyond the confines of his immediate family; it brings the biography full circle, for this remark signifies, as does the preface, an appeal to the spiritual children of Dorchester, indeed of all New England, to continue under the leadership of their spiritual fathers. Then Richard would eventually be joined in heaven not only by his natural sons but also by the elect of Dorchester and by all the spiritual children of each succeeding generation of the Puritan fathers—all united eternally in the household of Christ, himself the Son of God, the Father (the subject of the sermon Increase preached on the death of Richard).

2

The success of *Life and Death* to some degree proceeds from the author's anonymous voice, or persona, as well as from his style and biographical technique. In surmising the motivation behind Increase's anonymity—he signed the preface in which he wrote "the Composer of this ensuing Relation is not willing that his Name should be published" (p. 37)—one might point to his own description of Richard's best characteristic:

> Some have thought that his greatest errour was, that he did not magnifie his Office, as he might and sometimes should have done. If a man must erre, it is good erring on that hand. *Humble enough, and good enough,* was the frequent Saying of a great Divine. And another observeth, *That every man hath just as much and no more true worth in him, as he hath Humility.* Austine being asked which was the most excellent grace, answered, *Humility;* and which was the next, answered, *Humility;* and which was the third, replied again, *Humility.* That indeed is Comprehensively All, being of great price in the sight of God. And if so, Mr. Mather was a man of much Reall Worth. (P. 63)

By suppressing his own identity Increase likewise evidences the virtue of humility. However, this quelling of the author's self may have a more subtle meaning. Increase's anonymity might be directly related to the image of the father that structures the biography as well as to the theme informing this motif.

The theme of the book, to repeat the point, concerns the progressive unfolding of divine will through the spiritual fathers of the Puritan community. In order to maintain the continuity of this sequence each father must in a sense continue to live among the following generation. This is particularly true in light of the fact that for the Puritans the revelation to which these fathers' lives and works give testimony remains constant throughout the vicissitudes of time. As a result, if such a continuity is to be preserved, each younger generation must imitate its spiritual parents—hence the Puritan interest in biographies. This concept is expressed in the first sentence of the book when Increase explains that Richard Mather's life is presented "for your Imitation in the Lord"; shortly thereafter he again remarks: "Your selves know that God made him Exemplarily Faithfull, Zealous, Patient, Humble, Holy: Follow him as he followed Christ" (p. 37). Later in the work, not only is the reader told that Increase's father was "a Pattern of Patience" (p. 59), but the reader is instructed by Richard Mather himself to think in terms of "the imitable and commended Example of Christ, and other faithful Servants of God" (p. 47).

As Richard's deathbed scene indicates, Increase is urged to carry on this tradition. He is to imitate his father as a minister and teacher of the Puritan family. Doubtless Increase did not escape the full impact of his father's wish "that his Sons after him might see by their Fathers Example, what it is to walk before God." To imitate his father would mean that, in some sense, his own voice and that of his father would become one and the same, at least regarding theological truth; for although God deals with New England progressively, the deity's timeless design is radically complete from the first. So, in relation to this design the individual voices of all the Puritan spiritual fathers are transformed into a collective voice, a Christic voice expressing the essential divine truth informing the lives and works of these ministerial agents.[14]

Herein lies the deeper dimension of Increase's anonymity. In *Life and Death* he achieves implicitly what he expresses explicitly about imitating exemplary figures; that is to say, by subverting the individuality of his voice and thereby keeping his narration of the biography relatively free from authorial intrusion, Increase completely identifies with his father. This identification did not come easily, but it was necessary as a resolution of Increase's experience of a psychological crisis at the time of his father's death.

Increase wrote the biography during what has been called a "time of stress," when subsequent to his father's death his "mood was one of passionate desire to do some last service before he, too, should be called to face trial by God."[15] Just how stressful for Increase was the time immediately after the death of his father, as well as the demise of his elder brother Eleazar in the same period, is dramatically revealed in article 15 of Cotton's *Parentator*, where we are told that in September, 1669, Increase suddenly became deathly ill in Northampton, where through the fall season he remained incapacitated and could not set in order his deceased brother's affairs. Upon his return to Boston he quickly became debilitatingly ill again and remained so through the entire winter. During these illnesses he was afflicted with melancholy and with nightmares.

Increase's protracted sickness at this time signals a psychological crisis in his mind as he faced his new, sudden responsibility of heading the Mather presence in New England. It was as if something in him, some dependency or some obdurateness of self, had to die in order for a new sense of self to be born. And indeed, by the spring of 1670 he recovered, edited some of his brother's sermons, and wrote the biography of his father. In this biography, a suitable companion to the sermon (on God, the Father) he preached on the death of Richard, Increase's reborn sense of self[16] affirms his new responsibility as head of the Mathers by merging his voice with his father's in order to arrive at a sense of sharing in the collective voice of Puritan divines as it had been manifested in Richard Mather's life and deeds. From this perspective anonymity actually means less a surrender of Increase's sense of self than his achievement of a true self, a self whose identity derives from the collective voice of the Puritan fathers throughout time.

Increase's anonymity is also related to the style he uses in *Life and Death*. The style is characteristically Puritan, a "plain style,"[17] which places it within the traditional voice of seventeenth-century New England doctrinal writings. This manner of writing had been advocated by his father, who often repeated a Latin proverb, "*Artis est celare Artem*" (p. 61). The writing style of a Puritan father, especially in sermons and other didactic works such as biographies, should be transparent, its artistry so disguised that the light of divine truth shines through without obstruction.[18] The style and language of *Life and Death* signify Increase's attempt to imitate his father—the language is drawn principally from Richard's own words—and to allow divine truth to reveal itself in the apparently artless narrative of the biography. Thus, appropriately and significantly, Increase echoes his father's literary standard when he speaks of *Life and Death* as a composition of "words of truth and plainness" (p. 39).

Increase's anonymity similarly relates to the techniques he employs in the biography. By relying on his father's own words—from his books, sermons, conversations, private meditations, and last will and testament—as well as on anecdotes and others' comments about his father, Increase actively represses any overt emotional response to the loss of his father and assumes a somewhat passive disposition that is appropriate to a transparent style of "truth and plainness."[19] The technique of allowing details to filter through his prose without embellishment allows Increase to become, like his father, an instrument of divine will and thus to identify with the collective voice of the Puritan fathers. By means of this identification Increase could begin to fulfill his father's wish to be imitated by his sons; and by doing so, he pays his father the highest compliment. As he remarks in his diary at the time: "I considered with myselfe that if I should write and publish my Fathers life, that would be a service not only honourable to my Father, but acceptable and honourable to the Name of God."[20]

Moreover, through this identification with his father in *Life and Death* he could achieve a sense of renewal at a time when he felt guilty and spiritually depressed. Then, symbolically assuming his father's role as a spiritual father, Increase is ready to assert his new self and heed his father's advice about taking "Care concerning the Rising Generation"; for in an effort to carry on his father's work and the paternal tradition to which it belongs, Increase resolved in his diary, after his father's death, to write "some discourses wherein the Rising generation should be especially concerned . . . for God's glory and the good of souls."[21] The full title of one of Increase's sermons, delivered about a year later, indicates his conscious effort to make good his resolution: *The First Principles of New-England, Concerning the Subject of Baptisme & Communion of Churches. Collected Partly Out of the Printed Books, But Chiefly Out of the Original Manuscripts of the First & Chiefe Fathers in the New-English Churches; with the Judgment of Sundry Learned Divines of the Congregational Way in England, Concerning the Said Questions. Published for the Benefit of Those Who Are of the Rising Generation in New-England.*

Increase's concern about the rising generation became particularly evident in his changed position on the halfway covenant. Instituted by the Synod of 1662 when New England churches were experiencing increasing difficulty in securing converts from the younger generation, the halfway covenant allowed that "if a person born and baptized in the church did not receive faith he could still continue his membership and have his own children baptized, by leading a life free from scandal, by learning and professing the doctrines of Christianity, and by making a voluntary submission to God and His church."[22] By this means, it was hoped, both parents and their children would be drawn closer to the church, their halfway membership providing an incentive for their eventual emergence as full members. Only full members could partake of the Lord's Supper. Richard Mather, as his son makes clear in the biography, firmly supported the halfway covenant. In fact, he had urged the measure as early as the Cambridge Synod (1646–48). Ironically, after his success in having the practice approved by the Synod of 1662, Richard's parish at Dorchester at first repudiated the practice, only adopting it during the ministry of Josiah Flynt, Richard Mather's successor.[23]

Equally ironic was the resistance expressed by both Increase and Eleazar Mather. Concerned with the purity of the church, Increase adhered to the practice of administering Baptism only to the children of members in full communion. Just when Increase changed his position is not clear; Norman Pettit and Mason Lowance, apparently relying on the identical publication dates of *The First Principles of New-England Concerning the Subject of Baptisme* and *A Discourse*

Concerning the Subject of Baptism, suggest 1675 as the the date of Increase's reversal.[24] Although both of these works were printed in 1675, they were written in 1671 and 1673 respectively, suggesting that Increase's change of position on the halfway covenant nearly coincides with the publication of his *Life and Death.* It is altogether likely that the biography prepared for, perhaps even eventually triggered, this change in his thinking.[25] If he were truly to follow in the footsteps of his father, if his voice were indeed to merge with the collective voice represented by his father, then he too must subjugate his arrogant resistance (which might have been a factor in the vague sense of guilt he felt at the time of his father's death) and humbly take up Richard's concern with the rising generation as embodied in his support of the halfway covenant.

It is reasonable, therefore, to think that to some extent the composition of *Life and Death* either crucially prepared for or perhaps even signaled the start of Increase's change of position on the halfway covenant. The chief clue lies in the touching deathbed scene in which Richard implores Increase to continue his father's defense of halfway membership as a vital means of caring for the next generation. Nowhere in the passage is Increase's former or new position on the subject revealed. Richard's request remains merely a request, and yet the explicit identification of the anonymous narrator with Richard implies Increase's own continuation of his father's appeal to recalcitrant Dorchester to accept the halfway covenant and, thereby, implies Increase's quiet, humble transformation into a member of the community of Puritan spiritual fathers.

Thus, just as the funeral speeches of his father were "taken up not with Praising the Dead, but with Instructing the Living" (p. 44), so, finally, is Increase's book. *Life and Death* is not merely a biography of one father but a testament to God's continuing call to the New England family through its spiritual fathers, even through Increase as he becomes one of them.[26] As a biography, however, it is a paragon of the genre as it would develop in late seventeenth-century Puritan America. The author's anonymity as well as the brevity, structuring motif, pervading theme, transparent style, and biographical technique of the book all contribute to yield an integrated work of art, one that conveys implicitly as a whole what it argues explicitly.

3

Cotton Mather's *Parentator* (meaning, observations in honor of a dead parent) differs from Increase's *Life and Death* in several ways, some more important than others. Whereas Increase's book is more strictly hagiographical in its omission of personal detail about Richard, Cotton's book is more full-bodied, including glimpses of Increase as a person, details about his setting, and even transcripts of some of his dialogues with others. Nearly fifty-five years had passed between the writing of these two books, and the sort of expectations of a reader of biography and his or her attitudes toward the genre had changed by the time Cotton wrote his book. In contrast to Increase, who had nervously to defend his book briefly by proclaiming it as no monument to Richard, Cotton can boldly announce: "All the World allows a SON, to Erect a Monument for, & Preserve a Memorial of, his Departed FATHER"; moreover, "The Splendor of the Monument, and the Value of the Memorial, should bear a Proportion to the Merit of the Subject" (p. 75). The times had changed, so that although each book typically emphasizes its subject as an exemplary model of piety, the authorial stances behind the two presentations differ.

Also different in the two books is the concept of the father. Increase wrote his biography (only his second book at the time) when he was thirty years old, and for him, becoming a ministerial father like his parent was an important stage in his vocation; but Cotton wrote his biography (among his very last publications) when he was sixty years old, and for him, the opportunity to be like his parent had already vanished. Indeed, references to fatherhood, actual and metaphorical, in Cotton's biography sound a sad, diminished note, a distant echo really, compared to their resonance in Increase's book. Increase relies on the image of the father to resolve a psychological crisis (the sudden need for him to become an influential Matherian ministerial father), whereas Cotton uses the image of the father to reflect on his own sense of displacement in a world perhaps increasingly insensitive to the role of ministerial fathers, but certainly (in his mind) insensitive to himself in that role. In Cotton's view, New England was receptive to Increase as a father figure, but not as receptive to him; it is no accident that he speaks of the *Parentator* as an appendix to *Magnalia Christi Americana* (p. 78) and that he elaborately defends the *Magnalia* in his introduction as "a well meant Essay to do Some Good in the World; And, if the World will not Accept it, I am not at all Disappointed: The Essay is made, and, Surely, my Judgment is with the Lord, and my Work is with my GOD" (p. 81).

Acceptance is indeed the issue, and of course Cotton was personally very disappointed in the lack of response he thought the world gave him and his writings, especially his *Magnalia*, which had been particularly abused by some critics. By 1724, Cotton had to contend with an increasing sense of loss: he was old and (he thought) near death, his father was dead, most of his children had died, his wife was insane (he thought),[27] his son "Cressy" was wayward, his hopes for the Harvard presidency were doomed, many of his favorite writings were unpublished, his financial debts were large, his anxiety over lawsuits was debilitating, his role in the smallpox epidemic was impugned—in short, an opportunity at age sixty to be anything like Increase, or Richard before him, simply no longer existed. Whereas Increase had as a part of the agenda for his biography the need to deal with his disagreement with his father about the halfway covenant, Cotton had as a main part of the agenda for his biography the need to deal with his imagined sense of his father's disappointment in him. Both fathers were dead, but Increase could at least change his theological position, while Cotton could do nothing to change his circumstances or his impression of his father's attitude toward him.

Cotton was always sensitive to others' response to him, but most especially to his father's. Apparently he was never certain just how his father felt about him as a Matherian successor. He remembered his father's reluctance, until he gave his consent in 1684, to have his son join him in his ministry to the North Church in Boston, in spite of enormous pressure from parishioners for Cotton's appointment there with Increase. Increase's resistance to Cotton's appointment might have had good reasons behind it, as David Levin suggests,[28] or it might have had disapproving reasons behind it, as Kenneth Silverman suggests.[29] Neither side can be persuasively argued because Increase's motives remain obscure. But as both Levin and Silverman agree, whatever were Increase's motives, Increase's resistance to Cotton's appointment was felt by Cotton to be an expression of his father's disapproval. So Cotton felt diminished in stature in terms of his perception, his imagined sense of his father's depreciation of him.

And he felt diminished by the times. Like Increase's book, Cotton's biography asserts a belief in a progressive providential unfolding of the continuity of the divine will, but in Cotton's work this belief is not identified primarily with the role of the ministerial father. Although he sees Increase as a divine agent, Cotton is less certain than was Increase about the manner and direction of providential design in regard to himself. If in 1679 Increase had to contend with "the Spirit of the World" wherein "there was a Sensible Decay of Real and Vital PIETY, and the Power of Godliness began sensibly to suffer some Abatements" (p. 128), the situation seemed even worse to Cotton in the still more secular world of the early eighteenth century. On 5 November 1723, for example, he complained to Thomas Hollis, Jr. that there was now "a fearful decay of Piety" in New England.[30] In Cotton's mind it seemed that whereas Increase and his fellow divines could do something in 1679, his own actions in 1723 and 1724 were by far less efficacious. Cotton's comfort, such as it was, lay in recognizing the conformity of his disappointments and tribulations to "the Discipline of the Cross," for Christ "no where Promised a Temporal Prosperity, unto a Life of Piety" (p. 129). His father's example of how "Humiliations . . . were only to Prepare him for Marvellous Exaltations" (p. 136) gave him courage, but it did not, so late in his life, give him much hope. In Cotton's mind the Mather heritage, from Richard to Increase to himself, had diminished, and he did not know for sure whether Providence was managing this decline for a greater good (which certaintly he could not at the moment see, but did wish for) or whether the fault for the decline, as he imagined his father thought, rested with Cotton, the heir.

All of which made Cotton defensive: his biography of Increase is at once a defense of his father and of himself, and it is meant (as was Increase's book) as much for himself as for a public audience. Increase hardly sounds a defensive note; there are only brief moments justifying the writing of the biography and dismissing the charge that Richard was not sufficiently active among the clergy. Cotton, in contrast, defends not only his father's preaching, infrequent changes of mind, and engagements in secular concerns (the last in article 24 and 26 is especially protracted because it applies to Cotton too), but also his own actions, particularly his writings, including the biography itself. A strange moment occurs early in the biography when Cotton feels the need to refute any possible challenge to his veracity; he reminds the reader that the author is "Responsible to [God], whose Eye [he has] Remembred" and that he has "also Vouchers in [his] Hands, for every one of the Articles, which any one shall be Welcome to see, whenever he Pleases" (p. 75). Of course Cotton's defensiveness becomes most pronounced when he turns to a discussion of the *Magnalia,* which he relates to the *Parentator* on two grounds: the latter is an appendix to the former, as we noted earlier; and "Dr. Mather was in some Regards, much of a Father to" the former work (p. 80). The lengthy defense of the *Magnalia* extends beyond Cotton's introductory remarks; that defense intrudes into the biography itself, where references to the church history necessarily recall to the reader that introductory defense (e.g., article 4 and 12).

4

Chief among the literary consequences of these various differences between Increase and Cotton, and between their books, is a matter of narrative voice. Increase subverts his individual voice to gain an identity with the collective voice of New England's ministerial fathers. For defensive Cotton this collective voice is much harder to discern, and such a subtle submersion of his own voice, aside from the issue of whether this act would be possible for him, might be completely ignored in early eighteenth-century New England. Increase found a new selfhood by subordinating his idea of himself to a providentially managed collective paternal agency; and in this way Increase gained a new sense of self after his protracted illness in 1669–70, when his old sense of self died. Cotton's personal experiences suggested that society was now much more obdurate than Increase's had been, that society was very hard-of-hearing when it came to listening to Cotton. In order to be heard Cotton felt constrained to assert himself.

This contrast results in different narrative voices in the two biographies. Whereas Increase virtually never intrudes upon his nearly transparent narrative, Cotton frequently takes center stage. Cotton's sense of self, quickened by defensive assertion, gives an opacity to his narrative. Intrusions occur not only in recurrent references to the *Magnalia,* but everywhere. Such comments as "I Have briefly dispatched one of the Promised Articles"; "Let my Reader, I beseech him"; "e're long you'l see the Reason of my Saying so"; "Tis the Writer"; "I must again ask Pardon"; "as I told you before"; "I have a Thousand Struggles in my mind, whether I shall proceed in it"; "as much as tis fit for me to give you"; "I think, there are Thanks due to me, for my forbearing to Tell the Story"; or "If I venture to say . . ." only typify how Cotton's *I* abounds in the biography, which is, after all, about himself as well as about his father. On at least two occasions Cotton reveals his self-awareness as a voice in the narrative: once in the Introduction when he says he has "Studiously laid aside that Care of Embellishing" and of "Salting [his] Sentences now and then with short, Instructive, and Unforced Intermixtures of something or other that I have Read"; and again on the first page of the narrative proper when he says that Increase deserves "a more Qualified Historian, than he whose Pen is now Employ'd upon it" (pp. 77–78, 85). Both disclaimers are properly humble, the second even conventional, but in fact in Cotton's book both draw attention away from the subject of the biography and direct that attention toward the author. The author is an abiding presence throughout the *Parentator.*

There is nothing anonymous about Cotton's narrative voice, but like the printing of his name at the end of the dedication of the book, his signature is written large throughout the work. If Cotton is to succeed his father, no quiet subordination of the self is appropriate. On the contrary, assertion of self is called for not only by the emerging philosophical spirit of the early eighteenth century (as evident, say, in Benjamin Franklin's later *Autobiography*) but also, and more importantly, by the increasing resistance (in Cotton's view) of New England society to the Matherian leadership and message that are now both totally Cotton's responsibility.

That Cotton cannot comfortably identify this responsibility with Increase's sense of the continuity of divine will through the agency of ministerial fathers is suggested by the failure of father imagery in the *Parentator* to provide an architectonic motif similar to that in *Life and Death*. But Cotton does find a substitute, one that reveals much about him as a narrator. In lieu of the image of the father, Cotton focuses on the image of the book.

Books figure everywhere in the *Parentator*. From the first, even in the dedication, the importance of books is emphasized by Cotton, who gently admonishes his Scottish colleagues to publish more than they have in past:

> I am not the only Person that have said it, and so t'will be the less Presumption in Me to say it; I have often thought it a Loss unto the World, that the Incomparable Pastors in the Church of Scotland, have their Pastoral Employments lying so hard upon them, that they have not much Liesure for the Writing of Books, for which there are so many of them, whose Talents are Extraordinary. . . . I cannot but think, that it would be Richly worth the while, for Ways and Means to be found out, that more of your Pens may be Employ'd for the Enlightening of a World, which is yet a *Dark Place*. (P. 73)

By way of instructive contrast Cotton points to New England ministers, who "now and then do some little matter, at the Writing of Books, and some small things do by the Press pass . . . into the World" (p. 73). Just as a concern with books figures prominently at the start of Cotton's biography, so too does it at the end of the work, where he concludes the last article with a complete chronological catalogue of Increase's books. At the end of this list Cotton appropriately quotes from the last book of the Bible: "Revelation XIV. 13. *They Rest from their Labours, and their Works do follow them*" (p. 213). "*Works,*" in Cotton's reading, refers to the deceased's former good deeds, especially those acts that resulted in the publication of books or works.

A concern with books not only frames the beginning and ending of Cotton's narrative; time and again, as in the instance of his praise of his uncle, Samuel Mather, part of his assessment (article 5) of the success and importance of a person is made in reference to that person's publications. This pattern is typified by Cotton's repetition of a detail from Increase's biography of Richard—Richard's propitious reading, on his deathbed, of a book by Thomas Goodwin (article 15); but the pattern especially applies to Increase, the subject of the *Parentator,* who is characterized not only as having spent long periods of time reading books (article 8), of which he kept a list, but also as having expended much of his energy in writing them. For instance, Increase's reading a book by Jonathan Mitchell saves him from persisting in an erroneous view of the halfway covenant (article 12). Consider, too, how often in response to a problem Increase is said to have written a timely work. This is apparent when Increase pens several documents on behalf of a proper charter for the colony, or earlier when during a single period of time, he writes the biography of his father, collects together the sermons of his brother Eleazar, and publishes a book for the rising generation. Perhaps the most dramatic example of his authorship of a timely work occurs during the witchcraft episode (article 28), when upon his return to his community, on the verge of self-destruction, Increase quickly writes *Cases of Conscience Concerning Evil Spirits Personating Men* (1693), which was a "Special Service" that "gave the most Illumination to the Country, and a Turn to the Tide" (p. 173). Similarly, Cotton reports that Increase believed the books he had published in England were as good as his presence there, and Cotton himself, who also hopes for the longevity of his books beyond his own life, always insists upon remarking "the useful Books which . . . [Increase] Published" (p. 189). Moreover, even when Increase did not publish a sermon, he could (and probably should) have, in Cotton's opinion; this point is clearest in Cotton's report that someone (was it Cotton himself?) once said that Increase "*never Preached a Sermon but what was worthy of the Press*" (p. 199).

Cotton's recurrent emphasis on the publication of books deserves close attention. What Increase discovers in his identification with the image of the father, Cotton tries to discover in books; that is, the continuity of divine will through the agency of ministerial fathers that is the locus of Increase's renewed sense of identity in *Life and Death* is displaced in the *Parentator* by Cotton's hope that the continuity of divine will is expressed through the agency of ministerial books. Unlike Increase at the age of thirty, Cotton could not at the age of sixty find a renewed identity in his place in the succession of Puritan ministerial fathers; the time for that possibility was gone, for Cotton felt himself to be a diminished heir of the Matherian heritage and felt himself to be close to death (he would in fact die within four years after the publication of the *Parentator*). He had to turn to something else to derive some comfort in his concern with self-identity, and he turned to books, of which he had written more than three hundred and fifty previous to the *Parentator.* Book writing was a primary feature of Cotton's life, and in his probing of his sense of identity in the biography of Increase he presents books as something that possibly evince the same sort of continuity that Increase posited in the image of the ministerial father.

For Cotton every book was a lasting *monument,* a word he uses in the introduction, as we saw, to describe his own biography. As his final catalogue of his father's writings and his quotation from Revelations indicate, books are what endure after the ministerial father passes away. Of Increase's publications Cotton says, "Thus does he Leave something behind him, that he may be doing of Good upon Earth, after he is gone to Heaven" (p. 209). Increase, in Cotton's mind, had a remarkably successful ministerial fathership in life and in books; and Cotton's life, in Cotton's mind, might not have been all it should have been as an agental father in life, but at least his books too, even if he had not been able to publish all of them, would be left behind after he died as monuments for doing providential good in the world, where after his death they might be more efficacious than he felt he had been during his lifetime. In the *Parentator* books become for Cotton a substitute for the life he should have led as an agental ministerial father,[31] and it is no small clue to his shift that at one point in the introduction of his biography Cotton metaphorically refers to virtuous men, like Increase, as "the Epistles of CHRIST unto the rest of Mankind" (p. 75). This is an image Cotton found in 2 Corinthians 3:3. But the biblical source of this image only reinforced Cotton's sense that one's life is like a written document, a book. Especially when a life, as he thought of his own, had not been appreciated in its time, the written record of it, in the books published during that life, remained for the world as a lasting monument.

Because for him a book represents the life of its author (whose life is like an epistle) and because for him books serve as monuments of instruction to those still in life after their authors have died, Cotton seems never to have realized that his emphasis on books was in effect a retreat from life. But for him this emphasis was something of an asylum. For him it became a retreat from his own disappointments in his present life, an evasion of the fear that he was at fault for the decline of the Matherian heritage during his ministry, and, in the specific instance of the biography of Increase, a sanctuary from the disappointment he imagined his father felt about him. Cotton, doubtless defending in part his own behavior, cannot help but unwittingly suggest that even Increase's bookish nature, as reader and writer, is something of a withdrawal from the world. He emphasizes a remark made to Increase by Jonathan Mitchell: "*My Serious Advice to you is, that you keep out of Company, as far as Christianity, and Civility, and Occasions will give you leave; take it from me, The Time Spent in your Study you will generally find Spent, most Profitably, most Comfortably, & most Accountably*" (p. 93). Then Cotton cites a maxim from St. Augustine, "*Non erit bonus Clericus qui non fuit Bonus Monachus*" (p. 93), meaning that one will not be a good cleric who was not a good studier in solitude. Indeed, when Cotton relates his father's daily routine (article 31) he emphasizes "the Work of the Study" from morning to even after midnight, for a usual daily total of sixteen hours spent there out of every twenty four. Cotton cannot avoid remarking the complaint of some of Increase's parishioners, that Increase was in his study, "some thought even to a Fault. More of his Pastoral Visits were wished for" (p. 181). Increase was of course a man much engaged in successful public activity, in religious and secular concerns; but in this picture of him as a man reading and writing books in his study, Increase's son finds something comfortable,[32] something akin to and justifying Cotton's own retreat from a world seemingly less receptive to him than it had been to his father. In the sanctuary of his study Cotton found asylum in the books he wrote there.

There are, beyond these observations, several subtle clues, quite beyond Cotton's ken, to the degree to which books figure as centrally in the *Parentator* as does the image of the father in *The Life and Death,* clues that serve as a key to Cotton's desire for a renewed sense of identity. Three intimations are particularly noteworthy.

The first occurs in the introduction, where Cotton defends *Magnalia Christi Americana* against its detractors by asserting that other readers have praised it too. Speaking of the mixed reception of this book, "whereto . . . [the *Parentator*] may pass for an Appendix," Cotton observes, "For the very same thing in the Heavens above us, is by some called, The Milky Way, and by others called, The Crooked Serpent" (p. 78). Of course Cotton intends a simple analogy: that just as some give the galaxy a pleasant or an unpleasant name, so, too, with the praise and epithets expressed regarding his work. But subtly, without realizing it, Cotton has equated his work with a galaxy, that is to say, with one of the greatest wonders of creation. And this inadvertent elevation of his book is only reinforced by the fact that the *Magnalia,* like its appendix, the *Parentator,* relates the lives of ministers, who by Puritan convention are described as stars (an image appropriated from Daniel 12:3). Even in the *Parentator* Cotton refers to Increase's mother's deathbed request that her son will join those ministers who "*shall shine as the stars forever and ever,*" to Increase's father as "Shining like the Sun in Gemini," and to Increase himself as a "Star, to Illuminate the Western Haemisphaere" (pp. 86, 96). When Cotton applies this analogy between a galaxy and his book, which contains ministerial stars just as the galaxy contains individual stars, he unwittingly elevates the monument of his own writings. Deep within his mind books seemed to be as monumentally awesome as a galaxy. This association ought not to be interpreted as an act of authorial egocentricity, but rather as an unconscious expression of the degree to which Cotton's books had become, at least late in his career, the center of his life, a possible vindication of his life, and even in some important sense an idealized substitution for and extension of his life.

The second hint to the primacy of books in Cotton's mind appears in a metaphor he fashions in article 9. Several pages earlier, in article 7, Cotton had poignantly detailed, with numerous passages from Increase's diary, how his father had suffered because of financial indebtedness, which Increase thought impaired his work as the spiritual father of his parish. Cotton had also experienced such indebtedness, but in *Parentator* the empiracality of the relationship between minister and parishioner gives way to a metaphor for the relationship between author and reader. In article 9 Cotton writes: "I am in my Readers Debt, for Three Paragraphs, which the Diary just now mentioned has bound me to; And I will go no further till I Pay what I Owe" (p. 105).

The third clue to the centrality of books, in lieu of the image of the father, in Cotton's biography occurs in what might be termed a psycholinguistic trace. It occurs in article 17, where Cotton relates Increase's uncanny ability to predict the future. On 19 November 1676, Increase had "a strange Impression . . . to Preach a Sermon on those Words, Zeph. III. 7. *I said, surely thou wilt fear me, thou wilt receive Instruction; So their DWELLING SHOULD NOT BE CUT OFF:* and Conclude the Sermon, with a Strange Prediction, That a Fire was a coming, which would make a Deplorable Desolation" (p. 126). And this prediction comes true, the fire even damaging Increase's own house and (Cotton, so sensitive to the value of books, quickly notes) his library. At the end of this account Cotton writes,

> I will not here Theologize, much less will I Philosophize upon the Original and Operation of those Praesagious Impressions about Future Events, which are often Produced in Minds, which by Piety and Purity and Contemplation, and a Prayerful and Careful Walk with GOD, are made more Susceptible of them[.] I am only to Observe, that this Holy Man of GOD, was no Stranger to them; and that I may dispatch at once all the Instances, that I think proper to mention until some while hence I

> foresee I shall be compelled unto some further Notice of them, I only add what in the Order of our Story should be Introduced here. (P. 127)

"Until some while hence I foresee" is a curious unguarded remark for Cotton to make in the paragraph following the account of his father's occasional ability to predict the future. The word *foresee* slips itself into his comments about himself as the writer of the biography, as someone who can look to the future of what he is going to write. It is a subtle moment of identification for Cotton; for just as Increase could predict the future, so too in some sense can Cotton.

Typically the psycholinguistic clue provided by *foresee* is two-sided. On the one hand, it does implicitly relate Increase and Cotton. Cotton's mind unconsciously confiscates this word in order to attain a moment of mutual identity with Increase, especially since Cotton's mind is full of self-doubt and of a sense of his father's disappointment in him. Cotton's mind craves this moment, and seizes it. But on the other hand, there is a negative feature to the use of this word at this moment in the biography; for clearly Increase had been able to make predictions in actual life, where he played so active a role "that one can scarce Write the History of his Life without Writing the History of his Times" (p. 128), whereas Cotton can only make predictions in the eventuation of his book.

What bridges these two sides, what keeps them in balance so as to cause no sense of discomfort as Cotton pens the word *foresee*, is the centrality of books in Cotton's mind. Since he elevates books to monumental, even galactic status, as a hopeful displacement for a disappointing life, as even an idealized substitute and extension of that life, then being able to predict what is to come in his book is a subtle, if tenuous, way of identifying adequately with his father, himself a bookish man according to Cotton. *Foresee* might be a two-sided psycholinguistic trace, simultaneously implying Cotton's sense of difference from and identity with his father, but finally it balances its ambiguous implications because it is applied in the context of the idealized life Cotton posits in books. For Cotton, books are all he has to show for his life; but for him books can be one's life, idealized. And so, late in his life, books, like the "monumental" biography he is writing about his father, become the abiding concern in Cotton's assessment of his identity as a agental Matherian ministerial father.

Life and Death and the *Parentator* may both be biographies, but they are two very different books. This difference is not merely a result of the fact that Increase's work was written in the seventeenth century and Cotton's was written in the eighteenth century. They are both as much about their authors as about their subject, and within this mutual concern lies their fundamental difference. Whereas Increase could, early in his life, locate his identity in terms of a continuity of divine will expressed through his succession as an agential ministerial father, Cotton, late in his life, could not do this because of his sense of diminishment and his uncertainty over whether the apparent decline of the Matherian heritage in his career was somehow part of providential design or was his own fault. Consequently, Cotton displaced Increase's emphasis on the image of the father with a hope that in the instance of his own seemingly less successful ministry the continuity of divine will is expressed through the agency of ministerial books, including not only Increase's but Cotton's publications as well. Through this hope that the longevity of his books would correspond to the longevity of Increase's personal influence on his time, Cotton managed to identify, as much as he could, with his father. This inner variance accounts for the difference between Increase's anonymous voice relating events in a transparent narrative without authorial intrusions and Cotton's signatured voice relating events in a dense narrative replete with defensive authorial intrusions. Whatever their differences, they are both remarkable books and fascinating examples of the art of New England Puritan biography.

Two Mather Biographies

THE LIFE AND DEATH OF That Reverend Man of God, MR. RICHARD MATHER, TEACHER of the CHURCH IN DORCHESTER IN NEW-ENGLAND.

Psal. 112.6. *The Righteous shall be had in everlasting remembrance.*
Heb. 13. 7. *Remember them who have spoken to you the Word of God.*
Rev. 14. 13. *Blessed are the dead which die in the Lord: they rest from their labours, and their works follow them.*

Ministri vita censura & cynosura.[1]

CAMBRIDGE:
Printed by S. G. and M. F. 1670.

TO THE
CHURCH
AND
INHABITANTS
OF
DORCHESTER in N.E.
Grace unto you from God by Jesus Christ.

Beloved in the Lord Jesus,

You have here presented to your view, and for your Imitation in the Lord, the Life of him that was to many of you a Spiritual (as to me a Natural) Father: Inasmuch as the greatest part of his time in the Ministry he was a Labourer in the Lord's Harvest amongst you; Also with you did he finish his course. There is therefore special reason why what is here done should be directed to your selves.

The Composer of this ensuing Relation is not willing that his Name should be published. But it is done by one who hath had the viewing of my Fathers Manuscripts; from whence, as well as from personal and intimate Acquaintance of many years continuance, and other wayes, he hath been truly furnished with the knowledge of what is here reported. And indeed the greatest part of the Story is known unto sundry amongst your selves.

What remaineth then, Brethren and Beloved in the Lord, but that we should be mindfull of what is by the Lord required, when the Scripture saith, *Remember them that have taught* (and not onely them that do teach) *the Word of God,* whose faith follow, considering the end of their conversation.[2] What that Doctrine of Faith is which your blessed Teacher did from the Lord instruct you in, I need not say; onely Remember it. Remember his Farewell Exhortation,[3] which is now in many of your Houses, and Oh that it were in all your Hearts.[4] And as for his Conversation, your selves know that God made him Exemplarily Faithfull, Zealous, Patient, Humble, Holy: Follow him as he followed Christ. So likewise pray that he may do who is

Boston Septemb 6.
N.E. 1670.

Yours in the Lord alwayes,
Increase Mather.

THE
LIFE & DEATH
OF
MR. RICHARD MATHER.

The Writing and Reading of the Lives of Worthy Ones, hath been by some accounted amongst the most profitable works of men under the Sun. The Labours of some Learned amongst the Gentiles this way have not been altogether without benefit, witness what is done by Plutarch, Laertius, Philostratus, Eunapius, Pliny, &c. albeit they are to be read with judgement.[5] But especially the faithful Description of the Lives of those who have been Eminent Teachers in the Church, hath been to the great advantage of after-Ages. Many have reaped benefit by reading Dorotheus his *Collection of the Lives of the Prophets, Apostles, and Seventy Disciples of Christ:*[6] And (not to speak of the Labours of Gennadius, Epiphanius, Isidore, and Prochorus of old) among later Writers, Shopfius his *Academia Christi,* and Tossanus concerning the Lives of the Fathers, and Melchior Adam concerning the Lives of all our Modern Divines,[7] as farre as he could by any means come to the knowledge thereof. The pains which Mr. Clark hath taken in publishing the Lives of many of our English Worthies,[8] hath been profitable to not a few: And great pity it is that more should not be done that way. If the Lives of Brightman, Parker, Ames, Burroughs, Hooker,[9] &c. were published to the World, it might be of generall advantage. Nor is it to be doubted but that there have been many famous in their Generations, whose Memories are buried in the dust, for want of some one to undertake this office, whereby their Names might have been perpetuated to Posterity.

Vixere fortes ante Agamemnona
Multi: Sed [omnes] illachrymabiles
Urgentur ignotiq[ue], longa
Nocte; Carent qxia vate Sacro.[10]

But it must needs be in it self a thing pleasing to God, that his grace towards and in his Servants, and the wonders of his Providence about them, should be kept in remembrance. Therefore some have written their own Lives. So did (not to mention Josephus, Bellarmine, Cardan) amongst our Worthies, Junius, Collinus, Buchanan; and of our own Nation, Bale, Burton, Hall, Bodly, &c.[11] And the like did this Reverend Man who is to be the Subject of the ensuing Discourse essay to do; and proceeded therein to the 39th year of his Age, but finished not what he had purposed. It remaineth therefore that some other should do it, which we shall in following words of truth and plainness endeavour to do.

There is in the Parish of Winwick in the County of Lancaster, a small Country Town or Village called Lowton: In which Village Richard Mather was born Anno 1596. His Parents Thomas and Margarite Mather were of Ancient Families in Lowton aforesaid, but by reason of some unhappy Mortgages they were reduced unto a low condition as to the World. Nevertheless, God so disposed their hearts, that they were willing to Educate this their Son in good Learning: Concerning which he (after that the Lord was pleased to bestow not onely Learning but Grace upon him) hath sometimes expressed himself, saying, *By what principles and motives my Parents were chiefly induced to keep me at School, I have not to say, nor do I certainly know: But this I must needs say, that this was the singular good Providence of God towards me, (who hath the hearts of all men in his hand) thus to incline the hearts of my Parents; for in this thing the Lord of Heaven shewed me such favour, as had not been shewed to many my Predecessors and Contemporaries in that place.*

Now his Parents being strongly bent in spirit to have their Son a Scholar, they sent him to Winwick School, which was about four miles distant from his Fathers house. In the Winter season they boarded him at Winwick; but such was his desire after knowledge, that in the Summer he travelled every day thither. Whil'st he was thus at School he met with no small discouragement, for that the School-master under whom he was, although he had an excellent faculty for teaching in Grammar-Learning, and many were trained up by him, so as to be sent unto Oxford and Cambridge, for Instruction in higher Studies; yet was he very severe and partial in his discipline. Junius was almost quite discouraged from his Studies, when being a School boy his Master would beat him eight times in a day whether in fault or in no fault: The like Magisterial harshness caused him of whom we write, earnestly desire that his Father would take him from School, and dispose of him to some other Calling. Himself afterwards, when he had waded through these Difficulties, would say, *God intended better for me, then I would have chosen for my self; and therefore my Father, though in other things indulgent enough, yet in this would never condescend to my request, but by putting me in hope that by his speaking to the Master, things would be amended, would still over-*

rule me to go on in my Studies; and good it was for me to be overruled by him, and his discretion, rather then to be left to my own affection and desire. But Oh that all Schoolmasters would learn Wisdome, Moderation and Equity towards their Scholars, and seek rather to win the hearts of Children by righteous, loving, and courteous usage, then to alienate their mindes by partiality and undue severity, which had been my utter undoing, had not the good Providence of God, and the Wisdome and Authority of my Father prevented. But thus was that of the Poet made good:

Multa tulit fecitq[ue], Puer sudavit & alsit
Qui cupit optatam cursu contingere metam.[12]

After that he had spent sundry years in this School, some Popish Merchants coming out of Wales to Warrington, which is two miles from Winwick, were inquisitive whether there were not any pregnant Wits in that School whom they might procure for Apprentices. Presently Richard Mather was mentioned to them as a pregnant Youth: Whereupon application was made accordingly to his Father, who was inclineable to accept of this Motion, because now his Estate was so decayed, that he almost despaired of bringing up this his Son as he had intended. But here the Finger of Divine Providence was observable; for when his Father was ready thus to part with his Son, and the Childe to go, the Lord raised up the heart of his Master, to be importunate with his Father still to keep him at School, professing that it was great pity that a Wit so prone to Learning should be taken from it, (as indeed it was) or that he should be undone by Popish Education. The Perswasions of the Master so farre prevailed, as that his Scholar was still continued under him, untill the fifteenth year of his Age.

It was a mercy to him, that whil'st he was yet in his Minority, he enjoyed the publick Ministry of one Mr. Palin, then Preacher at Leagh, of whom he would say, that the remembrance of that man was Comfortable and Honourable in his thoughts, even in his old Age, though his knowledge of him was in his Childhood: He then observed such a plain, powerfull, and piercing efficacy in Mr. Palins Ministry, as was not to be seen in the common sort of Preachers in those dayes, by means whereof some Illumination, though not a th[o]rough-Conversion, was wrought in him.

Having been thus long kept at School, he was called to leave his Fathers Family. The occasion whereof was this. At a place called Toxteth Park near Liverpool, there dwelt a wise and Religious People, who being desirous of the good of themselves and their Posterity, intended to erect a School amongst them, for the Education of their Children. It came into their mindes to send unto the Schoolmaster of Winwick, to enquire whether he had any of his Scholars whom he would recommend unto them for such a Service: who having received their desires, forthwith communicated the same to this his Scholar, and to his Father, to see if the Motion would stand with their acceptance. He was desirous rather to have gone to the University, but his Father closed with the Offer; whence it was in fine mutually embraced, so that he removed from his Fathers house to Toxteth (Anno 1611.) there to teach School. Nor is it any disparagement to his Worth that he was once a Schoolmaster; for very eminent Divines have been so, as of our own Nation Mr. Hieron, Mr. Whitaker, Mr. Vines,[13] not to mention others, but rather an Eminency; the like seldome known, that one should be found fit to be a Schoolmaster at fifteen years of Age: Yet the Lord helped him in those his young years to carry it with such Wisdome and Love and Gravity amongst his Scholars as was to admiration, so as that he was by them both loved and feared, beyond what is usual, even where there are aged Masters.

His being thus employed was more wayes then one advantagious to him: for by this means he became a more acurate Grammarian then Divines usually are. Being also diligent in his Studies whil'st he continued in this way of Imployment, he became a Proficient in other Arts, as in Logick, Rhetorick, yea and in Theology. Moreover, it afterwards appeared to be of God, that he was Called to such a Work in such a place, for there the effectual Conversion of his Soul unto the Lord, was wrought in his tender years, even afore his going to Oxford; whence he was preserved from those Corruptions which undid many of his Contemporaries, through the Temptation which in the University they met with. The means of his Conversion was partly by seeing a strange difference between himself and sundry in that godly Family, where Divine Providence had cast his Lot in Toxteth, viz. the Family of Mr. Edward Aspinwall, who was a Learned and Religious Gentleman. Now he observed that the way and walking of that holy man, was such as himself had not as yet been accustomed unto, which caused sad fears to arise in his Soul, lest haply he might not be in the way which leadeth unto Eternal Salvation. Also Mr. Harrison, then a famous Minister at Hyton, Preaching upon Job 3.3. concerning the necessity of Regeneration, and at the same time reading a Book of Mr. Perkins his, shewing how farre a Reprobate may go,[14] God blessed these three things not onely to Conviction, but to Conversion.[15] This was Anno 1614. The pangs of the New-birth were exceeding terrible to him, inasmuch as many times when they were at Meals in the Family where he sojourned, he would absent himself to retire under hedges and other secret places, there to lament his misery before God. But after some time, the Lord revived his broken heart, by sending the holy Spirit in the Ministry of the Word to apply the Precious Promises of the Gospel to his Soul.

Being thus become a New Creature, he was the more eminently a Blessing in the Family, and in the Calling which the Lord had disposed of him in: And such notice was taken of him, as that even from places remote Children were sent unto him for Instruction and Education; and many were, by the Lords blessing upon his Endeavours, fitted for, and sent unto the University. Some years having been past over in this way of Employ, he resolved *(σὺν θεῷ)*[16] to spend some time in one of the Universities, as apprehending that there, by converse with Learned men, and other Advantages not elsewhere to be had, he might gain more then by his private Studies in the Country. Accordingly he went to Oxford, and continued for some time there in Brazen Nose Colledge. Being there, he was variously affected: for it was a joy to him to finde many there who had been his quondam Scholars. It was also a joy to him that he had such leisure to follow his Studies, and by Disputations, Lectures, Books, Conferences with Learned men, &c. marvellous Advantages to obtain a Treasure of Knowledge. But his heart being afore this touched with the fear of God, the great Superstition and Prophaness which he was forced there to behold, was no small grief unto him.

Soon after his coming to Oxford, he came into Acquaintance with the Learned Doctor Worall, who was helpful to him in directing him as to the course of his private Studies. Amongst other things, he advised to reade the Works of Peter Ramus;[17] which counsel he followed, and saw no cause to repent of his so doing. But before he had spent so much time in Oxford as he could have wished that he might have done; the People in Toxteth, whose Children had been taught by him, sent to him, desiring that he would return unto them to instruct not so much their Children as themselves, and that not in meer Humane Literature, but in the things of God. This Call, after due Consideration, for weighty Reasons he accepted of. Being then returned to Toxteth, he Preached his first Sermon November 30. 1618. There was a very great Concourse of people to hear him, and his Labours were highly accepted of by the judicious: Such was the vastness of his Memory, as that the things which he had prepared and intended to deliver at once, contained no less then six long Sermons. The people having had some taste of his Gifts, were the more importunate in their desires that he might continue amongst them. And because that could not be without Episcopal Ordination, they urged him to accept thereof: Not having at that time so th[o]roughly looked into that part of Ceremonious Conformity as afterwards, he yielded unto the Motion; and accordingly was Ordained (with many others on the same day) by Doctor Morton then Bishop of Chester, after the Mode of those Times. The Ordination being over, the Bishop singled out Mr. Mather from amongst the rest, saying, *I have something to say to you betwixt you and me alone.* Mr. Mather was then afraid lest some Informations might have been given in to the Bishop against him because of his Puritanism, thereby to prejudice him; but it hapned to be otherwise: for when the Bishop had him alone, *I have* (saith he) *an earnest Request unto you, and you must not deny me; It is that you would pray for me: for I know* (said he) *the Prayers of men that fear God will avail much, and you I believe are such an one.* Nevertheless, after that the Lord gave him to see the evil of the sin of Conformity in the whole latitude of it, (for as to the substance of Conformity, even from his first entrance upon the Ministry he saw the evil thereof, and was by Divine Grace kept from being stained therewith) his Conforming (although it was at the desires of his people) to accept of this Ordination from the Prelate, was no small grief of heart to him. Many years after, one of his Sons taking notice of a torn Parchment in his Fathers Study, enquired what it is; unto whom his Father replied, That he received that when he was Ordained by the Bishop: *And* (said he) *I tore it, because I took no pleasure in keeping a monument of my sin and folly in submitting to that Superstition, the very remembrance whereof is grievous to me.*

Being as hath been related, setled in the Ministry at Toxteth, he resolved to change his single condition: And accordingly he became a Suitor to Mrs. Katharine Hoult, Daughter to Edmund Hoult Esq; of Bury in Lancashire. She had (and that deservedly) the repute of a very godly and prudent Maid. The Motion for several years met with Obstructions, by reason of her Fathers not being affected towards Non-comformable Puritans: But at last he gave his Consent that Mr. Mather should marry his Daughter; the Match therefore was Consummated Septemb. 29. 1624. God made her to become a rich Blessing to him continuing them together for the space of above 30 years. By her God gave him six Sons; four whereof (viz. Samuel, Timothy, Nathaniel and Joseph) were born in England, and two (viz. Eleazar and Increase) in New-England. After his Marriage he removed his Habitation three miles from Toxteth, to Much-Woolton, having there purchased an House of his own; yet he was wont constantly Summer and Winter to Preach the Word at Toxteth upon the Lords-dayes. During his abode there, he was abundant in Labours in the Gospel: For every Lords-day he Preached twice at Toxteth, and once in a Fortnight on the Third day of the Week he kept a Lecture at the Town of Prescot. Also, faithful and powerful Preaching being then rare in those parts, he did frequently Preach upon the Holy dayes (as they are called) being often thereunto desired by godly Christians of other Parishes in that Country: And this he did, not as thinking that there was any Holiness in those times (or in any other day besides the Lords-day) beyond what belongs to every day; but because then there would be an opportunity of great Assemblies, and it is good casting the Net where there is much Fish: for which cause it might be that the Apostles Preached mostly in Populous Towns and Cities, and also (which suiteth with what we are speaking) on the Jewish Sabbaths after their abrogation as to any Religious tye upon Conscience for their observation. Yea and besides all this, he often Preached at Funerals. It is true that Cartwright, Sherwood, Hildersham, and many other Renowned Non-Conformists, have scrupled Preaching Funerall Sermons;[18] Also in some Reformed Churches that practice is wholly omitted, yea and Decrees of Councils have sometimes been against it; but that hath been chiefly upon account of that Custome of Praising the dead upon such occasions, and that many times untruly: Which Custome (as many Learned men have observed) is Ethnicall, having its rise from the Funeral Orations of the Heathen. Publicola made an excellent Oration in Praise of Brutus, which the People were so taken with, that it became a Custome that Famous men dying should be so praised, and when (as Plutarch saith in the Life of Camillus) the Women amongst the Romans parted with their Golden Ornaments for the Publick Good, the Senate decreed, That it should be lawful to make Funeral Orations for them also.[19] *Hinc mortuos laudandi mos fluxit quem nos hodie servamus* Pol. Verg. *de Rer. Invent. lib*.3. *cap*. 10.[20] Nor indeed was this Rite practised in the Church before the Apostacy began. *Vide Magd. Cent*. 4. Capt. 6.[21] wherefore this faithful Servant of the Lord avoided that practice, his speech at Funerals being taken up not with Praising the Dead, but with Instructing the Living concerning Death, the Resurrection, the Judgement to come, and the like seasonable Truths. Thus did he Preach the Word, being instant in season and out of season, reproving, rebuking, exhorting, with all long-suffering and doctrine. In his publick Ministry in England he went over 2 Samuel, Chap. 24. Psalm 4. and Psalm 16. Proverbs, Chap. I. Isaiah, Chap. I. and Chap. 6. Luke, 22 and 23 Chapters. Romans, Chap. 8., 2 Epist. to Timothy; 2 Epist. of John; and the Epistle of Jude.

After that he had thus painfully and faithfully spent fifteen years in the Work of the Ministry, He that holds the Stars in his right hand,[22] had more work for him to do elswhere; and therefore the rage of Satan and wrath of men must be suffered to break forth, untill this choice Instrument had his mouth stopped in unrighteousness. The Lecture which he kept at Prefect caused him to be much taken notice of, and so was the more unto the Adversaries of the Truth an object of Envy. *Magnam famam & magnam quietem eodem tempore nemo potest acquirere.* Quint.[23] Wherefore Complaints being made against him for Non-Conformity to the Ceremonies, he was by the Prelates Suspended. This was in August, Anno 1633. Under this Suspension he continued untill November following: But then, by means of the Intercession of some Gentlemen in Lancashire, and by the influence of Simon Byby (a near Alliance of the Bishops) he was restored again to his Publick Ministry. After his Restauration he more fully searched into, and also in his Ministry handled the Points of Church-Discipline. And God gave him in those dayes not onely to see, but also to Instruct others in the Substance of the Congregationall-Way, which came to pass by his much reading of the holy Scriptures, and his being very conversant in the Writings of Cartwright, Parker, Baynes, and Ames.[24] But this restored Liberty continued not long; for Anno 1634. Bishop Neal (he who was sometimes by King James pleasantly admonished of his Preaching Popery, because by his carriage he taught the people to pray for a blessing upon his dead Predecessor) being now become Archbishop of York, sent his Visitors into Lancashire; of whom Doctor Cousins (whose Cozening Devotions Mr. Pryn hath made notorious to the world)[25] was one: These Visitors being come into the Country μετὰ πολλῆς φαντασίας,[26] kept their Courts at Wigan; where, amongst many other unrighteous proceedings, having Mr. Mather convened before them, they passed a Sentence of Suspension against him, meerly for his Non-Conformity to the Inventions of men in the Worship of God. It was marvellous to see how God was with him, causing a Spirit of Courage and of Glory to rest upon him, and filling him with wisdome when he stood before those Judges, who were not willing that he should speak for himself, or declare the Reasons which convinced his Conscience of the unlawfulness of that Conformity which they required. Concerning the Lords presence with him at that time, himself doth in a Manuscript left in his Study thus express it: In the passages of that day, *I have this to bless the Name of God for, that the terrour of their threatning words, of their Pursevants, and of the rest of their Pomp, did not so terrifie my minde, but that I could stand before them without being daunted in the least measure, but answered for my self such Words of truth and soberness as the Lord put into my mouth, not being afraid of their faces at all: which supporting and comforting presence of the Lord I count not much less mercy, then if I had been altogether preserved out of their hands.*

Being thus silenced from Publick Preaching the Word, means was again used by Mr. Mathers friends to obtain his Liberty; but all in vain. The Visitor asked how long he had been a Minister? Answer was made, That he had been in the Ministry fifteen years. And (said he) how often hath he worn the Surpless? Answer was returned, That he had never worn it. What (said the Visitor, swearing as he spake it) preach Fifteen years and never wear a Surpless? It had been better for him that he had gotten Seven Bastards. This was a Visitors judgement. *ὀμςὲν ῾μγιες.*[27]

Wherefore the case being thus, he betook himself to a private life: and no hope being left of enjoying Liberty again in his Native Land; foreseeing also *(Sapiens Divinat)*[28] the approaching Calamities of England, he meditated a Removall into New-England. The principall Arguments whereby he was Convinced that he had a Divine Call to engage in so great and hazardous a Design, he drew up together, and put them into form. Which because they are of weight, and because Posterity may thereby see what were the swaying Motives which prevailed with the First-fathers of N.E. to venture upon that unparallell'd Undertaking, even to Transport themselves, their Wives and Little ones, over the rude Waves of the vast Ocean, into a Land which was not sown; We shall therefore here insert them.

"Arguments tending to prove the Removing from Old-England to New, or to some such like place, to be not onely lawful, but also necessary for them that are not otherwise tyed, but free.

ARGUMENT I.

Propos. "To remove from a corrupt Church to a purer, is necessary for them that are not otherwise tyed, but free: as appears,

"1. If a purer Church be a better gift then a corrupter Church, the aforesaid Removing mentioned in the Proposition, is necessary.

"The reason of the Consequence is, Because we are commanded to choose the best gifts, I Cor. 12.31.

"But a purer Church is a better gift then a Church more corrupt. *Ergo.*

"2. If we should not unnecessarily endanger our selves to be corrupted, then the Removing mentioned in the Proposition, is necessary.

"The Reason of the Consequence is, Because by staying voluntarily in places corrupt, we do endanger our selves to be corrupted, I Cor. 5.6. Eccles. 9.18.

"But that is forbidden by the sixth Commandment. *Ergo.*

"3. If we ought not to behold evil voluntarily, then the Removing mentioned in the Proposition, is necessary.

"The Reason of the Consequence is, Because by staying voluntarily in corrupt places, when we are free to remove, we do behold evil voluntarily.

"But that we ought not, Psal. 119.37. *Ergo.*

Assumption. "But to remove from England to N. E. or some such like place, is to remove from a corrupter Church to a purer. *Ergo.*

ARGUMENT II.

Propos. "To remove from a place where the Truth and the Professors of it are persecuted, unto a place of more quietness and safety, is necessary for them that are free.

This appears by these Arguments; *viz.*

"1. That which hath a Divine Commandment for it, is necessary. But so it here, Matth. 10.23.

"2. That which hath the imitable and commended Example of Christ, and other faithful Servants of God for it, is necessary, Mat. 11.29. I Pet. 2.21. I Joh. 2.6. Phil. 3.17.

"But to remove from Persecution hath the imitable Example of Christ, Matth. 2.14 & 12.15. Luke 4.10. Joh. 8.59, & 10.39. And of other faithful Servants of God, viz. of Elias, I Kings 19.3. Moses, Exod. 2.15. Paul, Acts 9.25. *Ergo.*

"3. If not removing from Persecution when a man is not otherwise tyed, but free, be a Tempting of God, an exposing of ones self to unnecessary danger, and so against the sixth Commandment; Then the removing mentioned in the Proposition of this second Argument, is necessary.

"But the former is true. *Ergo.*

"4. If not removing from Persecution when a man is free, be a wrong to the Church, then the Proposition is true.

"The Reason of the Consequence is, Because we ought not to wrong, but to seek the benefit and salvation of the Church and Elect of God, as far as is in us, I Cor. 10.33. 2 Tim. 2.10.

"But not removing as aforesaid is a wrong to the Church, because it depriveth the Church of the benefit of such a mans life and pains, as might if he had peace and liberty, be profitable to the Church; whereas a voluntary staying in places of Persecution, &c. doth hinder profit and benefit which the Church might receive by such a man.

"5. Because a mans frailty is oft-times more then he knoweth of, and in a time of triall will utter it self, as appears by the Professors revolted in the Palatinate. This infirmity of mans Nature made Ridley to counsel those that were not taken to avoid the Realm; and Mr. Bradford on the same ground giveth the same counsel to Erkinald Rawlins and his Wife. *Acts & Mon.* Vol. 3. pag. 518 & pag. 319.[29]

Assumpt. "But to remove from Old England to New, is to remove from a place where the Truth and Professors of it are persecuted, to a place of more quietness. *Ergo.*

ARGUMENT III.

Propos. "To remove from a place where we cannot enjoy all the Ordinances of God, needful to the well being of Churches and particular Christians in regard of their Spiritual estate, unto a place where we may, is necessary for them that are free.

"1. Because we are commanded to seek all Spiritual blessings, with all the means of the same, Matth. 6.33. Josh. 6.27 Col. 3.1.

"2. Because the Spouse of Christ will not rest seeking her Beloved, till she finde him in the fullest means, Cant. 1.7. & 3.1,2,3.

"3. Because there is none of the Ordinances of God, but they are needful and profitable for the preservation and growth of Churches and Christians in grace. To think any of them not needful, or not profitable, were to disparage the Wisdome of him that appointed them.

"4. Because if it be necessary to remove for the enjoying of some of Gods Ordinances, it is necessary to remove for the enjoying of all, and in the want of any one.

"The Reason of the Consequence is, Because it cannot be shewed from Scripture, at what Ordinance a man is set at liberty from seeking any further by removing. And another Reason is, Because as some are not of necessity to the being and estate of a true Church, or a true Christian, no more are any: And as some are necessary to the well-being of a true Church and a true Christian, even so are all.

Assumpt. "But that the Removal is necessary for the enjoyment of some of Gods Ordinances, as for Preaching of the Word, will not be denied. *Ergo.*

ARGUMENT IV.

Propos. "To remove from a Church where the Discipline of Christ is wanting, to a Church where it may be enjoyed, is necessary to them that are free.

"1. If Discipline be an Ordinance of Christ, then the Removing mentioned in the fourth Argument, is necessary.

"The Reason of the Consequence is, Because the voluntary wanting any Ordinance of Christ is sinful.

"Besides the third Argument shewed, That Removal for the enjoying of all Gods Ordinances, is necessary to them that are free.

"But Discipline is an Ordinance of Christ, Matth. 16.19, & 18.17. *Ergo.*

"2. If Discipline be a part of Christs Kingdome, and a necessary and effectual means for preserving the Church, and the other Ordinances from corruption; then the removing mentioned in the Proposition is necessary.

"The Reason of the Consequence is, Because the voluntary wanting any part of Christs Kingdome, any necessary and effectual means to preserve the Church from Corruption, is sinful, Luke 19.14,27. Psal. 2.3. Second Petition in the Lords Prayer.

"But Discipline is a part of Christs Kingdome, a necessary and effectual means, &c. Isa. 9.6. I Cor. 15.24. *Ergo.*

"3. If removing from a Family where is no Government or good order for suppressing of sin and wickedness, to another where is, be necessary for one that is free; then the removing mentioned in the Proposition of this fourth Argument is necessary.

"The Reason of the Consequence is, Because there is one and the same Reason for both.

"But removing from such a Family is necessary for one that is free, Because a voluntary staying in places of danger is a Tempting of God. *Ergo.*

Assumpt. "But to remove from Old England to New, is to remove from a Church where the Discipline of Christ is wanting, to a Church where it may be enjoyed. *Ergo.*

ARGUMENT V.

Propos. "To remove from a place where the Ministers of God are unjustly inhibited from the execution of their Functions, to a place where they may more freely execute the same, is necessary to them that are not otherwise tyed, but free.

"1. God hath sometimes commanded a removing in such a case as this, Mic. 2.6,10. Acts 22.18.

"2. The godly have practised a removal in such a case, 2 Chron. 11.14,16. Acts 13.46.

"3. The Ministers gifts and talents should not be idle, but be imployed for the Churches profit, I Cor. 12.7. I Pet. 4.10.

"4. The sin of inhibiting the Lords Ministers, is a forerunner of some sudden and grievious Judgement, Isa. 30.10,13. when it is for no cause, or for trifles, Isa. 29.31.

Assumpt. "But to remove from Old England to New, is to remove from a place where the Ministers of God are unjustly inhibited, to a place where they may more clearly execute their Functions. *Ergo.*

ARGUMENT VI.

Propos. "To remove from a place where are fearful signs of Desolation, to a place where one may have well-grounded hope of preservation, and of Gods protection, is necessary to them that are free.

"1. Because it is the property of a wise man to foresee the plague, and to hide himself, Prov. 22.3.

"2. Because God hath commanded to remove in such case, Mic. 2.10. So Lot was commanded to go out of Sodom, before the destruction thereof, Gen. 19.

"3. Because there are commended Examples of them that have done this; as of Noah retiring into the Ark, Lot leaving Sodom, The godly leaving Jerusalem, a little before the last destruction thereof by the Romans, and going forth to Pella. See Brinsley in *True Watch,* Part 3. pag. 76.118. Cartwright on Prov. 22.3.[30] and Junius on Revel. 12.14.[31]

"4. Because Nature teacheth to seek ones own preservation.

"5. Because the sixth Commandment teacheth the same, and maketh voluntary staying in places of danger to be a degree of Self-murther.

Assumpt. "But to remove from Old England to New, is to remove from a place where are signs of fearful Desolation, to a place where one may have well-grounded hope of Gods protection.

"This Assumption is made good by the proof of two things: First, That in Old England there are many signs of fearful Desolation. Now signs of Desolation are such as these, and whether they be found in England, let it be considered.

"1. Abundance of sin and sinners, Hos. 4.1,2. Jer. 5.9.

"2. Impunity of sin and sinners.

"3. General Security, 1 Thess. 5.2,3. Matth. 24.38, Luke 17.28,29. Zeph. 1.12.

"4. The taking away of Gods dear and faithful Servants, Isa. 57.1.

"5. Not profiting by former Judgements, Amos 4.6, 7 &c.

"6. Warnings by the Lords Ministers, Amos 3.7. Isai. 44.26.

"7. Examples of Gods wrathful Judgements on others no worser sinners, Jer. 7.12. Rom. 1 1. Mr. Brinsley sheweth at large, That the same sins which brought the Captivity of 70 years on Judah, do as much abound in England as ever they did in Judah, and that therefore we may certainly expect desolation for our sins, unless course were taken speedily by general Repentance and Reformation to pacifie the Lords wrath. In 3d Part of *True Watch*, throughout the whole Book, and more especially in pag. 493 & 503, &c.

"The other thing to make good the Assumption, is, That in New-England one may have well-grounded hope of Gods protection, and for that there are these Reasons:

"1. The Promise of God to preserve Churches and Christians which purely observe his Word and Ordinances, faithfully execute Justice and Judgement, &c. For which, see these places: Isa. 4.5,6. 2 Cor. 15.2. Revel. 3.8,9,10. Isa. 52.17 & 54.17.

"2. The Example of Gods protecting and preserving such in former time, as 2 Chron. 17. 3,4,9,10. As long as Israel kept and walked in Gods wayes, no Enemy was able to prevail against them, &c.

"3. No instance can be given to the contrary, when God ever suffered any people to perish that did purely observe his Ordinances, and execute Justice and Judgement, untill by their defection and sin they had forfeited their happiness, and made themselves naked, and caused their Shield to depart from them. *Ergo.* &c.

AN ARGUMENT CONCERNING MINISTERS ONELY.

"To remove from such a place where the Pastors of the Congregation cannot exercise the Lords Discipline by Ruling and Governing their own Flocks by Censuring those that ought to be Censured, &c. to a place where they may do it, is necessary for them that are free.

"1. Because they are commanded to fulfill their Ministry, and to perform all the parts of their Pastoral Office, Coloss. 4.17. 2 Tim. 4.5. And this of Administring the Keyes of Discipline is one, Matth. 16.19.

"2. Because Christ hath no where dispensed with them in any part thereof.

"3. Because God hath reproved them that have failed to do this, Rev. 2.20.

"4. Because Parents and Masters are bound to remove if they were in such Commonwealths, where they might not be suffered to Rule and Govern their own Children and Servants. The Reason whereof is, Because they are bound to preserve their Children and Servants from being overthrown, if it be in their power; but where such restraint is, they are in danger to be overthrown.

"Now the Consequence of the Reason is, That then Ministers being free, are bound to remove, if they be in such place where they may not govern their own Flocks.

"The Reason of which Consequence is, Because of Parents and Masters over their Children and Servants, and of Pastors over their Congregations, there is *par Ratio*, That if one be bound in case aforesaid to remove, the other are bound in the like case to remove also."

These Arguments were thus presented to the Consideration of some godly Ministers, and other Christians in Lancashire, at several Meetings for that end. Nothing was satisfactorily said to take off the strength of these Reasons: But many were thereby perswaded that his Call to New-England was clear, yea even his own people at Toxteth, who did so dearly love his Person, and highly prize his Ministry, yet thought he was now Called of God to leave them. And hereunto he was the more inclined, by some Letters of Mr. Cottons and Mr. Hookers who were lately arrived in New-England,[32] and wrote (as then there was cause) very encouragingly unto godly people to come after them. Mr. Hooker in one of his Letters had this Expression; *In a word* (saith he) *if I may speak my own thoughts fully and freely, though there are very many places where men may receive and expect more Earthly Commodities, yet I do believe there is no place this day upon the face of the Earth, where a gracious heart and a judicious head may receive more spiritual good to himself, and do more temporal and spiritual good to others.*

Being then fully satisfied concerning the clearness of his Call for New-England, after many Prayers, and extraordinary seekings unto God, he engaged upon the Transportation of himself and Family thither. His parting with his People and other Friends in Lancashire, was like Paul's taking his leave of Ephesus,[33] with much sorrow, many tears being shed by those who expected to see his face no more in this world. This Journey was begun in April 1635. when he travelled to Bristol in order to taking Ship there. In this Journey he was forced (as sometime Brentius was)[34] to change his outward Habit that he might travel incognito, because Pursevants were designed to Apprehend him; but by this means he escaped them. From Bristol he set Sail for New-England May 23. 1635. The Lord, after manifold Trials of Faith and Patience, brought him in safety to the desired Haven. It is seldome known, that a man designed in Gods Eternal Counsel to special Service for his Name, doth not at one time or other experience Eminent Deliverances of Providence: So it was with this Servant of the Lord not once nor twice. Sundry eminent Salvations from deadly Dangers did the Lord vouchsafe unto him in his Childhood, which he would speak of in his old Age: But the most remarkable and memorable of all other, was that which hapned to him on the mighty Waters, where he that sits upon the Floods, and stilleth the raging of the Sea when the Waves thereof roar, and whom the Winds obey, shewed himself wonderful in goodness: for when the Vessel was upon the Coasts of New-England, there arose a fearful Storm (which the Americans are wont to call an Hiracano) by means whereof they were in no small danger; And had not the Lord strangely turned the Wind in an instant, they had all perished upon the Rocks which were just before, and within sight of them in the Ship. The Relation of this observable Providence we shall here set down in Mr. Mathers own words, left written by himself in his Journall from Lancashire to New-England. Thus he writeth concerning it.

August 15. 1635. The Lord had not yet done with us, nor had he let us see all his Power and Goodness which he would have us take the knowledge of: And therefore about break of day, he sent a most terrible Storm of Rain and Easterly Wind, whereby we were in as much danger, as I think ever people were. When we came to Land, we found many mighty Trees rent in pieces in the midst of the Bole, and others turned up by the Roots, by the fierceness thereof. We lost in that Morning three Anchors and Cables, one having never been in the Water before; two were broken by the violence of the Storm, and the third cut by the Seamen in extremity of distress, to save the Ship and their and our lives. And when our Cables and Anchors were all lost, we had no outward means of Deliverance but by hoysing Sail, if so be we might get to Sea, from amongst the Islands and Rocks where we had Anchored: But the Lord let us see that our Sails could not save us neither, no more then the Cables and Anchors, for by the force of the Wind and Storm the Sails were rent asunder, and split in pieces as if they had been but rotten Rags, so that of divers of them there was scarce left as much as an hand-breadth that was not rent in pieces, or blown away into the Sea: So that at that time all hope that we should be saved, in regard of any outward appearance, was utterly taken away; and the rather, because we seemed to drive with full force of Wind directly upon a mighty Rock standing out in sight above water, so that we did but continually wait when we should hear and feel the doleful crashing of the Ship upon the Rock. In this extremity and appearance of Death, as distress and distraction would suffer us, we cried to the Lord, and he was pleased to have compassion upon us: for by his over-ruling Providence, and his own immediate good hand, he guided the Ship past the Rock, asswaged the violence of the Sea and of the Wind. It was a day much to be remembred, because on that day the Lord granted us as wonderful a deliverance, as I think ever any people had felt. The Seamen confessed they never knew the like. The Lord so imprint the memory of it in our hearts, that we may be the better for it, and be careful to please him, and to walk uprightly before him as long as we live. And I hope we shall not forget the passages of that morning untill our dying day. In all this grievous Storm my fear was the less, when I considered the clearness of my Calling from God this Way. And in some measure (the Lords holy Name be blessed for it) he gave us hearts contented and willing that he should do with us and ours what he pleased, and what might be most for the glory of his Name, and in that we rested our selves. But when news was brought us into the Gun-room that the danger was past, Oh how our hearts did then relent, and melt within us! we burst out into tears of joy amongst our selves in love unto our gracious God, and admiration of his kindness, in granting to his poor Servants such an Extraordinary and Miraculous Deliverance. His holy Name be blessed for ever!

Thus farre is Mr. Mathers Relation of this signal Providence, as left written with his own hand. And this is the more to be taken notice of, because the lives of several Choice Instruments of Gods Glory, were then saved: For not onely Mr. Mather himself, but two of his Sons, who are now faithfull Ministers of God, were in that Vessel; and so likewise was that Worthy Minister of Christ Mr. Jonathan Mitchell, the Faithful and Famous Pastor of the Church of Cambridge in New-England, he being then a Childe of Eleven years of Age.[35] Also this Deliverance is the more remarkable, in that several Vessels were cast away in that Storm. A Ship called the *Angel Gabriel*, which set out from Bristol with the Vessel wherein Mr. Mather was, being then at Anchor at Pemequid, was broke in pieces; and the very same strange and sudden turn of Wind which saved the Vessel wherein Mr. Mather was, ruined the other which came from England at the same time. Also there was then a Ship, going between Piscataqua and the Bay, which was cast away in this Storm, and all the people therein lost, except two that were spared to report the News. And amongst others in that Vessel which then perished, there was a precious Minister of the Gospel, viz. Mr. Avery,[36] who with his Wife and five Children all perished. This Minister (though it be a Digression, yet the Story being so worthy of remembrance, let it here be recorded) every moment expecting that the next Wave would be a Wave of Death, lifted up his eyes to Heaven, saying, *Lord, I cannot challenge a Promise of the preservation of my life, but according to thy Covenant I challenge Heaven:* Which he had no sooner spoken, but a Wave immediately came and swept him away, and so wafted him to Heaven indeed. And by the way let it further be noted, That this which hath been mentioned is the onely Vessel which miscarried with Passengers from Old England to New; so signally did the Lord in his Providence own the Plantation of New-England.

But (to digress no further) this Storm being allayed, the Lord brought them safe to an Anchor before Boston, August 17. 1635. Mr. Mather abode with his Family for some Moneths in Boston; and both he and his gracious Consort joyned to the Church there.

Being thus by a mighty hand and an out-stretched Arm brought into New-England, Motions from sundry Towns were soon presented to him, desiring that he would imploy the Talent which the Lord had enriched him with, for the work of the Ministry amongst them. At the same time he was desired at Plimouth, Dorchester, and Roxbury. Being in a great strait in his own minde which of these Invitations to accept of; Considering that in difficult cases Counsel is an Ordinance of God, whereby he is wont to discover his will, he therefore referred himself to the Advice of some judicious Friends; amongst whom, Mr. Cotton and Mr. Hooker were chief, who met to Consult of this weighty Affair; And their Advice was, That he should accept of the Motion from Dorchester. Which being accordingly accepted of by him, he did (by the help of Christ) set upon that great Work of Gathering a Church; the Church which was first planted in that place being removed with the Reverend Mr. Warham to Conecticot.[37] There was an Essay towards Gathering a Church April 1. 1636. but by reason that the Messengers of Neighbour-Churches were not satisfied, concerning some that were intended Members of that Foundation,[38] the Work was deferred untill August 23. when a Church was Constituted in Dorchester according to the Order of the Gospel, by Confession and Profession of Faith; and Mr. Mather was chosen Teacher of that Church.

Being thus again setled in the Lords Work, he therein continued unto his dying day; the Lord making him an Eminent Blessing not onely to Dorchester, but to all the Churches and Plantations round about, for the space of near upon Four and thirty years.

It is a true Observation which many from Luther have taken up, *viz.* That three things make an able Divine.

1. *Meditatio;* Study. Such an one must give himself to Reading and Meditation.

2. *Oratio;* Prayer. A man of God must be a man of Prayer, even

ever & anon upon his knees before God: And *benè Orasse est benè Studuisse.*[39] Bradford the Martyr and Cartwright the Confessor, studied kneeling.

3. *Tentatio;* Temptation. As when Christ was to enter upon his Publick Ministry he was grievously tempted; so it is wont to be with his Servants, and so it was with this good man. The Lord having great Service for him to do, he must undergo great Temptations, that he might be the better fitted for that whereunto he was called.

Wherefore before, and for some years after his accepting Office-Relation in Dorchester, he was in much Spiritual distress by reason of uncertainties concerning his own Eternal estate. He did (as in wisdome he was bound to) keep these troubles secret from men, onely he revealed the distress of his Soul to that great Divine Mr. Norton, then Teacher to the Church in Ipswich,[40] unto whom (under Christ) God gave the tongue of the Learned to speak a word in season, whereby his Soul was Comforted, the Lord giving him to see that he was walking to Heaven in the same way that David, Asaph, Heman, &c.[41] had gone before him.

During the time of his Pilgrimage in New-England he under-went not so many Changes, as before that he had done; for he never removed his Habitation out of Dorchester, albeit he had once serious thoughts that way, by reason that his old people in Toxteth, after that the Hierarchy was deposed in England, sent to him, desiring his return to them: But Dorchester was in no wise willing to forgoe their interest in him, therefore he left them not. Nevertheless, he did in New-England (as in a Wilderness might be expected) experience many Trials of his Faith and Patience. That which of outward Afflictions did most agrieve him, was the Death of his dear Wife, who had been for so many years the greatest outward Comfort and Blessing which he did enjoy: Which Affliction was the more grievous, in that she being a Woman of singular Prudence for the Management of Affairs, had taken off from her Husband all Secular Cares, so that he wholly devoted himself to his Study, and to Sacred Imployments. After he had continued in the State of Widowhood a year and half, he again changed his Condition, and was Married to the pious Widow of that deservedly Famous Man of God Mr. John Cotton; and her did God make a Blessing and a Comfort to him during the remainder of his dayes.

Old Age now being come upon him, he was sensible of the Infirmities thereof, being in his latter years something thick of Hearing: Also (as it was with great Zanchy)[42] the sight in one of his Eyes failed, seven years before his Death. Yet God gave him Health of Body and Vigour of Spirit in a wonderful measure, so as that in fifty years together, he was not by Sickness detained so much as one Lords-day from Publick Labours. Which continued Health (as to Natural causes) proceeded partly from his strong Constitution of Body, and partly from his accustoming himself to a plain and wholsome Diet. *Bona Diaeta est potior quovis Hippocrate.*[43] He never made use of any Physician, nor was he ever in all his life sick of any acute Disease. Onely the two last years of his Life he was sorely afflicted with that Disease which some have called *Flagellum Studiosorum, viz.* The Stone, which at last brought him to an end of all his Labours and Sorrows.

Concerning the Time and Manner of his Sickness and Death, thus it was. There being some Differences in Boston, Counsel from Neighbour-Churches was by some desired, to direct them in the Lord what should be done: Accordingly the Churches sent their Messengers; and Dorchester Church, amongst others, sent Mr. Mather their aged Teacher, who Assembled in Boston, April 13. 1669. He was, because of his Age, Gravity, Grace and Wisdome wherewith the Lord had endowed and adorned him, chosen the Moderator in that Reverend Assembly. For divers dayes after his being thus in Consultation, he enjoyed his Health as formerly, or rather better then for some time of late. But as Luther when Assembled in a Synod was surprized with a violent Fit of the Stone, whence he was forced to return home, his Friends having little hopes of his life; so it was with this holy man. For April 16. 1669. he was in the night, being then in his Sons house in Boston, taken exceeding ill through a totall stoppage of his Urine. The next morning he therefore returned home to Dorchester. Great was the favour of God towards him, that he should be found about such a blessed Work as then he was ingaged in, for the Lord found him sincerely and earnestly endeavouring to be a Peace-maker. His being thus taken when at a Synod, brings to minde that of the German Phoenix;

Viximus in Synodis, & jam moriemur in illis.[44]

Now as usually Providence so ordereth, that they who have been speaking all their lives long, shall not say much when they come to die: Blessed Hooker in his last Sickness, when Friends would have had him answered to some Enquiries which might have made for their Edification after he was gone, he referred them wholly to the things which he had taught them in his health, because then he had enough to do to grapple with his own bodily weakness, &c. Neither did this good man speak much in his last Sickness either to Friends or to his Children. Onely his Son who is now Teacher of a Church in Boston, coming to visit his Father, and perceiving the Symptomes of Death to be upon him, said unto him, *Sir, if there be any speciall thing which you would recommend unto me to do, in case the Lord should spare me upon the Earth, after you are in Heaven, I would intreat you to express it.* At the which, his Father making a little pause, and lifting up his eyes and hands to Heaven, replied, *A speciall thing which I would commend to you, is, Care concerning the Rising Generation in this Country, that they be brought under the Government of Christ in his Church; and that when grown up and qualified, they have Baptism for their Children. I must confess I have been defective as to practise, yet I have publickly declared my judgement, and manifested my desires to practise that which I think ought to be attended, but the Dissenting of some in our Church discouraged me. I have thought that persons might have Right to Baptism, and yet not to the Lords Supper; and I see no cause to alter my judgement as to that particular. And I still think that persons qualified according to the Fifth Proposition of the late Synod-Book, have Right to Baptism for their Children.*[45]

His bodily Pains continued upon him untill April 22. when in the Morning his Son aforementioned, coming to visit him, asked his Father if he knew him; to whom he Replied that he did, but was not able to speak any more to him: Whereupon his Son saying, *Now you will speedily be in the joy of your Lord;* His Father lifted up his hands, but could not speak. Not long after his Son again spoke to him, saying, *You will quickly see Jesus Christ, and that will make amends for all your pains and sorrows:* At which words his Father again lifted up his hands; but after that he took notice of no person or thing, but continuing speechless untill about 10 h. P.M. he quietly breathed forth his last. Thus did that Light that had been shining in the Church above Fifty years, Expire.

As some of the Lords precious ones have had a reall apprehension and praesense of their approaching Dissolution imprinted on their Spirits; so it is noted of Ambrose and of Gorgonia of old; and of Gesner, Melancthon, and Sanford among Modern Divines:[46] Thus it was with this holy man some time afore his departure. The last Text which he taught from, and insisted long thereon, was that 2 Timothy 4.6,7,8. *I am now ready to be offered, and the time of my departure is at hand; I have fought a good fight, I have finished my course, I have kept the Faith: Henceforth there is laid up for me a Crown of Righteousness, which the Lord the righteous Judge will give me at that day; and not to me onely, but unto all them also that love his appearing.* And the portion of Scripture which before that he had insisted upon, was Job 14.14. *All the dayes of my appointed time, will I wait till my change come.* The Lord found his blessed Servant so doing. Also the last private Conference-Meeting which he was at in Dorchester, he had prepared to speak from those words, 2 Cor. 5.1. *For we know that if our earthly house of this tabernacle were dissolved, we have a building of God, an house not made with hands, eternall in the Heavens:* But bodily pains prevented him from speaking what was in his heart to have expressed; the Lord intending that he should no more speak of, but see that place which he had so much and so often thought on, and long prayed and longed to enjoy.

He was, especially in his last Sickness, a Pattern of Patience. For although extremity of pain, without any acute Disease, was that which brought him to his Grave, yet he did never so much as once cry out from first to last; and it was very rare to hear him so much as groan (but never grumble) under his dolorous Griefs. In this Sickness, whereof he died, he was much delighted in reading Doctor Goodwins *Discourse about Patience,*[47] in which Book he read till the very day of his Death. Once in his Sickness, his Son saying to him, that inasmuch as several small Stones were come from him in his Urine, now possible he might have some ease; his Father answered with an affecting earnestness of expression, *As for that matter, the Will of the Lord be done.* Such was his grace and patience. And at the same time his Son saying to him, *God hath shewed his great faithfulness unto you, having upheld you now for the space of more then Fifty years in his Service, and imployed you therein without ceasing, which can be said of very few men upon the face of the whole Earth.* His Father replied, *You say true; I must acknowledge the mercy of God hath been great towards me all my dayes: but I must also acknowledge, that I have had many failings and the thought of them abaseth me, and worketh patience in me.* When any one asked him how he did; his usual Answer was, *Far from well, yet far better then my iniquities deserve.* Thus did he (like old Austin[48] who died reading the Penitential Psalms) keep up a spirit of Repentance to the last.

As he was a man faithful and fearing God above many, so the Lord shewed great faithfulness unto him, both in making him serviceable unto the last, yea and continuing the vigour of his Spirit, and power of his Ministry. Few men, though young, are known to Preach with such vigour as he did but ten dayes before his death. Also the Lord was faithful and gracious to him, in respect of his Children. It was a special token of Divine favour unto some of the Ancients, that their Sons after them succeeded in the Ministry; so was it with the Fathers of Gregory Nazianzen, Gregory Nyssen, Basil, Hilary, &c.[49] And the Lord cheered the heart of this his Servant in his old Age, by giving him to see most of his Sons imployed in the Ministry many years before their precious Father's decease. He left four Sons in that Work;

one of whom, *viz.* Mr. Eleazar Mather, late Pastor of the Church at Northampton in New-England, went to his rest about three Moneths after his Father, with him to sound forth the praises of God amongst the Spirits of just men made perfect. The other three are yet surviving, *viz.* Mr. Samuel Mather, Teacher of a Church in Dublin; Mr. Nathaniel Mather, late Minister of Barnstable in Devon, and since in Rotterdam in Holland; and Increase Mather of Boston in New-England.

Concerning his Judgement. Touching matters of Faith and Doctrine, his large Catechism which contains the Summe of the Body of Divinity, doth sufficiently manifest his Orthodoxness to the World.[50] Indeed he was a strenuous opposer of the Errours of the Times. Touching Worship and Discipline, he was for the true Congregational-Way, in opposition to both the Extremes of Brownism on the one hand, and Presbyterianism on the other hand. As for Brownism, he was of the same apprehension with Mr. Dod and Mr. Cotton,[51] That God is not wont to make choice of men infamous for gross Vices (as that Brown and Barrow were)[52] to be the Discoverers of momentous Truths. And to manifest that he was farre from the Errour of that Way, he hath left a judicious Manuscript, proving that although Power, i.e. Priviledge and Liberty doth belong to the Fraternity, yet that Rule is proper to the Presbytery of the Church. As for Presbyterianism, his Printed Books in Answer to Mr. Herle and Mr. Rutherford,[53] shew how farre he was distant from that Perswasion. Also some years before his Death, he prepared for the Press an Elaborate Discourse, Entituled, *A Plea for the Churches of New-England;* divided into Two Parts: The former being an Answer to Mr. Rathbands *Narration of Church-Courses in New-England;* The other containing Positive Grounds from Scripture and Reason, for the Justification of the Way of the Churches in New-England.[54] Not many weeks before his death a Friend acquainting him, that some reported that he had declared himself to be a Presbyterian; He replied, *You tell me a strange thing: I have written Books in Defence of the Congregationall-Way, as differing from the Presbyterian, and doth any one say I declared my self for that Perswasion? It is nothing so.* At the same time it being said to him, that he had the principal hand in the Platform of Discipline, and had he not changed his judgement from that? His Answer was, *No, not in any one particular that I know of.*

His way of Preaching was plain, aiming to shoot his Arrows not over his peoples heads, but into their Hearts and Consciences. Whence he studiously avoided obscure phrases, Exotick words, or an unnecessary citation of Latine Sentences, which some men addict themselves to the use of. Mr. Dod was wont to say, *That so much Latine was so much flesh in a Sermon:* So did this humble man look upon the affectation of such things in a Popular Auditory to savour of Carnal wisdome. The Lord gave him an excellent faculty in making abstruse things plain, that in handling the deepest Mysteries he would accommodate himself to Vulgar Capacities, that even the meanest might learn something. He knew how to express χαινὰ χοιμ͡ῷς χ[αι] χοινὰ χαινῷς.[55] He would often use that Saying, *Artis est celare Artem.*[56] And much approved that of Austin; *If* (said he) *I preach Learnedly, that onely the Learned and not the Unlearned can understand and profit by me; but if I preach plainly, then Learned and Unlearned both can understand, so I may profit all.* He was Mighty in the Scriptures: Whence Mr. Hooker would say of him, *My Brother Mather is a mighty man.* Also his usuall way of Delivery was very Powerful, Awakening, and Zealous; especially in his younger years, there being few men of so great strength of body as he, which together with his natural fervour of Spirit, being sanctified, made his Ministry the more powerful. And the Lord went forth with his Labours to the Conversion of many, both in England and in New-England. Yet though his way of Preaching was plain and zealous, it was moreover Substantial and very Judicious. Even in his beginning times, Mr. Gillebrand (a famous Minister in Lancashire; and the more famous, for that though he did exceedingly Stammer in his ordinary discourse, he would Pray and Preach as fluently as any man)[57] once having heard him Preach, asked what his Name might be? And answer being made that his Name was Mather; *Nay* (said Mr. Gillebrand) *call him Matter, for believe it this man hath Substance in him.* Yea, such was his Solidity of Judgement, that some who were his Opposites, yet did therefore greatly respect and honour him. Doctor Parr (then Bishop in the Isle of Man) having heard Mr. Mather was Silenced, lamented it, saying, *If Mather be Silenced I am sorry for it, for he was a solid man, and the Church of God hath then a great loss.*

Because he was esteemed eminently Judicious, therefore amongst the Reverend Elders in New-England, he was much improved in Managing the Controversies then under Debate about Church-Government. The *Discourse about the Church-Covenant,* and the *Answer to the XXXII. Questions,* both written Anno 1639.[58] although they pass under the Name of the Elders of New-England, Mr. Mather was the sole Author of, as Mr. Cotton in his *Answer to Baily,* pag. 70 and *Answer to Williams,* pag. 63.[59] and Mr. Nathaniel Mather in his Epistle to the *XXI. Questions concerning Church-members and their Children,*[60] have truely related. And when there was a Synod called to Convene at Cambridge, Anno 1647. that Reverend Assembly desired three Elders to draw up A Modell of Church Government against the next Session, *viz.* Mr. Cotton, Mr. Mather, and Mr. Partrich.[61] The Printed Platform of Discipline is for the substance of it the same with that which was Composed by Mr. Mather. It might be said of him, as was said of that blessed Martyr, *that he was sparing in his Diet, sparing in his Speech, most sparing of all of his Time.* He was very diligent both as to duties of general and particular Calling, which are indeed the two Pillars upon which Religion stands. As to his general Calling; He was much in Prayer, especially in his Study, where he ofttimes spent whole dayes with God in suing for a Blessing upon himself and Children, and upon the people to whom he was related; and upon the whole Country where he lived. The Requests which upon such occasions he put up to God in Jesus Christ, and also how his heart was moved to believe that God heard him, he left (many of them) in writing amongst his private Papers, I suppose that so himself might have recourse upon those Experiences in a time of darkness and Temptation; also that his Sons after him might see by their Fathers Example, what it is to walk before God. Now what a loss is it to the world when such a Righteous man is taken away! Well might Philo and Jerome weep bitterly,[62] when they heard of the death of any such men, because it portended evil to the places where they had lived, and served God. As he was much in Prayer, so he was very frequent in Hearing the Word. It was his manner to attend several Lectures in Neighbour-Congregations, untill his Disease made him unable to ride; yea and usually even to his old Age (as did Mr. Hildersham) he took Notes from those whom he heard, professing that he found profit in it.

As to his particular Calling, he was even from his youth a hard Student. Yea his minde was so intent upon his Work and Studies, that the very morning before he died, he importuned those Friends that watched with him to help him into his Study: They urging that he was not able to go so farre, he desired them to help him and try; which they did: but ere he was come to the door of his Lodging-room, *I see* (saith he) *I am not able, yet I have not been in my Study several dayes, and is it not a lamentable thing that I should lose so much time?* After his entrance upon the Ministry, he was not onely in England (as hath been said) but in New-England abundant in Labours: for except when he had an Assistant with him (which was seldome) he Preached twice every Lords-day; and a Lecture once a fortnight, besides many occasionall Sermons both in Publick and in Private. Also he was much exercised in answering many practical Cases of Conscience, and in Polemical, especially Disciplinary Discourse. In his Publick Ministry in Dorchester he went over The Book of Genesis to Chap. 38.[63]

Psalm 16. The whole Book of the Prophet Zechariah. Matthews Gospel, to Chap. 15. I Epist. to Thess. Chap. 5. And the whole Second Epistle of Peter; his Notes whereon he reviewed, and Transcribed for the Press, not many years before his decease.

Notwithstanding those rare Gifts and Graces wherewith the Lord had adorned him, he was exceeding low and little in his own eyes. Some have thought that his greatest errour was, that he did not magnifie his Office, as he might and sometimes should have done. If a man must erre, it is good erring on that hand. *Humble enough, and good enough,* was the frequent Saying of a great Divine. And another observeth, *That every man hath just as much and no more true worth in him, as he hath Humility.* Austine being asked which was the most excellent grace, answered, *Humility;* and which was the next, answered, *Humility;* and which was the third, replied again, *Humility.* That indeed is Comprehensively All, being of great price in the sight of God: And if so, Mr. Mather was a man of much Reall Worth.

It hath been the manner of some, in writing Lives to insert the Wills of those whose Lives and Death they have described. The last Will and Testament of him, whose Life and Death hath thus been related, breathing forth a most humble, holy, and gracious Spirit, we shall here subjoyn the Preface and Conclusion of it. It was written with his own hand Octob. 16. 1661. And beginneth as followeth.

I Richard Mather, considering the certainty of death, and the uncertainty of the time thereof; and withall knowing it to be the will of God that a man should set his House in order before he depart this life, Do make this my last Will and Testament in manner following. First of all, I acknowledge the rich and wonderful Grace and Mercy of Almighty God, whose hands have made me and fashioned me, and who took me out of my Mothers Womb, that having made me a Man, who might have made me a Beast or other Creature; He hath also by his good Providence preserved the beeing and comfort of my life all the dayes of my Pilgrimage untill now, even for the space of these Sixty five years: During all which time, he hath not suffered me to want either food or raiment, or the service of any creature, which hath been requisite for my comfortable subsisting in this World; which I acknowledge to be the bounteous gift of Him who is Lord of all Creatures, and the High Possessor of Heaven and Earth. Next of all, and more especially I am bound to give Thanks and Praise to Him whil'st I have any beeing, that I being a Childe of Wrath by Nature as well as others, and being born in a place of much Profaneness and Popery, he hath of his abundant grace vouchsafed to draw me out of that woful estate of Sin and Ignorance wherein I lay, and to make himself and his Christ known unto me by the Gospel, of which grace I was most unworthy;

and in his great patience and mercy to bear with my manifold and great offences, both before and since the time of his gracious Calling of me, though for my unworthy walking in many particulars, I might justly have been for ever rejected of him. Yea and such hath been his rich grace, that he hath vouchsafed to put me an unworthy creature into the Ministry of the Gospel of his Son, that I should not onely know and profess the same (which is unspeakable mercy) but be also a Preacher of it unto others. In which Imployment if any thing hath been done which hath been pleasing unto him, or any way beneficiall to any Childe of his, it hath not been I that have done the same, but the grace of God which was with me. For I must needs acknowledge to the praise of his Patience and Grace, That in my poor Ministration for the space of these Forty two years and upwards, I have been much defective in Wisdome and Watchfulness over the peoples Souls, in Purity, in Faithfulness, in Uprightness, Meekness, Humility and Zeal: And because of these, and many other my defects and offences against the Lord, I stand in much need this day of mercy and forgiveness through his Christ, and have no cause to look for any acceptance either in this or in another World, for any Righteousness of my own, either as touching my Ministry or otherwise, but disclaiming all thought of that kinde, my onely trust and hope is to be accepted of him, and (when this life shall end) to be saved in his Heavenly Kingdome meerly by his Free-grace, and the Obedience and precious Passion and Intercession of his dear Son. And concerning Death, as I do believe it is appointed for all men once to die; so, because I see a great deal of unprofitableness in my own life, and because God hath also let me see such vanity and emptiness even in the best of those Comforts which this life can afford, that I think I may truely say, That I have seen an end of all perfection: Therefore if it were the will of God, I should be glad to be removed hence, where the best that is to be had doth yield so little satisfaction to my Soul, and to be brought into his presence in glory, that there I might finde (for there I know it is to be had) that satisfying and All-sufficient contentment in him, which under the Sun is not to be enjoyed. In the mean time I desire to stay the Lords leisure. But thou, O Lord, how long! Now concerning my Outward Estate, sith the Earth is the Lords and the fulness thereof, the habitable World, and all that is therein; to him therefore belongs the praise of all that I possess in this kinde: And for the portion thereof which he hath given unto me, it is my minde and will, if so it please his Highness, that after my decease the same may be disposed of as followeth, &c.

Having thus graciously expressed himself, he proceeds to the disposal of his Temporal Estate; which being of private Concernment, we shall not here trouble the World therewith. But after the disposal of that, he concludeth with a most Solemn Charge to his Children; with the rehearsall whereof we shall finish. It is in words following.

Concerning my Son Timothy, with all the rest of my Beloved Sons, as I hope God hath already made them partakers, at least sundry of them, of his saving grace in Christ, for which I and they have cause to be endlesly thankful; so I think it not amiss, for the furtherance of their Spiritual good, to lay upon them this serious and solemn Charge of a Dying Father, That none of them presume after my decease to walk in any way of sin and wickedness in one kinde or another, or in a careless neglect of God, and the things of God, and of their own Salvation by Christ: for if they shall so do (which God forbid) Then and in such case I hereby testifie unto them, That their Father which begat them, and their Mother which bare them, with all the Prayers which they have made, and Tears which they have shed for them, their Example, their Admonitions and Exhortations which they have administred to them, together with this my last Will and Solemn Charge; All these will rise up against them as so many Testimonies for their Condemnation at the last day. But I have better hopes of them; And do hereby declare unto them, That if they shall seriously repent of their sins, Believe on the Lord Jesus, and by his grace walk in all the wayes of God, and as becometh the Gospel of Christ; as this will be to the Honour and glory of Him that made them, so it will redound to their own unspeakable comfort and benefit in this and in another World: and their Father that now speaketh unto them, with their dear Mother now with God, shall exceedingly rejoyce in the day of Christ, when we shall receive our Children unto those Everlasting Habitations; and shall see not our selves alone, but those also that have proceeded and come forth out of our own bowels, to have their part and portion in that Eternall Glory. In desire and hope that it may be so, I commend them all to the Lord of Heaven's Blessing: And let the Blessing of God in Jesus Christ, be poured out and remain upon them all for evermore. Amen.

FINIS

PARENTATOR

MEMOIRS
of
REMARKABLES
in the
LIFE
and the
DEATH
of the
Ever-Memorable
Dr. Increase Mather.
Who Expired, August 23. 1723.

2 King. II. 12.
My FATHER, *my* FATHER.

Boston: Printed by B. *Green*, for *Nathaniel Belknap*, at the Corner of Scarlets-Wharff. 1724.

To the Illustrious University of Glasco[w].

Honourable, Venerable, and much Esteemed.

It was not possible for me to be long undetermined, unto whom I should apply my self, in doing the part of a PARENTATOR, when I Remembred what Acknowledgments I owe, to the Learned Body, before which I am now appearing. Unto whom can I so agreeably present my FATHER as to my MOTHER; even to that Ancient and Famous University, whose Favours have so Cherished me, that they have rendered me as, A man whom his MOTHER Comforteth?

It is no small Intimation, how much the Truth which is according to Godliness is acknowledged in the Exemplary Church of SCOTLAND, That the Name and Worth of an OWEN[1] is considered in it as it is, and his Writings are so much Recommended unto your Students. And, I hope, ANOTHER, who was of his Evangelical Principles, Exhibited in the History of his Life and Death, will also find some Regards with you. Yea, there have been some very Expressive Testimonies of His having already done so. And if you now see me helping my Aged Parent into the Senate of Illustrious Men, you would no more tax it as a Fault in me, than you would in an Antoninus.[2] But yet I have done it in such a manner, that after the first Paragraph I drop the Relation, and speak not only in the Style but also with the Faith, of an unrelated and Uninterested, and Unbiassed Historian; putting on the Historian, I act the part of the Honest Levite, who said of his father, *I have not seen him.*[3]

The Renouned Church of SCOTLAND, in which I cannot but believe, that the Glorious Lord Looking down from Heaven, the Habitation of His Holiness and of His Glory, upon it, beholds those things that are very pleasing to Him, is doubtless an House of His Glory; and as he has Glorified it, so He will do it yet more abundantly.

A CHURCH which does Rejoice in this Distinguishing Blessing of Heaven unto it, That it made a more Thorough Work, & stop'd less than others at halfing of it in the Reformation, at the entrance of Antichrist into his last Half-Time, & more thoroughly came out of the Romish Babylon;[4] And has ever since been in Singular Conflicts to hold fast that which it has Received, and let no Man take away its Crown. It's Motto has been, *With great Wrestlings have I Wrestled, and I have prevailed!*[5]

A CHURCH, which after it has undergone a Finishing Stroke of

Persecution with such Barbarous and Inhumane Cruelties, for Four times Seven Years together, as were hardly ever equalled among all the vile things done under the Sun, the Burning Bush has not been Consumed; but the Professors of the Truth have after all been found more Numerous and more Powerful than they were before, and able to bring about a Revolution, which was indeed the Lords Doing, and ought forever to be Marvellous in our Eyes! The Persecutors are by a mighty Hand of GOD Wonderfully turned out of Doors; And the Historical Pen of a Meritorious Woodrow, following what has been done by the Polemical Pen of an Astonishing Jameson[6] (who has pull'd a Temple down like another Sampson) it may be hoped, has clap'd an Eternal Bolt upon them.

A CHURCH, wherein the Excellent Wisdom found in the Servants of GOD, which upon just occasions knows how to Bury in Oblivion the lesser Differences arising on Various Temptations, and coalesce in the Common Cause of all True Protestants, has in it something that is Great and Just and Generous, and not every where to be met withal, *Where is the place of such understanding, which is hid, from the Eyes of almost all the Living.*[7]

And where is the Church under Heaven that can shew a MINISTRY, more Faithful, more Painful, more Zealous, or under a Stricter Government? Unto which doubtless, the Abdication of an Uninstituted and Unwarrantable Oversight, and of that whereof our Wickliff[8] long ago declared, *That it was not only contrary to the New-Testament; but also the Effect of Imperious Pride,* may, (as it has done in other places also that have Dethroned that Idol) more than a little Contribute.

A CHURCH, which that so nothing that would add unto the Perfection of its Beauty may be wanting, improves continually in a Spirit of kind Forbearance, and sweet Charity, and Brotherly Affection towards Dissenters in Smaller matters, while Genuine PIETY is Conspicuous in them: and goes further than some others who boast they have need of nothing, in Conforming to that Golden Rule, To Receive all that CHRIST receives to the Glory of GOD. Indeed, what can be more Unexceptionable than a Sanctuary measured by the *Golden Reed,*[9] which knows no other Measures for Admission, but only that PIETY, which Qualifies for the Kingdom of GOD, and wherein all the Children of GOD are United Brethren!

Where is the CHURCH, in which the Sabbath of the Lords-Day is more Carefully & Suitably Celebrated? The Sabbath, of which the Power of Godliness is kept or lost according to the Celebration? The Rest of GOD is Glorious in it, & will make it Glorious!

A CHURCH wherein the SOCIETIES formed for the Propagation

of Religion, do fairly serve the cause of Pure & Undefiled Religion; and their Wisdom dwells with the Prudence, which finds out the Knowledge of Well-Advised Inventions to do the Best Good that can be done unto & among the Sons of Men; and such things are done, as may give a full Satisfaction unto those who send in their Bounties from all parts unto their Treasury, that their Money is not Misapplied, but that their Bountiful Oblations will be such Sacrifices as GOD, thro' His CHRIST, will be Well-Pleased withal; and their Substance never better Bestowed, than in this way of Laying up good Bills of Exchange for the time to come. Their Missionaries have the right Spirit of the Gospel, and not of a party in them: and are the Angels that carry the pure Maxims of the Everlasting Gospel with them.

To do any Service for such a CHURCH, tho' the doer of it should be ranked among the lowest Nethinims,[10] were an Honour, which I know one, who is as Ambitious as he is Unworthy of. And if the little Book which now goes over to you,—Alas, That he who sends it, can't go with it!—may be so Honoured, as to be in any sort useful to the best Interests among you, I am in the glad Circumstances of the Man who sees his Desire Accomplished.

Among those who Compass the Camp of the Saints, and are as Disaffected unto you, as Good Men are Well-affected, there is a set of Strange Men who assault you and insult you, with Imagining a Vain Thing, wherein the Reformed Churches in these Parts of America, & on the whole Continent of Europe have aequally with You, an Attempt made upon them; The Men who try to shake the Minds of the Faithful, with Cavils at The Validity of a Presbyterian Ordination: The Men who crying up the Necessity of an Episcopal Ordination, do as your Worthy Champion Willison[11] Expresses it, advance a most Unmerciful Opinion, which Unchurches almost all the Protestant Churches in the World, and which does the greatest Service that can be done to the Church of Rome, and the Kingdom of Satan; Inviting People to turn Papists, or Hardning them in their Vices and Immoralities. What these Men mean at This time of the Day,—'Tis Unaccountable?—In the mean Time, we are not left Uninformed, That even about the Beginning of the present Century, very Notable Treatises Published in Germany, Complain of Emissaries creeping in among the Churches there, who upon the Intention of carrying people back to Rome, do hold forth unto them, That the Protestant Ministers are meer Laymen for the want of Episcopal Ordination; and as the Acute Voigtius expresses it, *Multis etiam illustribus animis persuadere Conati sunt, non esse Legitimos quos haberemus Ecclesiae Ministros.*[12] To stop the Mouths of these gainsayers, whom they call,—What I will not say?—we find such Eminent Persons as a

Joachim, Hildebrande, a Seckendorf, a Bebelius, an Osiander,[13] & other great Men within these very few Years, appearing, to Allow indeed, that they have not Bishops of a Distinct order from their Presbyters; but then to Maintain that they do not Want them, and that the Sacred Scriptures know nothing of them, and that the Primitive Churches were Strangers to them; and that none but, *Pontificij, et Hierarchici in Anglia,*[14] do Dispute the Validity of our Presbyterian Ordination. But this is not altogether so Unexpected, as it may be to find, that even in France it self, the Doctors of the Sorbon have lately Published Instruments, Decrying and Condemning of Episcopacy, declaring it an Usurpation, and asserting in strong terms the old Aerian Heresy, as it was called, & all that Jerom writes upon it.[15] The Translators Dedicate these things to the Arch bishop of Canterbury; assuring him, that very many of His Clergy are come into the same Sentiments, & Admiring at it, that in France those who are yet called Roman-Catholicks, are gone further from Rome, than some who go by a better Name, after a Struggle of Two Hundred Years to get rid of Popery. And yet this is not altogether so Unexpected, though it may be owned also somewhat Unaccountable! For tho' the very Life and Soul of the Papacy be in its Prelacy, yet the Force of Truth has brought a Confusion of Tongues on the Builders of it[16] and extorted sometimes from the Papists themselves those Confessions which many that call themselves Protestants may be Confounded at. You know what their Master of Sentences has Pronounced on the Identity of Episcopus and Presbyter; and the Original & occasion of the former. And you know where to find it expres[s]ly asserted even in the Canon Law it self; That there are no more than Two Offices in the Church, the Presbyterate, and the Diaconate. But now, besides the many Rational Confutations given to the folly of these Men, it may be hoped, there will be a very Sensible one, from our Glorious Lord Owning and Crowning the Ministry of His Appointment in His Churches, with a Success that shall be Remarkable! And when it is Observed, that the Good Men, full of the Holy SPIRIT, shall have the Hand of the Lord with them, and many shall be by the Blessing of GOD upon their Labours Turned unto the Lord, their Call and their Character will no longer [be] made a Question of. Such will more and more Issue from the Happy Nursery of Glasco[w]: Yea, Great will be the Army of them that shall go forth from thence with Sufficient Authority as well as Capacity to Publish the Word which our Ascended Lord has given for us.

But will you give me leave Humbly to Propose, that by Writing, as well as by Speaking, they may do more of the Good Work, which their Hand finds to do!

I am not the only Person that have said it, and so t'will be the less Presumption in Me to say it; I have often thought it a Loss unto the World, that the Incomparable Pastors in the Church of Scotland, have their Pastoral Employments lying so hard upon them, that they have not much Liesure for the Writing of Books, for which there are so many of them, whose Talents are Extraordinary. And, if I may Presume to say so, I cannot but think, that it would be Richly worth the while, for Ways and Means to be found out, that more of your Pens may be Employ'd for the Enlightning of a World, which is yet a *Dark Place*,[17] and greatly need Illuminations; and that your Admirable Boid, and Calderwood, and Rutherford, & Dickson, & Durham, and Galaspy, and Hutcheson, & Ferguson,[18] and some others [other] Stars of their Magnitude, may never want Equal Successors among you.

We in these American Colonies are under the same Disadvantage:—Which yet hinders not, but that we now and then do some little matter, at the Writing of Books, and some small things do by the Press pass from us into the World. Among these Essays, there is one that now Humbly Prays for a kind Reception with you. And this the rather, because tis from the Distance of a great and wide Sea, that the Fruits of the Land are brought as a Present unto you. Mean Things brought from a far distant Country, are Usually Well-accepted on the meer account of their being so: and as Well-esteemed as Great Things produced nearer Home. I suppose an Ear of our Indian Corn, or a string of our Indian Peag,[19] would find some Acceptance with the Curious among you. And if this Composure be never so Mean, yet you will cast a benign Aspect upon it, for This very cause, It is American: And it comes from a Thousand Leagues beyond your *Ultima Thule*.[20] Yea, I Promise my self, that there is yet a more considerable Thing, to Bespeak of some Hospitality to the Stranger: It is Christian: And it is Calculated for the Meridian of the Real, Vital, Solid Christianity, by which you Live, and in which is the Life of your Spirit.

The World is Appris'd of and may be justly Surpriz'd at, the Methods taken and Studies follow'd at the Frederician University in the Lower Saxony, & the Divine Appearances there, which are so Miraculous, that whosoever is Wise, wilt Observe those Things. The Glascuan University will also be (as the Glauchian) a Pattern to the rest of the World, in which the Recovery and Regulation of Schools to Answer their Chief End in Living to GOD, & Knowing of CHRIST, & being made Wise unto Salvation, is one of the most Important Things that can be Wished for. And Heaven will so Smile upon that Mother in Israel, that after an Arrival to near Six Hundred Years of

Age, O Daughter of GOD, Thou shalt continue as Fruitful as ever. Yea, The Children which thou shalt have shall Say again in thine Ears, *The Place is too strait for me.*[21] The Glascuan University shall be a River, the Streams whereof shall make Glad the City of GOD, as long as the Cluyde[22] shall Comfort and Adorn the Beloved City of Glasco[w]. With such Prayers and Hopes here now Subscribes,

Your most Obliged

Cotton Mather.

Boston, New England.
October 1. 1723.

Introduction.

All the World allows a SON, to Erect a Monument for, & Preserve a Memorial of, his Departed FATHER. Antiquity proceeded so far in this Concession, that it Produced the Teraphim, wherein People kept the Images of their Ancestors, and Wickedly Consulted their Manes by them.[23] At the same time there is an Allowance also given, that the Splendor of the Monument, and the Value of the Memorial, should bear a Proportion to the Merit of the Subject. If the Parent be a Man of Worth, it is on all Hands Agreed, that the Commemoration may be Proportionable.

This is what Legitimates, and even Encourages, that which is now a doing. And yet I Solemnly Declare, That my Pen should not have been Employ'd on this Occasion, if I had not been verily perswaded, That it would be a Thing Acceptable to the Glorious GOD, and Serviceable very many ways unto the cause of PIETY, to Exhibit the Conduct of His Providence in the Life of a Good Man, and the Exemplary Methods taken by such a Man, to do Good in the World. THIS is the Mark I would perpetually Aim at; And if it has been Determined, That the Name of an Historian shall be, Vertues Secretary, I know not how the Pen of an Historian can be better Employ'd, than in Reporting the Vertuous Tempers and Actions of the Men that have therein shown forth the Vertues of our Blessed REDEEMER, and been the Epistles of CHRIST unto the rest of Mankind. Nor indeed has Mankind generally found any sort of History more Useful and more Grateful, than what has been given in the Lives of Men that have been distinguished by an Excellent Spirit. The Best of Books does very much Consist of such an History!

For the Sincerity and Veracity with which the History which we are now going to, is carried on, I am Responsible to HIM, whose Eye I have Remembred, I hope, Constantly upon me, while I have been Writing of it. But I have also Vouchers in my Hands, for every one of the Articles, which any one shall be Welcome to see, whenever he Pleases.

I confess, It is a Lamentation, and it shall be for a Lamentation, That so much False History is Imposed upon the World. Many others, besides Vopiscus, have Detected it and Bewailed it, That among all the Celebrated Historians, it may be proved, *Neminem non esse aliquid Mentitum;*[24] Or, as it had been said long before him,

All are Lyars. The Old Gentleman whom they call, The Father of History (notwithstanding Harry Stephen's[25] unlucky Apology for him) as truly be called, The Parent of Fable. But what a Fabulous Generation have come after him?

No man has with more Justice Complained of the Iniquity Chargeable upon Historians, especially upon a Black-sould Heylin[26] and his Brethren on both sides the Alps, than our Venerable Baxter;[27] And no Man could more truly say, *I Hate and Abor Lying,* than he. But yet even He himself was taxeable with some Wrong Representations in his, *History of his Life and Times:* Among which, what he gives of Dr. Owen, has been Happily Corrected, and should be Forgotten.

How many Excellent Men, and more Precious than *the Golden Wedge of Ophir,*[28] have been strangely Sambenito'd[29] by Partial, Prejudiced, Passionate Historians, and handed down unto Posterity in Vile Characters, which will never be wiped off, until the Resurrection of the Just! Such I really take Montanus as well as Origen,[30] to have been among the Ancients. But among the Moderns, there has been an exceeding great Multitude, which no Man can Number. Indeed Luther and Calvin,[31] and some other Buffeted Hero's, have had their Vindicators: But who dare appear in the Vindication of ______ or so much as to say, *Tis Pitty that they are not Vindicated!* Who is there I beseech you, Syrs, Who so Hardy and so Honest, as to take the *Athenae Oxonienses,*[32] of a Wood, and so take the Poison out of the Lamprey, that the Books being Freed from the Spiteful Scoffs and Lies which he forever Loads the Best of Men withal, may be Read with Safety and become (as without them they might be) an Useful Performance? This Author I may the more particularly mention, because Dr. Mather was the Person from whose Generous and Communicative Goodness, he Obtained very much History of those Brave Men, whom he forever Skorakizes;[33] and therein basely Deceived and Defeated the Expectations of the Gentleman whose Communications he so much Subsisted on. But O great Burnet,[34] Give thou the Character of the Scribler; tell what a Tool of Rome, he appears to be!

It is not more Shameful than Certain, That Historians very Commonly Write as Tools of a party, to which every one may see, they are as much Addicted, as Fabius and Philimus[,] the two Opposite Writers of the Carthaginian War, were to Theirs.[35] What a Credible Writer of History, was Paulus Jovius, a Bishop; with whom the Execrable John Basilovitz is cryed up as *A Good and Devout Christian;* and of whom they tell us, that he brag'd he had one Pen of Gold, for his Friends, and another of Iron, for them that had not purchased his

Favours;[36] and the more impartial Thuanus affirms, *Ad Gratiam et in Odium Scripsisse, et Venalem Calamum habuisse, sere Omnibus persuasum est.*[37] But how many more may this be Affirmed of? If the Reformed in France might once make their just Remonstrances, against such Historians as a Florimond de Remond, or a Varillas,[38] I am sure, their Brethren the Non-Conformists in England, may make the same concerning some English Histories, that must pass for Uncontradictable Things. The *True History* of a Lucian,[39] has as much Truth in it as they have, when some Affairs & Persons come in their way! The Motto to be Inscribed on Them is, *Omnia pro Tempore, nihil pro Veritate.*[40] The Time and not the Truth, Governs the Pen in all the Motions of it. And of these I know some that will Venture to say, *Many have done vitiously, but thou Eachard, in some things Excellest them all: Except a Collier may be a Rival to thee.*[41] In the mean time, would not the Dissenters be more Wise for their Generation, if more Effectual care were taken, to transmit more Faithful Records unto Posterity? Consider of it, take Advice, and Speak your Minds!

The History now before us, is not like much in the Life of a Cyrus,[42] a feign'd Pourtraiture of, A Man to be wished for, but Written, *Ad fidem verae Historiae.*[43] And tho' people have usually a Pardon ready, for the Liberty taken by Josephus as well as Livy and others,[44] to form Speeches and Harangues, which never were any where but in the Imagination of the Historians, yet so much Liberty as That, would be a Crime in the Apprehension, of him that is at Work in what is now a doing: I have kept close to matter of Fact, just as it was: I am not more fond of Obtaining any Testimony than that. *Thou dost Faithfully whatsoever thou dost.*[45]

I am no Pretender to what some have been Commended for, The Art of good Narrative. And therefore, as for the Style of this Narrative, I will make no Excuses, till you, Gentlemen-Criticks, first can show your Patent for your Criticising, and who Constituted You to be Censors for the rest of Mankind; and until you are better agreed among yourselves, upon the Rules of Criticising; for I cannot Learn that there are any Two of you, but what are Intolerably Severe and Cruel in your Censures upon one another. I acknowledge, That I am too liable to an Infirmity, of Salting my Sentences now and then with short, Instructive, and Unforced Intermixtures of something or other that I have Read of; but as I was upon Reforming it, I stumbled upon a Passage in a Letter of Monsr[.] Tournefort unto the Lord Pontchartrain, *You gave me leave to insert some touches of Erudition, to heighten the Subjects treated of: And I fancy such Additions will make them the less tiresome:*[46] And this a little hardened me. However, having Exhibited the Lives of about Seventy Ministers, all Published in one Volumn,[47] and the Characters of near Twenty more, at several times in more Separate Publications, it can't well be expected, that I should be very Liberal in dealing out those intermixed Embellishments, which make a Narrative less Tedious to the Sons of Erudition: or have my Speech Seasoned with so many Grains of Salt as it use to be. And yet I can truly say, I have Studiously laid aside that Care of Embellishing: I have drop't a World of what some would count Ornaments, which while I was Writing Offered themselves unto my Mind; Resolving upon a Plain, Simple, Honest Narrative of matters which alone would by being so Remarkable afford a continual Feast unto the Readers. And indeed there is a Truth in what Pliny says, *Honeste factis Veritas Sufficit.*[48]

But having mentioned a Book (that is to say, The *Magnalia CHRISTI Americana,*) whereto this [biography] may pass for an Appendix, I think I have here a proper Occasion to take some Notice of the Fate which it has mett withal. For the very same thing in the Heavens above us, is by some called, The Milky Way, and by others called, The Crooked Serpent.

The BOOK being Written with a Variety of Projection and Contrivance, to serve that Real, Vital, Solid PIETY, which seems now almost wholly to have left the Earth, (O Glaucha, Do thou yet retain it!) and give some Account of Men and Things, which cannot be given without Exposing the Persecuting Spirit of some that Hate to be Reformed; I could not be so weak, as to Imagine, That Impious People, or such as are no better than meer Formalists in Religion, would forbear their Invectives against it, and their endeavours to bring all possible Contempt upon it. The Introduction to the History Sufficiently foretold it, and also Signified how much the Breast of the Author, *Trebly Oak'd and Brass'd,*[49] was prepared for it.

I cannot but Wonder at the kind Reception which that Work has found in Scotland, and in Ireland, and in many parts of England; And the Complements which I have received upon it, (even equal to what a Salust could have had from his Milton[50]) from as Competent Judges of Writing as any of them, whose Malice against the Design of the Work has disposed them to decry it. It would be a Trespass upon the Laws of Modesty in me to recite them: And I must ask Pardon, if I do so far Trespass, as to let the World know, just this one little part of my Buckler;[51] That the Famous and Acute Mr. Alsop,[52] in an Assembly of Ministers, when some were Proposing to make an abridgment of that History, said upon it: *It is a very improper Proposal; Tis Impossible to Abridge it! You Injure it, if you go to do it. There is nothing Superfluous in it: Instead of talking about Epitomizing of it, go do as I have done; Read all of it no less than twice over: No man that has A Relish for Piety or Variety can ever be weary of Reading it.* I would not have said so much, if Bad Neighbours had not forced me to it! The Apology will be made for me, that was made for Lubbertus, when some of his Adversaries Compelled him to notify the Public with a little part of what Regards had been paid him, *Effraenis Adversarij Maledicentia Modestissimae Animae Expressit.*[53]

But it is no wonder at all to me, that the Poor Book has met with some that have thought it proper to let the World see, that they look upon it as an Object of their Enmity. And among these none has more Signalized the Enmity, or more put the Third Chapter of Genesis in Execution, than one John Oldmixon, in a Book Entituled, *The English Empire in America.*[54]

Tho' I have had first and last, such a Number of Pamphletts thrown at me, that if I had been Vulnerable, I might appear stuck as full of Darts as the man in the Signs of the Almanack; yet upon considering the sorry and silly Stuff which they have Consisted of, and the Despicable and Stercoreous[55] Quality of the Scriblers, and Remembring that Lyes have no Legs, and what I had Learnt about the Treating of Insolent men with Humility, and Angry Men with Meekness; I have still tho't, the Twenty-sixth of the *Proverbs* and the Fourth, a full Answer to them: *Sile, et funestam dedisti Plagam!*[56] I have had so much Better Work to spend my Precious Time in; that I don't call to mind, I have ever once yet, Published a Direct and Formal Answer to any of them all, but instead thereof and once and for all, I gave to the Public my, *True Way of Shaking off a Viper.*[57] Yea, and I would now also have Excused Oldmixon too, (with as much Disdain as I have done, a Dirty and a Drunken STREET, or a Whiting that can spawn a Volumn of Lies at once without Blushing at them; Or the rest of the Unregardable Sons of Darkness) if the Venerable Person for whom I am now doing an Act of Piety, had not been Assaulted by him with such rude and coarse Indignities, that I must have been a very Dumb Son indeed, if I did not break my Silence upon it.

What the Scorner more Particularly bestows his Flouts upon, is Dr. Mather's PREACHING. Strange! His PREACHING! Of all things,—His Preaching!—Yes He says, This Mather "Preached often in Dissenters Meetings in London; His Style was more Affected and Quaint than those of the Nonconformist Teachers, who are most Famous in that Way; and would Confirm all that has been said (which was with Derision enough) of the Harvard-Eloquence, if any of his Sermons had been Printed." What is this, but Folly in the Exaltation of it! So many Scores of his valuable Sermons, which tis true, have more of the Bible (A Book not so much for thy Relish, Oldmixon!) than of the Stage-play in them, have been Printed, that it is not in the Power of any Allatrations[58] to depreciate them.

And, Since a late Publisher of some Venemous Things, which he calls *Laconicks*, has been so kind unto the Dissenters, as to make this Observation, *The Presbyterian Divines have been observed of late, to preach after the manner of the Church of England Men; But without setting up for a Prophet* (says he) *I dare Venture to affirm, that this will be their Ruine:* I will take leave to say, (and Venture to Advise) That if the Nonconformists would more Preach after the manner of Dr. Mather, and be so Affected and Quaint (if it must be called so,) as to have much of the Sacred Scripture well Explained and well Applied in every Paragraph of their Sermons, and the State of Souls reached with Skilful and Pungent and Adapted Searches into it: It would be no Disservice to the Kingdom of GOD.

After such a FATHER has been so Insulted & Abused, it will be rather an Honour than otherwise unto the SON to bear him Company. Oldmixons Chief Rage is at the Church-History of a Country, which also Dr. Mather was in some Regards, much of a Father to. And of this Church-History, to pass by his Grin, that the Book is cram'd full of—Acrosticks; Whereas, Reader, if thou find so much as one Acrostick in all the Book—Let the Book be treated as *The English Empire in America,* is like to be!—I say, to pass by this, the Accuser would have it Believed, *That the Church-History is very Trivial in the matter of it.* Yes, by all means! The Marvellous Works of GOD in Producing and Maintaining & Afflicting and Relieving of Colonies in a Matchless manner Formed upon the Noble Intentions of Pure and Undefiled Religion: The Wise Measures taken by the Best of Men, to Establish that Religion, and the bright Patterns of Living up to it, seen in the Lives of such Men; and as choice Materials as a Church-History can be composed of; These are Trivial Matters! Come then, let us go to Master Oldmixon for Important Matters. It is a Trouble unto me, to descend unto any thing so Ludicrous; But it is he and not I, that must Answer for it. In his *History,* wherein he rails at ours, you shall find whole Pages Consecrated unto Long, Long Tiresom[e] Relations, of some that he singles out as the more Curious Events; He calls 'em so. These Curious Events are, "That a couple of Starved Indians (at Hudsons-Bay) went a Fishing—and then, a Hunting,—and met with only two Moose,—and—how t'was—and how the Geese flying away to the Southward, in October, the People there (such their Segacity!) knew that hard Weather was Approaching;—and in November, (O Marvellous!) it Snow'd.—And then,—a Long tedious Narrative, how they catched Partridges, (not Woodcocks!)

yes, (An Exploit that should be told unto future Generations) Four Men in a Weeks Time killed Six & Twenty.—And then (A terrible Thing happened, as much to be Remembred as the Sicilian Earthquakes:) in December, a Boy had his Feet hurt with the Frost."—And an Hundred more such Curious Events, is this History set off withal. These it seems are the Important Matters, that are most worthy of a Room in History. A Church-History furnished, as aforesaid, has only Trivial Matters for you!

But I shall be truly guilty of Trivial Matters, if I make thus free with the Patience of the Reader; and I shall only detain him from far Better Matters, if I go on to Answer the Rest of this Mans Impotent Cavils at a Work, for which after all, I have little to say but this! That it is a well meant Essay to do Some Good in the World; And, if the World will not Accept it, I am not at all Disappointed: The Essay is made, and, surely, my Judgment is with the Lord, and my Work is with my GOD!

Nevertheless, Concerning the Work of him who thus turns aside, I owe so much Duty to Truth, and Service to Men, as to let the World be Apprised of it, That as Antonius Augustinus Affirms of Guevara, who was Historiographer to the Emperour Charles V, *Ea Comminiscitur quae nec visa nec Audita mortalibus:* He is always Inventing things that no Mortal but himself ever dream't of; This I do affirm concerning this Historiographer to Sir Some body else; He is for History another Guevara. And I do here Publickly make this Declaration;

In Reading Eighty six Pages of what this Wretched and worse than Careless Writer has given us about New-England, I noted down with my Pen, the more Gross, Evident, and Notorious Fals[e]hoods—which I Observed in it, Omitting many lesser matters which cannot be Justified: And upon casting up the Number, of these Fals[e]hoods I found them to be above the Number of Eighty-seven. These Fals[e]hoods are many of them the more Inexcusable, because the History of New-England which he decries with so much Foolish Malignity, had in those very points given him a Truer Information. And for many of them, tis Impossible for him to find any Author, but his own Romantic Brain. O Palaephatus,[59] Thou hast nothing so Incredible. Unhappy Collection! In which there are so often more Lyes than Pages! Miserable Age! How do thy Historians put upon thee!

I suppose this is that Oldmixon, who wrote a play ca[l]led, *Amyntes,* whereof the late Writer of, The History of the more Celebrated Play-Writers, has left this upon lasting Record; *It met with Ill Success.* And it is a pity, he should Succeed any better in Writing of

English Empires. I am not alone in my Complaints of this Miserable Romancer, who even in a[n] Old Irish Family of Quality would scarce have been thought worthy to Supply the Office of a Story-Teller. The Ingenious Beverly in his Well-Composed *History of Virginia,*[60] Declares that he found Oldmixon's Account of that Country (just as I found his Account of New-England) so very Faulty, that he laid aside all thoughts of Correcting it; it being Bad beyond all Possibility of Amending it. He Stigmatizes him as a *Faithless and a Fruitless Historian;* And says, *It would make a Book Larger than his own to Expose his Errors*[.] And indeed, as he has dealt with New-England and with Virginia, so his Dealings with New York are such, that when any Gentleman of that Province will Please to Oblige their Country with a True History of it, he will certainly join with Us, in just Castigations upon such a Wretched Scribbler. But I have now done with him!

Reader, I am Heartily Sorry, that thou shouldest find such a Creature Chained at the Porch; when thou art Entring into a Structure, where Thirty Four Articles like so many Apartments, will afford thee, I hope, some agreeable Entertainment; My *Parentalia* will be the Banquet unto which thou hast here my Invitation.

Let us lose no more Time; There are some REMARKABLES Waiting for us.

REMARKABLES
of
Dr. Increase Mather.

Article I.
The SUBJECT of the History.

The Church of God is now to be Entertained with an History of a MAN, whose Life had in it many Memorable Things, which are Worthy to be Recorded and Reported, and have the Memory of them kept alive, by a more Qualified Historian, than he whose Pen is now Employ'd upon it. But if since the Days of Josephus, the World has more than once allow'd an Eminent Person to Write his Own Life; and better Men than a Cardan, even a Junius, an Hall, a Baxter, to say nothing of a Thuanus, have unexceptionably done it; (an Austin too has e'en almost done so:) and had a Goodwin and an Owen done so, we had been furnished with some Antidote against some of the Lies, that Croak in our English Chronicles;[61] Most certainly, it may now be allow'd a Son, to Write the Life of his Father. I shall before I have done, find such a Pattern of a Son Writing the Life of his Father; as will raise my Action, if it be at all well done, unto the Honour of being some Reward of a Sons doing so. In the mean time, I think it enough to say, my dear Friend Mr. Matthew Henry did it.[62] I never heard any Blame cast on the Greek Lady, who used her Pen, to tell the Story of her Father, nor does any Body that I know of, blame Nazianzen,[63] for his Panegyric upon his Father; But I might single out him the rather to be Mentioned on this occasion, because the Term of a Patriarch, (afterwards Applied unto an Ecclesiastical Dignity, and Station, which the Gospel knows not, and which Introduced what we all know in the West,) was first Innocently used in an Oration of Nazianzen upon his Deceased Father: and it was with the same Innocency that the very Term was commonly used in the Language of our People, whenever Dr. INCREASE MATHER was at any time in his latter Years Discoursed of.

The Place Distinguished by the Birth of this Eminent Person, was Dorchester, of New-England; the Wilderness where his Father flying with his Family from *the Face of the Dragon,*[64] Arrived Four Years before. The Time was, June the Twenty-first, One Thousand Six Hundred Thirty and Nine. His Father was Mr. Richard Mather; a Reverend and Renoumed [renowned] Minister, (in Lancashire, before the Transplantation to New-England) and one of the greatest Instruments in Explaining and Maintaining those Principles of Evangelical

Piety and Purity and the Congregational Church-Discipline, on which the Churches of this Country were first Established. His Life being Published in the Church-History of this Country, as well as in Clark's Collections,[65] I shall here say no more concerning him.

His mother was Mrs. Katharine Holt; a Gentlewoman Honourable for her Descent; but much more so, for her Vertue; and that for which a Woman is most of all to be Praised. She was a Woman of Uncommon Devotion, and in her Importunate Prayers for this her Son, she (like another Monica)[66] became Twice a Mother to him. She sometimes told her Son, while he was yet scarce more than an Infant, but very much her Darling, That she desired of the Glorious GOD only two Things on his behalf; the one was, The Grace to Fear and Love GOD; the other was, the Learning that might Accomplish him to do Service for GOD; both of which it was her strong Perswasion (She told him) that GOD would bestow upon him. *Child,* said she, *if GOD make thee a Good Christian and a Good Scholar, thou hast all that ever thy Mother Asked for thee.* As the Lad grew up she Taught him, (as her Lemuel)[67] all that was Good. But among her Instructions, it is to be Remembred, That she mightily In[c]ulcated the Lesson of Diligence upon him, and often put him in Mind of that Word, *Seest thou a man Diligent in his Business: He shall STAND BEFORE KINGS; he shall not stand before mean men.*[68] I said, It is to be Remembred; and e're long you'l see the Reason of my saying so. When he was about Fifteen Years Old, she Died Marvellously Triumphing over the Fear of Death, which thro all her Life, she had been Afraid of; and with that Word in her Mouth, *Eye hath not Seen, Ear hath not heard, nor hath entred into the Heart of man, the things which GOD has prepared for them that Love Him.*[69] On her Death-Bed, she Earnestly Exhorted him, to Resolve upon Serving of CHRIST in the Work of the Ministry: and Advised him often to consider on that Promise, *They who turn many to Righteousness, shall shine as the stars forever and ever:*[70] Which left a great Impression upon him; and the Remembrance of the Invaluable Mother that gave him the Advice, was Precious to him all his Days.

If a pretty late Abortion might have Passed for a Birth, it might have been said of this Gentlewoman, she was a Mother of Seven Sons. But without That, and allowing one of the Seven to have so disappeared, the Number of the Sons, which GOD bestow'd on this Happy Pair, amounted unto six: Whereof one Dyed in his Childhood; and Four Proved Useful, and Faithful & Famous Ministers of the Gospel. INCREASE, was the Youngest of them; Whom his Father called so, not with Regard unto any of the Celebrated Names-sakes in Antiquity, whereof tho' there were some no better than they should be, yet One at least, who is mentioned in the Conclusion of the Second Epistle to Timothy, has a good Reputation in the Church of God; but because of the never-to-be-forgotten Increase, of every sort, wherewith GOD favoured the Country, about the time of his Nativity. And if he might have had an Hebrew instead of an English Name, I suppose it must have been a Joseph, which is of the like Significancy. Had he been Indisputably a Seventh Son, yet he would not have Countenanced the Foolish, Profane, Magical Whimsey of the silly People which furnishes the Seventh Son, with I know not what Uncommon Powers; T'was among the Vulgar Errors always derided with him. However, we shall hear of Strange Things done by him, and for him. I am apt to think, some Readers will anon say, *We have seen Strange things to Day.*[71]

Article II.
An Early Conversion to Serious PIETY.

If it might be allow'd unto Dr. More,[72] to say it of himself, *That he had as a Fiery Arrow been shot into the World, and he hoped, he had hit the Mark:* Such an Expectation may be Allow'd now to be raised for Dr. Mather; and we shall see how the Arrow Flies and Shines and Speeds in its Motions.

While he might yet but pass for a Namesake to *Matherellus,* he was a Lad, that Lov'd his Play well enough; and yet there was no Lad in the School of his Age that could hold pace with him for his Book: He was (with his Brother Eleazar who was two Years Older than he) Admitted into the College at the Age of Twelve. After he had Lived about a Year at the Colledge, his Parents fearing that some things there might not well suit his Weakly Constitution, (for so they took it:) and willing to have him under a more than Ordinary Inspection and Instruction, sent him to Live with the Famous Mr. Norton,[73] at Ipswich; and with him he removed unto Boston A. C. 1653. continuing several Years a Pupil under him.

He had been hitherto, a Lad (tho' free from any Scandalous Outbreakings of Immorality, yet) nothing more than outwardly Moral; One *Walking in the Vanity of his Mind;*[74] and a Stranger to the Dispositions of Serious Piety; one Alienated from the Life of GOD, and Unmindful of the Great Work and End, which they that Live unto God, must have their Mind above all things concerned about. But the Glorious GOD having made him a Chosen Vessel, and intended him for His Instrument in Turning many to Righteousness, made an Early Siezure on him, and betimes took him under the

Sanctifying Operations of His Holy SPIRIT. That Sincere and Thorough Turn to GOD, and Righteousness, was now Produced [in] him, which made a Conspicuous Change upon him, and fixed him in the Ways of PIETY all the rest of his Days: Yea, the Work, diverse from the Life of Nature, when it came to the Age of Threescore Years and Ten, so far was it from Enfeebled and Impaired, that it was then in its brightest Vigour, and most near unto Perfection. The Words of our Famous Perkins,[75] will be a very Agreeable Preface to what we are going to be Entertained withal. "It is meet, that they who are to Convert others, should be Effectually Converted themselves. John must first Eat the Book, and then Prophesy. The Ministers of the Gospel must first themselves Eat the Book of GOD; which is indeed done, when they are not only in their Minds Enlightened, but their Hearts are Mollified, and brought into Subjection to the Word of CHRIST. Unless CHRIST be thus Learned Spiritually and Really, Divines will speak of the Word of GOD, as Men Speak of Riddles, and as Priests in former times said their Matins, when they hardly knew what they said." But now Behold, our Mather, under the Work which was to fit him for Service here, and for Heaven hereafter!

I shall chuse to give his own Relation of it.

"The great Care of my Godly Parents, was to bring me up in the Nurture and the Admonition of the Lord; Whence I was kept from many Visible out-breakings of Sin, which else I had been Guilty of; and whence it was, that I had many good Impressions of the Spirit of GOD upon me; even from my Infancy. Nevertheless, I Swam quietly in a Stream of Impiety and Carnal Security for many Years together, till it Pleased the Lord in the Year 1654. in Mercy to Visit me with a sore Disease, which was Apprehended to be the Stone: out of which (perhaps the Strangury) I was quickly Recovered. For this Happy Sickness I have many a time blessed the Lord; and I hope, I shall Bless him forever. For He made it the Means of the first Saving Awakenings of my Soul. I was brought now to have Real Thoughts of Death, and see Eternity before my Eyes; And then I could Remember what I had many a time heard from the Word of GOD, concerning such Sins as I had not yet thoroughly Repented of. After I was Recovered, the Arrows of GOD still stuck fast in my Heart, and I was followed with sore and grievous Troubles in my Mind for several Months together; that what in the World to do with myself I knew not: But the Terrors of GOD were so heavy upon me, that I Resolved I would no more Live in any known Sin; and Examining my own Heart, I could not find any Sin, which I was Heartily willing to part with: And I set upon the Practice of Duty, and that Constantly, and that in Secret Devotions too, which before these Distresses of my

Soul, I had not made Conscience of. Nevertheless my Wounded Conscience Remained with me; and GOD set my Sins in Order before me, and brought unto my Remembrance many Sins that I had forgotten, with all their Circumstances and Aggravations. He shewed me the Vanities of my Childhood, and made me to Possess the Iniquities of my Youth, in such a manner that my Heart sometimes was even Sinking and Dying at the sight of it. I resolved, that I would Afflict my Soul, and seek unto GOD, by Fasting as well as by Praying, that He would Pardon all the Sins that were brought unto my Remembrance, and all the other Sins that I had been Guilty of. This course I took, (at Dorchester, shutting myself up in my Fathers Study, when he was gone abroad upon a Public Occasion, and not to Return for a Day or Two:) and I wrote down those Particular Sins which lay most of all upon my Conscience, and spread them before the Lord in Secret, after the manner of Hezekiah Spreading the Blasphemy of Rabshakeh[76] before the Lord; and I begged of GOD, that he would Pardon them. At this time I thought with myself, that if all the World were mine, I would freely part with it, to have my Hard Heart taken away from me: And I Pleaded hard with GOD that Promise, which says, *That He will take away the Heart of Stone, and give an Heart of Flesh.*[77] But I still thought, my Heart was as hard as a Stone. Thus my Soul Continued in the New Birth; And very sore were the Pangs of it. Sometimes I was afraid, I was Guilty of the Unpardonable Sin. But upon Discours[e] with my Father about the Nature of that Sin, I became Satisfied, and found that I had never been Guilty of the Great Transgression. And I thought my Sins were too Great to be Pardoned. But Reading a Book of Mr. Hooker's, Entituled, *The Doubting Soul drawn to Christ,*[78] I was Induced to believe, That my Sins were Capable of a Pardon, and that the Greatness of Sin could not hinder the Mercy of GOD. (Psal. XXV. 11.) I was brought not to doubt of GOD's Ability to Save and Pardon me. But still I did much doubt of His Willingness to do it. And I was foolishly ashamed to Acquaint any Body with my Troubles; I was loth to let any one know, that *my Iniquities were gone over my Head, and as an heavy Burden too heavy for me:*[79] Till at last, not being Able to hold or bear any longer, the Hand of GOD Pressing me so sore, I Acquainted my Father with some of my Soul-Distresses, and (Living at Boston) I wrote unto him, how it was with me, & Begg'd him to Pray for me. I Resolved upon setting apart another Day, to be Spent in Secret Prayer with Fasting before the Lord; and the Lord made it an Happy Day unto me; A Day I shall never forget while I have any Being! On the Day of our Anniversary Election, the Greatest Anniversary Solemnity of the Countrey, the Scholars which

Boarded at Mr. Nortons, being all Abroad on their Diversions, I took this Opportunity of a Private Chamber; and shutting the Door I spent all the Day, in Pouring out my Complaints unto the Lord. Towards the Close of the Day, being full of Extremity of Anguish in my Soul because of my Sin, it was put into my Heart, that I must go and throw myself down at the Feet of my Saviour, and see whether He would Accept of me or no; Resolving, that if He would Accept of me, then I would be His; but if not, then I would Perish at His Feet. So I came before Him with those Words of Esther, *If I Perish, I Perish.*[80] *Yet,* (I said) *Lord, if it must be so, I am resolved to Perish at the Feet of thy Mercy. It is true, I am a Dog, and indeed unworthy of so much as a Crumb; I have been a great Sinner; Yet I am resolved, I will not Offend any more, but be Thine, and be Thine only, and be Thine forever!* And while I was thus Praying and Pleading, those Words of CHRIST were darted into my Mind, *Him that cometh unto me I will in no wise Cast out:*[81] Which Promise I Pleaded with the Lord. After that, I had some Comfortable Perswasion that my Sins were Pardoned, and that the Lord would shew me Mercy. And thus I went on Comfortably and Walked with GOD! But after some time, Mr. Norton shewed, That a Man might Forsake his Sins, and have been in some Sorrow of Heart for them, and yet not be truly Converted unto GOD. This Word stuck deep into me; And I was afraid, that though I had been in Unspeakable Sorrow for my Sin, and thence had Forsaken it, yet my Conversion might not be Sound. But then, hearing my Father Preach on that, *The whole have no need of a Physician, but the Sick,*[82] I thought the Sermon was Preached wholly for myself. My Father shewing, That where there was New and True Obedience, and where the Heart was Changed from the Love of Sin to the Love of God, it Argued Conversion; Examining myself, I thought it was so with me. My Father also Answered a Scruple that was in my Heart: For I feared, my Faith was not Right, because it was not so much some Word Preached, but Affliction that was the first means of my more Effectual Awakening. He shew'd how the Conversion of Menasseh[83] was Accomplished. Sometime after this, Mr. Mitchel[84] Preaching on Joh. I. 47. *Behold, An Israelite indeed:* He Pres[s]ed much to Self-Examination! Laying down several Characters of Sincerity: As, When GOD in CHRIST is become the Rest of the Soul; And when there is no known Sin Lived in, or Duty Neglected; And when the Heart is for GOD Chiefly, Wholly, Universally. I set myself upon Serious Examination by these Marks, and found that my Heart went along with the Word. So I went on cheerfully in the Ways of GOD; And if in any thing I have been Overtaken with a Fault, the Lord has given me to see it, and Mourn for it, and Turn from it."

O Nicodemus,[85] don't Laugh and Scoff at these things. This Fanaticism, as you call it, Verily, tis That which brings into the Kingdom of GOD! Such a Thing there is, as Regeneration, and a thing it is of the Greatest Consequence in the World, though you should not find the Term in the Dictionary.

Behold, the Preparation of the Sanctuary, with which a Young Man was Prepared for the doing of Good Work about the House of his GOD! Young Men who rush into the Evangelical Ministry, taking it up only as a Trade which they are to Live by, while they have no Experience of a Sanctification for as well as by the Truth upon them; what are they but the Miserables to whom (as in the Fable of Origen)[86] the Sixteenth Verse of the Fifteenth Psalm, is the first of the Texts which might justly occur unto them to be Preach'd upon! The Words of Dr. Joseph Woodward,[87] Writing an Account of his Excellent Father, are not Unworthy to be Cited for the Period. *That Mouth ought to be well Purified with the Coals of the Altar, which is to be the Mouth of the People unto GOD! And that Breast ought to be Purified seven times, which is to bear the Names of the People of GOD in the Presence of GOD, and turn away the Wrath of GOD from them, through the Lord Jesus Christ, the Chief Shepherd. Until this step be made Good in any Church, there will be Infinite Disorders, and no Effectual Reformation.*

Seventy Years after the Good Work thus begun upon him, Dr. Mather caused his Grand-sons to Transcribe this Relation of it, and he made the Perusal of it, and the Remembrance of this his Early Consecration to GOD, a Rich Cordial to him, in his Lingring Passage through the Valley of *the Shadow of Death*,[88] which he was then called unto.

Article III.
First Appearances.

When the Year Arrived, wherein he should have Proceeded Batchelour of Arts, there was for I know not what Reasons of State, an Order Procured, That the Class whereto he belonged, & some others also, should be detained a good part of a Year longer at the College, than of right thcy should have been. This gave so great a Dissatisfaction, that no fewer than Seventeen of the Scholars withdrew from the College without any Degree at all; Some of whom nevertheless proved afterward very Considerable in the Service of the Churches. However the Father of this Young Man (though greatly Troubled, as diverse others of the Overseers were, at this Hardship on the Students,) would not have him take his Name out of the College-Register, which had been done by others. And when he afterwards Travelled with a Testimonial, which Expressed the Year of his Admission, and not of his Graduation, and elsewhere Claimed the Next-Degree, he found some Reward of his Patience. In the Year 1656. he took his First Degree; At which time the Praesident, who was deep in the Dark Principles with which the Stagyrite[89] has for many Ages Tyrannized over Humane Understanding, upon a Dislike of the Ramaean Strains[90] in which our Young Disputant was carrying on his Thesis, would have cut him Short; but Mr. Mitchel publickly Interposed, *Pergat, Quaeso, nam-doctissime disputat.*[91] But in the Year, 1657. he took a Greater; For on his Birth-Day, he Preached his First Sermon, at a Village belonging to Dorchester. And on the next Lords-Day he Preached in his Fathers Pulpit at Dorchester: When the whole Auditory were greatly Affected with the Light and Flame, in which the Rare Youth Appear'd unto them: Especially was his Father so, who could scarce Pronounce the Blessing, for the Tears which from the Blessing he had himself now so Sensibly Received, he was thrown into.

Article IV.
A Voyage to Europe; With various Occurcences [Occurrences] in Several parts of it.

At this Time, his Eldest Brother, Mr. Samuel Mather, (that great Man, whose Life makes a very considerable Figure in the *Magnalia Christi Americana,*) being one of the Principal Ministers in Dublin, wrote unto his Father, to Encourage his [Increase's] going over unto him. He had a strong Inclination that way; and Obtained his Fathers Acquiescence in it. At his going away, his Venerable Father Wept over him abundantly, (and the Son also did not want for Tears on the Occasion) and with much Solemnity Blessed him, and Advised him to Remember his own Sermon which he had Preached the Lords-Day before; adding, *That if he Heard well of him, and if he Proved Faithful to CHRIST, the Joy of it would lengthen out his Life*, who was now Sixty One Years of Age. At his going off, many Gracious and Generous People in Dorchester, Assisted him with Private Presents, for his Voyage; of whose Names and Gifts he kept an Ingenuous Record, which afterwards he sent unto his Father, with desires that the Thanks of both might be returned unto them. At this time, taking his leave of our Incomparable Mitchel, he had this Advice from him for his Farewel; *My Serious Advice to you is, that you keep out of Company, as far as Christianity, and Civility, and Occasions will give you leave; take it from me, The Time Spent in your Study you will generally find Spent, most Profitably, most Comfortably, & most Accountably.* Father Austin would no doubt have given the same Advice, with whom it was a Maxim, *Non erit bonus Clericus qui non fuit Bonus Monachus.*[92] When our SAVIOUR would make One a Good Speaker, He first of all *takes him aside from the Multitude.*[93]

He sail'd from New-England, July 3. 1657. and in Five Weeks reached England. On August 24. he went from London for Lancashire: Where his Fathers old Friends received him, with a Singular and Mutual Satisfaction. In September, he Sailed from Liverpool to Dublin, and in Twenty four Hours arrived there. His Brother, who had not seen him for Seven Years, found it Necessary to be Convinced by the Letters he brought with him, and by Questions of Infallible Discovery, that he was indeed what he was. But now he became also as a Father to him: And on his Advice he Entred his Name in Trinity-College. In October he fell Sick of the Measles; at which very time, his Brother Eleazar, with whom he had always been brought up, as with a Twin-Brother, lay Sick of the same Disease, at a Thousand Leagues Distance from him: And the Month after, the Small-Pox Arrested him, from which it Pleased GOD Graciously to Recover him. In the Year, 1658. June 24. When he was Nineteen Years of Age, he Proceeded Master of Arts in Trinity-College; having first Performed the Exercises required by the Statutes of that University. The Proctor & some of the Fellows, who were Prelatically Disposed, gave him all the Discouragement they could, or durst; because of his being what they called, A Praecisian.[94] Nevertheless the Scholars were so Pleased with the Wit and Sense and Polite Learning brill[i]ant in his Exercises, that they Publickly Hummed him; which being a Complement that he had never heard Paid unto any one before, at first had like to have given too much Surprise unto him, All the Seriously and Piously Disposed Scholars in the College Loved him; And none more than the Memorable Doctor Winter, who was the Provost of the College, and who had a Son (Mr. Josiah Winter) that was unto him as a Jonathan unto his David.[95] By the Influence of the Provost, he was chosen a Fellow of the College: but he did not Accept it. Motions came to him from diverse Places, to come and Preach the Gospel unto them; and the Lord-Deputy and Council particularly Assigned him to Marahfelt; Whither being on his Travel, he was taken so very Sick on the Road, that he was forced back to Dublin. The Irish Air proved so Disagreeable to his Constitution, that he resolved for England; though the Lord-Deputy very kindly assured him, That he should not go over to England for want of Encouragement in Ireland, while he should be in any Power there. I will take the Occasion to say: This was that Admirable Man, the Lord Henry Cromwel, who in the time of his Government acquitted himself with so much Wisdom and Justice, and Goodness, and a Conduct so Unexceptionable, that when he Voluntarily retired unto his own Estate in England, upon the Changes coming on, he was not known to have one Personal Enemy in the World.[96] Mr. Mather had also an Invitation to Sedwells in Exon, (Procured by another Elder Brother[,] Mr. Nathanael Mather, then a considerable Minister in those Parts,) by which his resolution for England, were Confirmed: Where he Arrived in July. 1658.

At London, he became Acquainted with that Man of a Thousand, Mr. John How, who was then a Chaplain to the Lord-Protector; and not only then, but also Thirty Years after, gave to Mr. Mather such a Character of that Mighty Man, as was altogether the Reverse of what some Histories and Chronicles, have given of him. He now perswaded Mr. Mather to lay aside his purpose for Sedwells, and go to Great Torrington in Devonshire, where he had formerly himself Resided and Laboured. So he spent the following Winter there, Preaching the Gospel to a great Assembly and with a great Acceptance; only he spent One Month with his Brother Mr. Nathanael Mather, who was then a Preacher greatly Admired at Barnstable. On the Death of the Lord-Protector, Mr. How returned unto his Old People at Great Torrington; At which time Colonel Bingham, then Governour of Guernsey, sent him an Invitation to become a Chaplain unto the English Garrison there. He went thither in April, 1659. where he Preached every Lords-Day in the Morning at the Castle, in the After-noon at the Town, called Peters-port, where many of the French people who understood English, were his Auditors. Here he set himself to do good; And particularly, Observing the Lords-Day to be much profaned, he Preached on the Fourth-Commandment, with such Power and Success, that it Produced a considerable Reformation in the Island.

It was not long before his Friends in England pressed his return thither. A Church in Sandwyche sent him an Invitation with all their Names unto it; requesting him to Accept the Pastoral Charge of them. This he Declined for some Reasons; whereof one was, That the Congregational Church in the City of Glocester, where that Excellent Man Mr. James Forbes was now shining, procured for him a Legal Title to a place called, St. Maries. Thither *He that holds the Stars in his Right Hand*,[97] brought him in December, 1659. And there he

Preached in the Forenoon at St. Maries; in the Afternoon at the Cathedral.

He was willing to have settled there [Glocester, England]. But he saw a Change of Times at the Door. Yea, as Young as he was, he then very Publickly Declared, (from Rev. XI. 2.) that *further Sufferings for the Faithful Witnesses of CHRIST were to be looked for.* In this View he returned unto Guernsey; where he had not been many Weeks before King Charles II. came in; And, what came in with him, every Body knows. When the King was Proclaimed, he openly Refused and Rebuked the Paganizing Rite of Health-dringing [drinking], which threatened on that occasion to drown all Sobriety: And anon, the King himself being by those whom he had Ensnared, Prevailed withal to Publish a Proclamation against that Practice, it Proved an Advantage unto this Young Reprover, and put some stop to Insults upon him. At this time, the matchless General Monk, sent a Demand upon all Commission Officers in those parts, to Subscribe a Paper, wherein they were to Declare, *That they Believed the Times NOW were and would be Happy.* But while some Old Men Dreamed Dreams, this Young Man saw a true Vision of the Times. He Declined a Subscription to the Vain Paper; and thereupon the Deputy-Governour, who greatly Valued him and Admired him, did so too. The Chaplain of Jersey, (one Ashton) who had the Character of a Naughty Person, Informed the Duke of Albemarle, that the Reason why there did not come such Complements from Guernsey as there did from Jersey, was, Mr. Mather being there. The Duke was violently Incensed, and in his Rage told the Governour, (Colonel Weaver, who was then at London,) that Mr. Mather should be sent for. But the Governour, though he was one of Monks appointing, and one that Mr. Mather had never seen, yet had his Heart so Disposed from above, that by his Means the Threatened Storm was diverted.

While he was in Guernsey, the Salary Allow'd him was One Hundred and Twenty Pounds Sterling a Year: and every one thought, he would now lose his Arrears, which were above One Hundred Pounds: the rather, because one Sharp, a Vile Hypocrite and Apostate (who had once been a Member of Mr. Griffiths Church) was become the Deputy-Governour, and Secretly did him all the Mischief he could, and returned the Muster-Roll without his Name in it. But when the matter was brought before the Commissioners at London, (where one Difficulty Pretended was, Crescentius, forsooth, could not be the same with Increase!) a Gracious Providence ordered it, that one Monsieur Martin, a Deacon of the French Church at Peters-port, hearing of the Question made about it, Appeared and Affirmed, that unto his most certain Knowledge, Mr. Mather was Officiating in Guernsey at the time then spoken of; and offered his Oath unto it. The Issue was, that this Faithful Servant and Seeker of GOD, was paid his Arrears before any other Man belonging to the Garrison. I will by'nd by [by and by] tell, of what Use this Occurrence was unto him.

Sr. Hugh Pollard now being made the Governour of Guernsey, Mr. Mather must either Conform to the Revived Superstitions in the Church of England, or leave the Island. So he took his leave of that Island, March 1. 1660. and the next Day came to Weymouth. For four Months he abode partly in Weymouth, partly in Dorchester, Preaching in many places, where he was desired; yea three or four times in a Week; but without any Maintenance, or any Recompence. His Friends in Dorset-shire, much press'd his Continuance with them there; but he foresaw what was a coming. He was offered a Living of no less than Four Hundred a Year, if he would Conform, and Read the *Common-Prayer.* This he could not; he durst not. Several Gentlemen urged him to Travel with them, into the Continent of Europe; And Mr. Samuel Bellingham obtained a Promise from him to Accompany him in such a Travel: But a sudden Emergency drove that Gentleman over to Holland, before the Time agreed for, which Released him from his Engagement.

In fine, all things Conspired for the moving of the Star, to Illuminate the Western Haemisphaere.

Article V.

A Return to New-England; and the Station assigned there.

Mr. Mather hoped for some shelter to be had, and service to be done, in his own Country, and proposed what once there had been little Hope for; To see his Invaluable Father before he Died. Wherefore on June 29[.] 1661. he sailed from Weymouth, in a Vessel Bound for Newfoundland. He arrived there in August: And staying the[r]e no more than Ten Days, a Vessel bound for New-England Opportunely Presented, in which he reached thither by the first of September. He came to Dorchester, very unexpected on a Saturday Evening; But the Tears of Joy mutually poured out, at his first Interview wi[t]h his Father!—His brother Eleazar was also just come thither, from a Remote place where he was now S[t]ationed in the Country; And the Comforted Old Patriarch, sat Shining like the Sun in Gemini, and hearing his two Sons, in his own Pulpit entertain the People of GOD, with Performances that made all People Proclaim him, *Art Happy Father.*

He had now Invitations to as many places as there are Signs for the Sun in the Zodiac, all Coveting of him, as one of the Best Gifts that could be bestow'd upon them. In the first Winter after his Arrival, he Preached Alternately the one Lords-Day with his Father in Dorchester, the other to the New Church in the North-part of Boston, which anon swept away the prize from the Twelve Competitors.

On March 6. 1662. he came into the Married State; Espousing the only Daughter, of the Celebrated Mr. John Cotton;[98] in Honour to whom, he did (as Dr. Lightfoot had before done in Honour to a Patron of the same Name) call his First-born Son by the Name of COTTON. She was a Gentlewoman of much Goodness in her Temper; A Godly, an Humble, and a Praying Woman, and one that often set apart whole Days for Prayer and Secret Interviews with Heaven. When she Died, which was Fifty two Years after, her Eldest Son did as much as Justice to her Memory, as her Inhibitions of all Embellishments upon her Character would Permit him, and Published it under the title of, *Maternal Consolations.*[99] But of him, there is no more to be Written. Tis the Writer.

Their second Son, was Mr. Nathanael Mather, who Died at the Age of Nineteen, an Instance of Uncommon Attainments in Religion and Erudition: deserving the Epitaph upon his Grave at Salem; *The Ashes of an hard Student, a good Scholar, and a great Christian.* His Life, Entituled, *Early Piety Exemplified,*[100] has had the Respects of three or four Editions paid unto it; and this Addition thereto, that no little part of the first Edition was bought by that Good Man, Mr. Philip Henry to give away; and the second Edition had a Praefatory and Panegyrical Attestation of that Bright Man Mr. Matthew Mead set before it.

Their third Son was Mr. Samuel Mather, at this time a Faithful and Useful Minister of the Gospel at Witney in Oxford-shire: A Writer of several Valuable Treatises; among which, his, *Vindication of the Doctrine of the Trinity;* and his, *Vindication of the Deity of the Holy Spirit;* and his, *Vindication of the Sacred Scriptures;*[101] do shine with a particular Lustre, and challenge a Room and a Name for him, among, The Blessings of the Age. They had also Seven Daughters, all of which, Liv'd to be Mothers, except one which Died in its Infancy.

And they had herewithal that Rare Felicity, of Hearts made glad with Hopes, that they saw all their Children Chusing the Things that Please GOD, and laying hold on His Covenant.

The North Church in Boston, had a Struggle of diverse Years, before they could Obtain a Conquest over his Aversion, to the Consummation of his Desired Settlement: Which was Principally Occasioned by some Views he had of greater Service elsewhere. At last, the Brethren of the Church kept a Day of Supplications unto Him who has all Hearts in His hands, to Pray that GOD would Incline him, and Perswade him, to Accept the Invitation which they had given him. From This Day, he felt another Biass on his Mind, and soon Complied with their Desires; and on May 27, 1664. he did with a great Solemnity, wherein his Father Publickly gave him his Charge, Accept the Pastoral Care of the Flock; with which, (Them and their Children,) he Continued Serving the Lord, with many Tears and Temptations, and keeping back nothing that was Profitable for them, for more than Threescore Years together.

Article VI.
Grievous Temptations Conquered.

Temptations were just now Mentioned. And the first Thing I will now Observe, shall be This. As when the Danite Hero was first entring upon his Public Actions, a Lion roared upon him:[102] So Mr. Mather had not long made his entrance upon his Public Services, before he felt singular Assaults from the Lion which goes about Seeking whom to fall upon. Our SAVIOURS Ministry begun with a Storm of Grievous Temptations upon Him; And many of His Faithful and Useful Servants have in their Condition, this Conformity unto His: In the Beginning of their Ministry they suffer Grievous Temptations from their Grand Adversary. Mr. Mather did so. The more Early Years of his Ministry were Embittered unto him, with such Furious & Boisterous Temptations unto Atheism, as were Intolerable to him and made him Cry out like Peter in the Tempest.[103] Vile Suggestions and Injections, tending to question the Being of the GOD, whom he Fear'd, and Lov'd, and was continually Praying to, where shot at him as Fiery Darts from the Wicked one, and caused him to go Mourning because of the Oppression of the Enemy. His Holy Soul suffered an Unutterable Anguish from this Blast of the Terribles upon him[.] From his Vehement Abhorrence of these Thoughts, and from his Groans for a Deliverance from them, and from the Cries of a Chast Soul under a Rape, which he made, when his Pious Mind was Affronted with them, (as well as from the Time and Way of the Vexations,) it was Plain, They were none of his own; they were plainly of a Satanic Original. But yet, the Trouble they gave him, was what Satan intended him; Inexpressible and Insupportable.

His great SAVIOUR indeed, who forever holds all the Fiends of Darkness in a Chain, had Wise and Good Ends in Permitting them to bring such a Fiery Tryal upon him: And no doubt, This among the rest. He was a Young Man every where Admired, and Applauded, and Accepted, and Flock'd after, and Uncommon Regards were from all Quarters paid unto him. Now these Colaphizations[104] were of notable Advantage, to prevent all undue and unsafe Elations; and keep him Humbly Wondring that the People of GOD should have any esteem for a Person, who felt in his Heart Cursed Motions towards that Horrible Thing, A Denial of the GOD that is above. I cannot Learn, that under these Temptations he found much Benefit by Disputing with them: though he took Delight in Reading Fotherby's *Atheomastix*,[105] and others who have shewn what they could Speak on GOD's behalf. Indeed, it puts too much Respect upon a Devil, to Argue and Parley with him, on a Point which the Devil himself Believes and Trembles. It is too much of Complement, if not Complaisance, unto Atheism, to Pour in Elaborate Confutations upon it. When we prove any thing, we prove something that is less known by something that is more known. But is there any Thing more known, than the Existence of that FIRST CAUSE, who in forming the Spirit of Man within him, has left upon our Spirit an Impression of a Return to Him: and be sure then for an Owning of him? Tis a First Principle; and we are assoon Conscious of GOD, as Conscious to our Self. Mr. Mather found the Cudgel, the most Proper Logick for these Temptations; and the best way of Answering them, to be by Rejecting them and Repelling them with all Possible Detestation as Infinitely Unworthy to be listned to: and with a most flat Contradiction of them, to form Thoughts that still carried in them, the devoutest Acknowledgements of a GOD, and Applications to Him. Thus he tired out the Adversary; and the Devil being so Resisted, anon fled from him. As to a Rational Satisfaction, the most that he received was this; As he Employ'd Incessant Prayers on this Occasion, so the Evident and Marvellous Answers of his Prayers, which he had seen in some other matters, did also help to bring him some Answers unto these. The Glorious GOD in some Strange Instances, (and the Relief of his Guernsey Distress was one of them,) had Enabled him to say, *This Poor Man Cried, & the Lord Heard him:*[106] And for him now to doubt the Existence of a GOD, whom he had found so nigh and so kind unto him,—it appeared unto him such a Monstrous Ingratitude, that he could not be Guilty of it! Yea, once I find him, as one Resolved upon throwing every Stone he could find, at the Head of the Dragon, recording such a Passage as this. *Being thoughtful about some heavy Afflictions upon me, I resolved that I would seek Help from GOD. This very thing serves me as an Help against Atheism; For if we have a Conscience, which in a Time of Distress, Directs us to go unto GOD for Help, surely, there must be a GOD for us to go to;* [Jer. II. 27.] In Remembrance of the old Wormwood & Gall, he much more than half an Hundred Years after, Published a little Discourse entituled, *There is a GOD in Heaven.*[107]

Article VII.
Further Temptations Encountred.

But since we are upon Temptations, here will be Perhaps as fit a place as any, to Introduce more of those things whereof Luther would say, They made up, with Meditation and Supplication, the Three Things which a Finished Divine must find his most Instructive and Effectual Tutors. The Temptations which we have spoken of, were no sooner gone off, but another sort were brought on, to keep the Servant of GOD in a Continual Warfare, and Enduring what a good Souldier of JESUS CHRIST must be call'd unto. The Churches of New-England are not the only Reformed Churches, that have been Chargeable with the Crime of Ingratitude unto their Ministries[.] The French Synods complained of it, as a Sin too Rife among them; Yea, they Declared, that the Ingratitude of People refusing to Contribute unto the Subsistence of their Ministers, threatned the Churches with a Total D[i]ssipation; which, alas, is now come upon them. No sooner was Mr. Mather got under the Engagements of a Settlement with his People, which they esteemed Sacred and Unreleasable and Indissoluble, but Presently they that had the Ordering of these things grew very slack in Answering their Engagements to support him with a Tolerable Maintenance. The Deacons of the Church were not Spirited like some that have Suc[c]eeded them; and the Leaders of the more Honest People also, were Men of a low, mean, sordid Spirit[.] By which means he was Reduced unto Wants and Straits, and such hard Circumstances as ought by no means to be Related, and if they were could scarce be Credited. For one of his Education, and Erudition, and Gentlemanly Spirit, and Conversation, to be so Creepled and kept in such a Depressing Proverty!—But, O thou Angel of the Church, We know who said, *I know thy Poverty, but thou art Rich!*[108]—In these Distresses, it was to little purpose for him to make his Complaint unto Man! If he had, it would have been basely Improved unto his Disadvantage. He writes upon it, *I had no other way, but to go unto the Lord JESUS; and make my Moan before Him, who I knew was willing that I should be Supported in His Service.* By these Temptations there was a strong Trial made, of his Patience, and of his Prudence, and of the Principles which Acted him in his Ministry; but being tried he came forth as Gold. He had offers of a Settlement, where he might have mended his Condition in the World; But he generously refused them, from a Fear lest the Way of Truth should be Evil-Spoken of. In the mean time, it was a wonder, that by having a Spirit broken with Unkind Usages, he was not perfectly killed; or at least, unhinged and unfitted for the Duties of his Ministry. It is a Reflection which I find falling from his Pen under this Oppression; "Little do People think h[o]w much they Wrong themselves, when they have Ministers among them, whose Hearts are set upon nothing but their Studies, and Spiritual Employments, that nevertheless shall not be Suitably Provided for, as to their outward Subsistence, and that Food and Raiment which while on Earth, they need as well as other Men." But now, see what can be Done, and what Born, and how, by PIETY Assisted from Above! See after what manner Unkind Usages are to be Encountered with! It may be of s[o]me use unto many Holy Witnesses of the Lord Prophesying in Sack-cloth, to Read the Conduct of this their Fellow-Sufferer under these Grievous Temptations, as I find himself Relating it.

On a certain Day he wrote: "Perplexed and Hindred much in my Studies, with the Sad and Sinking Consideration of my outward Wants; and that though they put me on more Expense and more Labour than formerly, yet there is not an Heart in Sundry of my People to consider it. The Lord Help me through my Temptations, enable me to Finish His Work, and hasten me to Himself.—Nevertheless, there are some of them that Respect me Dearly, and do much for me."

On another Day, thus. "Extremely Grieved and Distracted in my Studies, with the Thoughts of my Debts, and the Consideration of my People (some of them) not caring for my deep Sorrows in that Respect. Methinks, I could be Content to be Poor, I care not how Poor, so as I may be in a Capacity to Serve GOD without Distraction. But to be in Debt, to the Dishonour of the Gospel, is a Wounding, Killing Thought to me; Yea, so Grievous as that if it be not Remedied, in a little time it will bring me with Sorrow to my Grave. O Lord JESUS, pitty a Poor, Sinful, Wretched Creature, lest Dishonour come to thy Dear Name."

On another Day, thus. "Spent in Prayer with Fasting in my Study. I closed all with this Resolution. Lord, If thou will provide for me, and Answer my Prayers, I will Love thee, and Thank thee, and Serve thee. And, if thou wilt not Provide for me, I will yet Love thee, and Bless thee, and Serve thee. If thou will cast me off, I will not cast thee off. I deserve that thou shouldest cast me off, but Thou Lord, never Deservedst Ill at my Hands."

On anther Day, thus. "Miserably Perplexed with the sad Thoughts of my Debts, and the Unworthy Spirit, which is in some of my People that have no Heart to Relieve me in these my Sorrows, and that think every thing too much for me. So that I lose (which Kills me) much Precious Time, and am exceedingly hindred in the Work of the Lord. The Scripture Directs Ministers, to shew themselves Patterns of Patience and Long-Suffering. Conscience of that has made me bear thus long. But now I can bear no longer, my Grief is so Extreme. Oh! That the Lord JESUS, who hears my Complaints before Him, would either give an Heart to my People to look after my Comfortable Subsistence among them, or, if He has any further Service for me to do (who Desire Life only that so I may do something for Him who has done so much for me!) remove me to another People, who will take care of me, that so I may be in a Capacity to attend His Work, and Glorify His Name in my Generation; or give me a Sufficiency of Grace, that these Sinking Evils and Discouragements may not Overwhelm me; or, Hasten me to Himself, where no Temptation shall keep me from Serving Him with Freedom of Spirit. O Dear Lord JESUS, For thy Names Sake, Pitty, Hear and Help. Amen, my Lord, and Redeemer, Amen."

After some time of Waiting upon a GOD of Judgment, who was all this time Waiting that He might be Gracious, there arrived a Day, in which he Wrote thus. "This Day pouring out my Complaints into the Bosom of the Lord JESUS, I begg'd of Him, that He would not Punish any of my poor People, because of their Neglects of me, but Pardon them and Bless them; And that He who heard my Complaints before Him, and knew the Sorrows of my Heart, yea, and knew that I was therefore Grieved at my outward Wants, because I was thereby hindred from doing Him Service, and from Glorifying His Name, and the Name of the Father, and because I lose Precious Time, of which I would not lose any Particle, would pitty me when the World would not. After this, my Heart was at Ease; and I Believed, that the Lord JESUS heard me; only I Professed before Him, that I was Content to be Poor, and in Debt, and laid aside as a broken and useless Vessel, if He would have it so; Yea, to be any thing that CHRIST will have me to be. Now I am Satisfied; The Will of the Lord be done!"

And NOW arrived the time of his Deliverance! The Glorious ONE who knew the Works, and the Service and the Patience of this Tempted Man, ordered it, That several Gentlemen of good Estate, and of better Spirit, were become the Members of his Church;

Among whom a Remembrance is particularly due to Sr. Thomas Temple; as fine a Gentleman as ever sat foot on the American strand. These Persons were moved with a very just and generous Concern, when they understood how Unworthily their Meritorious Pastor had been dealt withal, and they took Effectual Care, that it should be so no more. It came to pass, that at length, he found such Filial Usages from his Church, as took away from him all room of Repenting, that he had not under his Temptations Prosecuted a Removal from them. Yea, they Supported his Family, when he, who once could scarce tolerably Cloath himself, made an handsom Appearance in the Courts of KINGS for Four Years together, and often did and got considerable Things for the Support of others that were Necessitous, and even relieved Parsons of the Established Church seeking to him in their Necessities. And in his latter Years, his Church, with a never-to-be-forgotten Gratitude, continued unto him his whole, and a large Salary for several Years together, while he much Intermitted his Publick Labours, and in the last of his Years he wholly ceased from them: And at the same time, they advanced considerably, for Gratuities to Reward the Labours of many Candidates who occasionally Supplied the Pulpit for him. They did also another thing, which will be told, at the End of our story; Yea, wherever this Book shall be Read, what they have done shall be spoken of, with a Memorial of them. It may be, I have been too long upon this Article. And yet, it shall not, it may not go out of my Hands, till I have Observed one thing more upon it; which is, That in the midst of these Distresses, I find him sometimes keeping of Thanksgivings; and the sense of some Sorrows did not so Embitter his mind, as to make him Insensible of the many Comforts which he also Received at the Hands of GOD; and on those Days he drew up Catalogues of the Favours which a Gracious GOD had bestow'd upon him.

Article VIII.
The Diary of a Time-Saver.

The Reader having been entertained with some, and likely to be with more, Passages Transcribed from his Diary, I will before I go a step further, give some Account concerning the Diary, and relate the Intentions and Ingredients of it; Glad, if it may be Directive unto any, with whom, The way of keeping a Diary, may be a matter of some enquiry.

Briefly then; The Diary, which he kept from the time of his Return to the New-English, to the Time of his withdraw to the Heavenly

World, consisted for the most part of none but very Brief Touches, on things which it might be of some Consequence for him afterwards to look upon. A main thing in it, was an Hint in two or three Words, how he spent his Time; and being of the Opinion that Large Records of that matter would be but a Mispence of Time, he would not ordinarily employ more than two or three Words upon it. And for the same cause, he kept not so large Records in his Elder as he did in his Younger Years. He noted sometimes particularly, what Books he Read, and sometimes only more generally Varios Authores. Sometimes he noted only, *Sermon,*—and sometimes added the Subject of it. Sometimes he noted, Visits given but not always, To whom. Sometimes he noted Visits received; but often Complained of the Interruptions he suffered by them. Sometimes he has Pathetically Written, *Eheu, Maximam Diei partem perdidi!*[109] He noted, when and where he Preaced, and who Preached for him, or with him. Sometime[s] he noted Grievances he met withal, which (if the Manes[110] will forgive me,) I would venture to say had better been wholly forgotten. Unto the Diary there belonged Three Articles more, which I think will deserve to make Three Paragraphs in our History.

There shall no more belong to this, but only, the Projection which he formed, for the Spending of his Time; and which he set down in such Terms as these.

"O Dear Lord JESUS; Thou that knowest my Works: Help! Help! Help a poor Creature, I earnestly Beseech thee, so to Improve his Time, as shall be most for thy Glory, the good of thy People, and the Rejoicing of his own Soul, in That Day, when I shall see Thee my Lord, and Speak with Thee Face to Face. Amen! Amen! Amen!

"My Purpose (by Thy Help, O Lord!) is to Spend my Time every Day as followeth:

"I. Day of the Week. Besides my Public Labours, attend Catechising, and personal Instruction in my Family.

"II. A. M. Read Comments. Study Sermon. P. M. Read some Authors. Study Sermon.

"III. A. M. Read Comments. Study Sermon. P. M. Endeavour to Instruct Personally some or other; (at least in the Summer Time.) Read Authors.

"IV. A. M. Read Comments. Study Sermon. P. M. Read Authors. Sermon.

"V. A. M. Read Comments. Study Sermon. After Lecture Endeavour among the Ministers, to Promote what shall be of Public Advantage.

"VI. A. M. Read Comments. Study Sermon. P. M. Read Authors, Sermon.

"VII. Read Comments. Prepare for Sabbath; (Committing Sermons to Memory.)

"Only Allowance must be given for Visitations, and Necesary Avocations, which cannot be foreseen.

"I am not willing to allow my self above Seven Hours in Four and Twenty, for Sleep: but would spend the rest of my Time in Attending to the Duties of my personal or general Calling."

Afterwards he Wrote; "In this Course I continued for some Time, but at last, thro' many unforeseen Things coming in upon me, I was forced to alter the Method of my Studies, as to some Particulars here set down; For I never intended to bind myself unto these Rules any longer than I should find myself capable of Attending thereto, or until I should know a better Method."

Article IX.
HEARTY Piety.

What I said about, the Three Articles, cannot be forgotten.

I am in my Readers Debt, for Three Paragraphs, which the Diary just now mentioned has bound me to; And I will go no further till I Pay what I Owe. Nor can I so well go on to Observe, as I design, the Order of Annal in our Story, till I have done with some Things, that were Incorporated all along into it.

One of them was This. An Heart Serious, was one of the Main Strokes occurring there. When that Great Man, (who might on many Accounts be justly called) Grotius,[111] had his Death Approaching, one asked him, what was the best Advice which one of his great Erudition and great Experience, could leave with a Surviver? His Answer was, *Be Serious.* Dr. Mather was an Uncommon Follower of that good Advice; and though he knew how to be Pleasant in such Company as he might safely use a Facetious and an Innocent Freedom withal, yet he maintained a Serious Temper of mind, and such a Gravity as made all sorts of Persons, wherever he came, to be struck with a Sensible Awe of his Presence, as much as any ever were of a Roman Cato's;[112] Yea, If he Laughed on them, they believed it not. It was commonly thought of him, He was a Man of GOD, and his Countenance was like the Countenance of an Angel of GOD, very Venerable! And it was Commonly said, It was a very Edifying Thing, only to see him in our Public Assemblies; His very Countenance carried the Force of a Sermon with it. And this was not a Forc'd and a Starch'd Appearance, and a Tartuff[113] cover to a mind at the same time abandoned unto Levity: But the Guard which he kept upon his

Heart, and which was an Infallible Effect and Symptom of his having the true Fear of GOD planted there, was that which produced the Serious Aspect which had that Wisdom so shining in it. I cannot say, how many Thousands of Times, I find in his Diary, that Clause concluding the Hints of what he did, and where he was, in the Day; **Heart Serious**[.] By Heart Serious, he meant, an Heart which kept alive a Sense of his having the Eye of GOD upon him, with a Dread of Sinning against the Holy One; and an Heart Proposing an Obedience to GOD; Studious to Know and to Do, the Will of His Heavenly Father; and an Heart in a proper Frame to Entertain, all that the Glorious GOD should order to befal[l] him. When he found his Heart remit in the Vigour of these Dispositions, he Wrote, *Heart Various.* When he found his Heart considerably otherwise than he would have it, with a Sorrowful Heart he Wrote so. Yea, I find this among his other Entries. *Heart in a Serious Frame. till towards Evening, when a Gentleman that made himself too much an Object of Ridicule called me to Visit Sr. Thomas Temple; and by being in Company, though good Company, I lost the Good Serious Frame of my Spirit, and much Precious Time also. It is good, and no more than needs, to be always Watchful.* Anon his Heart became so Established in a due Frame of Piety, that in his latter Years, his Diary left off taking any further Notice of it.

Article X.
Jejunator, or, Days of Devotion.

I Have briefly dispatch'd one of the Promised Articles. The next is to report, that one of the most Copious Entries in the Diary, was upon what concerned the Days of Prayer, and more soaring Interviews with Heaven, which he kept with Fasting (even with Rigid Fasting) usually once a Month, (and sometimes oftner) as part of his Preparation for the Monthly Celebration of the Eucharist. Of which Days I find his Pen once dropping this Testimony, *I would not for all this Worlds Good, be without the Answer of those Prayers!* On these Days, his manner was, one while in Papers wholly assign'd unto that purpose, to note on One Column, *Causes of Humiliation;* on the Adverse Column, *Matters of Supplication.* Afterwards, he entred them, only in his Diary, without any Distinct Columns for them; and he never entred any where else, the like Enumeration, which he always made, of Matters, and Causes, for the Public Days also, which he kept in Conjunction with the People of GOD. And what he did for Fasts, he also did for Thanksgivings: For some such Days he kept also in Secret before the Lord; Affecting himself with the Various Mercies of GOD unto him, and Contriving special Returns of Obedience, wherein he was desirous to Glorify GOD. In these Registers one finds the very Spirit of PIETY in the true Breathings and Pulses of it. But the Public Spirit Conspicuous in them, and his generous concern for others as well as himself, and for the Town, and the Land, and the whole Church of GOD, was highly agreeable to the large Heart which GOD had Crown'd him with.

Besides these Things, he sometimes writ down what Hopes he had of having succeeded in his Prayers, and what Grounds he had for his Hopes. Of this it may be I shall tell you more another Time: At this Time, I will Illustrate it, with Transcribing of only Two or Three Passages.

At one time; "In the close of the Day Especially, my Heart was moved to Believe, that GOD would Accept and Answer my poor Prayers. First, because I drew nigh to Him; Therefore His Blessings will draw nigh to me. Secondly; Because the Things which I asked, and the Ends why I asked them, were for the Glory of GOD: Not for my own Sake, but for GOD's Sake. Thirdly; For the Honour of His Son JESUS CHRIST. Fourthly; Because nothing but my Sins which I this Day Confessed before the Lord, can hinder the Answer of my Prayers; But these cannot hinder, because they are done away in the Blood of CHRIST, who has Loved me, and given himself for me; which I know, for that I feel my Heart Loveth Him. Fifthly; Because there never was any Creature, who did Humbly seek unto the Lord for such Blessings as this Day I Pray'd for, that was denied by Him: And surely I shall not be the First whom GOD will deny! O Blessed forever be my dear GOD in JESUS CHRIST, who heareth Prayer."

At another time. "Some Fervency and Faith in the Performance of the Duties of the Day; so that I now Wait upon the Lord for a Gracious Answer, with a Spirit much Revived. I put the Answer of my Prayers, upon the Sincerity of my Soul before GOD, saying before the Lord, O my GOD, if I do not Sincerely Desire to Glorify thy Name, then Deny my Requests, and let me have no Answer of my Prayers. But if I do in Sincerity Desire to Serve and Glorify Thee, then have Compassion on me, and Deny me not, I pray thee. Upon these Terms let me go either with an Answer, or with a Denial. Therefore GOD will Answer me Graciously in His own Time. O my Soul, Wait thou on the LORD."

How he felt sometimes on these Days, I will Employ but one Passage more, to Intimate.

"May 8. 1672. I set apart this Day to Humble myself in Secret, as for other causes, so in special on the account of the Death of my dear Brother Samuel, the Tidings whereof came lately to me.

"In the Beginning of the Duty, the Lord melted my Heart; especially in the second time of my falling down on my Knees before Him. As I was Praying, that the Lord would Remember the Prayers which my Precious Brother had put up for me, when he was living in the World, and that He would give much of that Spirit unto me, which he caused so Eminently to rest on my now Blessed Brother; as I was thus Praying, my Heart was exceedingly melted, and methoughts, I saw GOD before my Eyes in an Inexpressible Manner, so as that I was Afraid I should have fallen into a Trance in my Study."

Article XI.
An Entrance into the Holiest of all.

I am still in Arrears, for the Diary: and I am thus to Answer them. I remember that Gregory Nazianzen, Speaking of the Prayers, which his Father poured out at the Celebration of the Eucharist, says nothing of a Lifeless Liturgy, but says, *They were Dictated by the Holy Spirit of GOD.* The Prayers made by mine, on the Eucharistical Occasions often were most certainly so! And now and then in the more Early Years of his Ministry, he made a short entry of such Flights as his melted Soul was transported to. You shall have a Scantling.

On a certain Day, he Writes: "I was this Day much Affected in Administring the Supper of the Lord: Especially in the last Prayer, saying, Now Dearest Lord, If ever there were poor Creatures in the World, that had cause to Love and Bless the Lord, we are they! We have done thee Infinite Wrongs; But thou hast forgiven us all those Wrongs, and dealest with us, as with thy Friends this Day. How can we but Mourn for the Wrongs that we have done unto thee! If we had Wronged an Enemy, and that in a small matter, we should be Grieved for it: But we have Wronged the Son of GOD; Wronged our SAVIOUR; Yea, we have killed Him. He had never come to the Cross, had it not been for our Sins, as we are the Elect of GOD. But the Blood that we have shed, has Procured our Pardon; as it did for the Jews that killed Him; So many of them as belonged unto thine Election. Yea, CHRIST Prayed for them, Saying Father, Forgive them! And so thou knowest, He has done for us. CHRIST hath said before thee concerning us, Father, Forgive them! If Children much Offend their Father, yet when any of them come and say, I am sorry for what I have done; I'll do so no more; Father, Be Reconciled unto me! Will not a Father then Forgive them? O our Father, we have sinned against thee; but we are sorry for it, and would do Iniquity no more; Father, Forgive us! Thou knowest our Hearts; Thou knowest that we could be glad if we might never have so much as one sinful Thought in our Hearts, nor Speak so much as one Unprofitable Word more, whilst we Live? Yea, This is the Thing that we would beg of Thee! If ever thou wilt hear the Cries of Poor Creatures, oh! Deny us not this Request. It is, O Lord, Let thy Holy Spirit Sanctify us Wonderfully!"

On another Day, thus. "I was this Day much Affected at the Table of the Lord, saying in Prayer unto Him there; Lord, we shall never Perish! They that Believe on thy CHRIST shall never Perish: And thou knowest, that we Believe on Him. Though [Thou] hast brought us to the Blood of Sprinkling; and therefore thou wilt bring us to JESUS, the Mediator of the New Covenant,[114] and we shall behold His Glory. We shall see our Joseph, our JESUS, in all His Glory, we shall behold our King Solomon, in all His Glory, yea, Solomon in all his Glory was not array'd like our JESUS. We shall see that Glory; yea, sit down with Him on the Throne of His Glory."

On another Day, thus. "I had some Quickenings at the Lords Table; Especially in Praying for much of the SPIRIT of CHRIST, and saying, Lord, we have one Argument to Plead with Thee; and it is a great one; yea, it will be a Prevailing Argument. It is, thy own dear Name, and the Glory of it. If thou will give us much of the Spirit of CHRIST, thy Great Name will then have much Glory from us."

On another Day, thus. "I had something Quickening at the Table of the Lord; Especially in the last Prayer, Saying; O Heavenly Father, and our GOD in our Lord JESUS CHRIST; we have Avouched Thee to be our GOD; And now we know that thou hast Avouched us to be thy People: Because thou hast given us thy Son, and thou wilt with Him give us all things: Father, We humbly expect from thee, that according to thy Covenant, even the New Covenant, thou wilt Forgive us our Iniquities. Such is the Grace of thy Covenant, that thou wilt not Impute our Infirmities to us, if they be our Burden[.] And thou knowest that they are so. We put the Answer of our Prayers upon That, and are willing to be Denied if it be not so. But thou that searchest all our Hearts, knowest that thou hast Created Such a Spirit within us. We are willing to be Delivered from all Sin, and we are willing to yield Holy Obedience to all thy Commands, though how to Perform, we find not. Father, Father, Deal with us as with thy Children."

On another, thus. "Quickened at the Lords Table; Especially in

Praying, that GOD would Remember His Covenant with our Children, saying before the Lord; Lord, Our Fathers, and our Mothers (as for many of us, we may say it) are now in Glory; and thou wilt bring us to be with them; and so thou wilt our Children after us. They, and We, and our Children shall together be Employ'd in thy Praises to all Eternity. In Speaking of This, Tears gushed from me before the Lord. I Trust, Prayer and Faith shall not be in vain. Oh! I have Prevailed, and I have Obtained Mercy for my Children. Amen, Lord JESUS."

On another, thus. "Quickenings at the Lords Table, especially in Praying for our Children, that GOD would Remember His Covenant with them: and saying, O Heavenly Father, Did not JESUS CHRIST make His Soul an Offering for the sins of our Children, as well as our sins? Did not He Dy, for our Children as well as for us? Therefore let thy CHRIST see His Seed; Let our poor Children be Converted unto Thee, that they may Glorify GOD with us in the World that is to come, and World without End."

Indeed the Prayers, and the earnest and mighty Pleadings, with which on the Sacramental Occasions, he commonly Wept before the Lord, on the behalf of his own, and his peoples Off-spring, were such as carried Evident Marks on an Heavenly Afflation[115] in them.

In his latter Years, he did not Record so many of these Heavenly Afflations, because they grew so frequent with him. And he also found a Truth, in what some Candidates of Heaven, Approaching to the Courts of the Lord, have Observed; That the Flights of a Soul rapt up into a more Intimate Conversation with Heaven, are such as cannot be exactly Remembred with the Happy Partakers of them. The Sublime Conceptions, and the flowing Expressions, of the Soul in such Heavenward Salleys are presently lost; and though the Feasted Soul would give never so much to recover them, they can by no means do it. The Spirit that made them, once being Retired, the very Remembrance of them cannot any more be Recovered.

O Disciple of Epicurus,[116] Let not a Vain Philosophy tell thee, That such Heavenly Afflations are nothing but a melting of the Brain by chance happening in a Warm Temper; and that they who Speak of GOD shining out upon them, only happen to be under Heats of the Brain, that rise and flow Copiously more at some times than at others; and so by Consequence, that the case of a Troubled mind Complaining of Desertious and Aridities,[117] is to be laugh'd at, as the Whimsey of a Brain happening to be under a Cloudy Vapour. It is true, Bodily Dispositions do often affect the mind; and Ministers are applied unto, when Physicians would be more properly and effectually called for. But they, who laugh at all Spiritual Operations upon the mind, are Ignorant, and Short-sighted Men, Sensual, not having the Spirit; And the many Volumns about such things Written by men of Renown in the Congregation of GOD, have not been all foolishly thrown away on a meer Mechanical and Chymaerical[118] Business, not concerned in them.

Article XII.
Second Thoughts on the Synod, in 1662.

There is now nothing to retard the Progress of our History: But having settled Mr. Mather in the Pastoral Charge of the North Church in Boston, and exhibited the Dispositions and Exercises, of a more General Application, which he had, not only in the First Years of his Ministry, but also pretty far into it, we may now proceed unto some Remarkable Affairs and Actions of his Life, in the Order wherein we shall find them occur unto us.

At the time of his Return to New-England, he found the Country deeply engaged in a Disputation, about the Church-State of their Posterity; wherein it is no wonder if the Political as well as the Ecclesiastical concerns of a Country founded on the Bottom of Religion, were affected. The Country soon became sensibly divided into, Synodalian; and Antisynodalian; & Mr. Mather from his Youth making a Figure wherever he came, he now did so on the Antisynodalian side. If I venture to say, He was in the Wrong, I shall anon shew so good Authority for my saying so, that He & the World, will Pardon me. The case was This. When our Churches were come to between Twenty and Thirty Years of Age, a numerous Posterity appeared, among whom there were Multitudes of well-disposed persons, who professed themselves desirous to Renew their Baptismal Covenant, and Submit unto the Church-Discipline, and so have their Houses also marked for the Lords: but yet they could not come up to that Experimental Account of their own Regeneration, which would Sufficiently Embolden their Access unto the Table of the Lord; and which the Churches required of them. Now for the Churches to make no Ecclesiastical Difference between those hopeful Candidates and Competants for the Eucharist; and Pagans who might happen to Hear the Word of GOD in our Assemblies; This was judged an Unwarrantable strictness, which would quickly abandon the biggest part of the Country, unto Circumstances by no means to be wished for. But on the other side, it was feared, that if all such as had not yet Exposed themselves by censurable Scandals found upon them, should be admitted unto all the Priviledges in our Churches, a Worldly Generation of Men, might before we are aware, carry all things into such a course of Proceeding, as would be too Disagreeable unto the Kingdom of Heaven which the Church is to represent unto the World. The Thing became a Considerable Controversy. On this Occasion, there was by the Direction of the General Court, a Synod of the Churches Convened at Boston, in the Spring of the Year, 1662. Who Agreed upon certain Propositions concerning the Subjects of Baptism, and Consociation of Churches, which being presented unto the General Court, an Order was there passed for the Publication and Commendation thereof unto all the Churches. The fifth of these Propositions, and what was most contested was, That *Church members who were admitted in Minority, understanding the Doctrine of Faith, and Publickly Professing their Assent thereto, not Scandalous in Life, and Solemnly owning the Covenant before the Church, wherein they give up themselves and their Children to the Lord, and Subject themselves to the Government of Christ in the Church, their Children are to be Baptized.* But there were several Eminent Persons in that Venerable Assembly, who were Jealous lest the Sacred Ordinance of Baptism should come to be Applied unto such Unmeet Subjects, as would in a while put an End unto New Englands Primitive and Peculiar Glory of Undefiled Administration: And some of these made very Public Exceptions, to the Synods Decisions. One of these was the President of the College, the Learned Mr. Charles Chauncey; who Published a Treatise, Entituled, *Antisynodalia Americana;* Which was Answered by the Worthy Mr. John Allin.[119] On the same side, with his Praesident, was Mr. Mather; who had (with his Generous, *Magis amica veritas*)[120] the Infelicity at the same time to Dissent from his own venerable Father [Richard]: However such was the Wisdom and Goodness on both sides, that there was no Diminution of their Delight in one another. The Famous Mr. Davenport wrote in Opposition to the Synod, what he called, *Another Essay for Investigation of Truth.*[121] But it was Accompanied with, *An Apologetical Praeface,* Written by Mr. Mather; wherein every one Confessed, the Best was done that could be done, on the side so Appeared for. They said—*Si Pergama Dextra Defendi poterant, etiam hac defensa fuissent.*[122] Now, to Answer Mr. Davenport, they Appointed Mr. Mather the Elder; who did it, like himself, Solidly, Nervously, and with such a Respectful Usage of his Antagonist, as to be, what I have heard my Good Old Mr. Higginson remark upon it, *A Pattern for all Ansiberers to the End of the World.*[123] But as a Match for Mr. Mather the Younger, they pitched upon that Matchless Mr. Mitchel, of whom our Great Baxter said, *That if there could be Convened an Oecumenical Council of the whole Christian World, that Man would be worthy to be the Moderator of it:* And he did his part also, like himself, Incomparably.

An Abridgment of what was offered both by the Apologist [Increase], and by the Answerer [Jonathan Mitchell], is exhibited in our, *Magnalia,* and is too long to be now Repe[a]ted. But the Effect of the Disputation is now to be Related: And my Good Authority for my saying what I did a while ago, is to be Produced, Mr. Mather found the Truth so Victoriously cleared by Mr. Mitchel, that he not only Surrendred himself a g'ad Captive thereunto, (which Mr. Mitchel had the Unspeakable Satisfaction to know before he Died) but also Obliged the Church of GOD by Publishing unto the World, a Couple of Unanswerable Treatises, in Defence of the Synodical Propositions: In which he Expresses very much of his Inexpressible Value for his Excellent Opponent and Conqueror, and uses about him the Words that Beza uses about Calvin,[124] *Since Mitchel is dead, Life is less Sweet, and Death will be less bitter to me.* And Pathetically Addressing and Advising his Antisynodalian Brethren, to be more Jealous of their Apprehensions, he uses these Words. *Brethren, I was once of your Perswasion; But Study, and Prayer, and much Affliction has brought me to be of another Belief than Once I was.* The Sentiments he fixed on, were, That we are to Distinguish between a Particular Church, as it is more Strictly taken for a Particular Corporation of Covenanting Believers, Entrusted by our Lord with the Keys of the Kingdom of Heaven; and as it is more Largely taken for that Special part of our Lords Visible Church, which doth subsist in this or that Particular place; And that a Membership of the Catholic Church, discovered by a Relation to a Particular Church, not in the former but in the latter sense, is the formal claim to Baptism; And so, the Qualifications in the Fifth Proposition give a Right unto it. Upon the whole, I shall only Repeat the Words of our *Church-History* on this Occasion. "If the Apologist were one who so Signalized a Modest sense of Second Thoughts unto the World, it can be reckoned no Disparagement unto him; until the Humility of Austin in his *Retractations,* or the Ingenuity of Bellarmine in his *Recognitions,*[125] come to be Accounted their Blemishes, or until Bucers, yea, and Luthers, change of their Opinions about Consubstantiation, & the Recovery of Zuinglius from Inclinations to Antipaedo baptism,[126] shall be Esteemed the Disgrace of those Renouned Men or, until Mr. Robinson[127] shall be blamed for Composing his Weighty Arguments against the Rigid Separation, which once he had zealously Defended." In fine, I will to this occasion apply the Words of the famous Dr. Owen to the froward Mr. Cawdry, to take off the charge of Inconstancy laid upon him, for his Appearing on the behalf of the Congregational Church-Discipline: *He that can Glory, that in fourteen Years he hath not altered nor Improved his Conceptions of some things, of no greater Importance than that mentioned, shall not have me for his Rival.*

Article XIII.
A Second Instance of Second Thoughts.

But that I may at once rid my Hands of All (if Two may be properly called All, for there were no more) Instances, wherein he found himself Obliged unto a Change of Sentiments, I am willing to do Justice unto the Cause of Truth, in one Article more; Which I may the rather do in this place, because it will be no great Anticipation or Dislocation in the Chronology of our Story.

"The great Light of Africa, was once of the same Judgment with the Antenicene Fathers,[128] (who express'd a just Abhorrence for the vile Method of Enforcing Religion by Persecution[)]; But, being willing to Justify some Violences, which the Catholicks of those Days thought it necessary to Employ against the Donatists,[129] his Judgment warped unto the Persecuting Side, and gave a Wretched Proof, that the Second Thoughts are not always the Wiser. What an Horror of Dependance on meer Humane Conduct must it Produce in our Souls, when we consider (what LeClerc has related,)[130] That the most Faithless and Bloody Tyrant that ever was in the World, could not be brought over to rescind all his Edicts in favour of the most Loyal Subjects upon Earth, until the Epistles of so great a Saint as Austin, unto Bonifacius and Vincentius, were shown unto him![131] And yet in those, and the other Epistles Published by the Archbishop of Paris, to justify the most Infandous[132] Persecution that ever was acted under the Sun, how Childishly does the Father argue? How trifling, how shallow, what little other than straitned Metaphors, are his Arguments? How little of Austin in them! And then anon, Conscience bestowing Rebukes upon him, how Importunate was he for the stopping of those Violences which he had Encouraged, and how Sollicitous to obtain Merciful Retrenchments and Abatements for them! Yea, in his Answer to CRESCONIUS,[133] he Expres[s]ly owns, *No Good Man in the Catholic Church allow'd the Punishment of Hereticks with Death.*"

A Perfect Reverse hereof, the Second Thoughts of Mr. Mather. New-England being a Country Planted by a People, whose Design it was to maintain, The Faith and Order of the Gospel, in Evangelical Churches, and therewithal transmit the same with all possible Purity down to their Posterity; And their Common Wealth being look'd upon, as an Institution of GOD for the Preservation of their Churches, and the Civil Rulers look'd upon as both Members and Fathers of them; there were Laws made which Inflicted Punishments on the Broachers of Pernicious Errors, and on such as made Invasions and Infractions upon the Ecclesiastical Constitution, which was esteemed the grand Gl[o]ry & Interest of the Country. The Zeal of the Good Men mightily urged for the Civil Magistrates using his Power, in Coercive Ways, to restrain all Attempts of Evil minded Men to Introduce any Apostasies or Deviations from the Religion, which was the Professed End of the Plantation. Toleration was decried, as a Trojan Horse profanely and perillously brought into the City of GOD. Plausible Outcries were made about, Antichrist coming in at the Backdoor of Toleration. It was a Maxim often Cited (but by none more, than them whose Resolution it was, to Tolerate next to nothing,) *To Tolerate all things, and Tolerate nothing, are both alike Intolerable.* Now, though Mr. Mather never went unto the Extremity that some carried the matter to, but greatly Disliked the Bitter Spirit he saw in some that carried all bef[o]re them; and little Approved some Unadvised and Sanguinary Things that were done by them who did all; particularly, the Rash Things done unto the Quakers. And indeed, it is a Thousand pitties, that the Unhappy Laws made in the Colony in those Days, ever should stand upon Record any where, when Some of them were never Executed, and All of them, were Disclaimed, and Renounced, and Repealed more than Thirty Years ago! Nevertheless, he joined with the Good Men, who did not care to hear of a Toleration for Seducers; and was for the Civil Magistrates Exerting his Power, as a Master of Restraint upon them. For this purpose, he wrote an Essay full of Erudition, and said all that could be said, on *The Power of the Civil Magistrate,* which yet he never Published. And it was well he did not! For, anon, he became fully Satisfyed, in the Declared Will of our SAVIOUR, That the Tares must have a Toleration: And indeed there was a Time, when Austin himself could say, about the Exterpation of the Tares,—*Nec quenquam Ecclesiae Filium debere arbitrari ad se hoc Officium Pertinere.*[134] He knew the Principle that generally Obtained among all Christians till the Days of Constantine, and was Asserted by many of the Fathers after him: Greatly decrying the Nonsense and Folly of Converting People with Penalties. He saw, That the Man who is a Good Neighbour and a Good Subject, has a Right unto his Life and the Comforts of it; and that it is not his being of This or That Opinion in Religion, but his doing of something which directly tends to the Hurt of Humane Society, by which this Right can be forfeited: And therefore, Blasphemies and Attempts to Poison People with Atheism and Profaneness, which Destroy the Ligaments of Humane Society, cannot Sue for a Toleration. He saw, That a Good Neighbour and a Good Subject, has a Claim to all his Temporal Enjoyments before he is a Christian; And he thought it very odd, that the Man should lose his Claim, from his Embracing of Christianity, and because he does not happen to be a Christian of the Uppermost Party among the Subdivisions. For an Uppermost Party of Christians, to Punish Men, in their Temporal Enjoyments, because in some Religious Opinions they Dissent from them, or with an Exclusion from the Temporal Enjoyments which would justly belong unto them, is a Robbery, whereof he could not but say, *It appears to me Unreasonable.* It became Evident unto him, That all the Sacrifices of Men unto GOD, nor Proceeding from a Conscience Perswaded, that He does Command them, & will Accept them: All Acts of Religion produced meerly by External Violence, are Detestable Things. He thought it not Enough to say, That such Sacrifices are no more Acts of Homage unto GOD, than a Log of Wood happening to fall before a Statue; but he tho't them rather Acts of Contempt upon His Infinite Majesty: For a Man to Do, in Religion, what his Conscience does not Approve, is for him to Deny the GOD that is Above: The most notorious among the French Persecutors themselves, have upon Occasion Confessed so! He became sensible, That the Example of the Israelitish Reformers, Inflicting Penalties on False Worshippers, would not Legitimate the like Proceedings among the Christian Gentiles. For the Holy Land of Old, was by a Deed of Gift from the Glorious GOD, Miraculously and Indisputably Granted unto the Israelitish Nation, and the Condition on which they held it, was their Observation of the Mosaic Institutions. To Violate them, was what carried a Rebellion in it, and was an High-Treason against the King of the Theocracy; An Iniquity to be Punished by the Judge! At the same time, Sojourners in the Land, were not Compelled unto the keeping of those Laws and Rites, which Moses had given to his People. Nay, & the Israelites themselves fell many of them into the worst of Herisies; yet, while they kept the Laws and Rites of Moses, the Magistrate would not meddle with them. The Haeresies of the Sadduces then st[r]uck at the Foundations of all Religion; yet we do not find that our SAVIOUR blamed the Pharisees for not Persecuting of them as they could have done. The Christian Religion brings us not into a Temporal Canaan; It knows no Designs; it has no Weapons, but what are purely Spiritual. Finally; He saw, that until Persecution be utterly Banished out of the World, and Cain's Club taken out of Abels Hand, as well as out of Cain's, tis Impossible to rescue the World from Endless Confusions: He that has the Power of the Sword will always be in the Right, and always assume the Power of Persecuting[.] In his latter times, he therefore look'd upon it, as one of the most Hopeful among the Signs of the Times, that People begun so much to be Ashamed of a Practice, which had been A Mother of Abominations. He came entirely into that Golden Maxim, *Errantis Paena doceri.*[135]

Now, Instead of Distinguishing (for Instance,) between, a Simple Anabaptism to be Tolerated, and (what the Angry Disciples would call) a Schismatical Anabaptism, which (it seems) might not be Tolerated, he went, and bore his part in Ordaining a Pastor to a Church of Baptists, in the Neighbourhood. And if he had seen any plead for the Persecution of Dissenters in yet greater Matters than those wherein these Brethren differ from us, Good Old Martin himself could not have appear'd more earnestly, than he would have done, to Discourage the Ithacian Spirit.[136]

Article XIV.
Sober Chiliasm.

About the Year, 1665. the World was Alarmed with Rumours of Motions among the Jews in several Parts of the World, that made some who were Waiting for the Consolation of Israel, to hope, that the Lord was going to set His Hand again the Second time, to recover the Remnant of His People, and assemble the Outcasts of Israel, and gather together the Dispersed of Judah. Mr. Mather Preached a Monthly Lecture, whereof all his Reward here was, that a Subscription was made and paid for the Support of a Godly Gentleman, an Elder of his Church, that lay some Years Confined and Languishing under a Palsey: And he took this Occasion, to give his Auditory some Elaborate & Judicious Lectures on that Mystery; Rom. XI. 26. *All Israel shall be Saved.* In those Lectures, he Declared, That he verily Believed the Motions then talk'd of would come to nothing; and that the Time for Favour, the Set Time, would not yet come on. But he maintained, That a Time would come, when the Israelitish Nation should be Converted from their Infidelity, and Restored unto the Possession of their Promised Land, and have a Glorious Kingdom of GOD erected among them, and thorough [through] them Extended unto the Gentiles. These Lectures were quickly afterwards Published in London; and they were not only Accompained [accompanied] with Praefatory Recommendations from such Eminent Persons as Mr. Davenport, and Mr. Greenhil, and Mr. Hook;[137] but also, tho' he were but a Young Man of about Six or Seven and Twenty, the

Renouned Mr. Caryl, when he Read the Book, pass'd that Judgment upon it, *That it was a Rare Thing to find any where a Conjunction of so much Learning & so much Piety, as there was in the Author of that Incomparable Treatise.* And it was a little Diverting unto him, above Twenty Years after, to meet with Gentlemen in London, who Complemented him, as having long ago read an Incomparable Treatise, Written (as they Supposed) by his Learned, and Pious, and Excellent Father, upon, *The Mystery of the Salvation of Israel.*[138]

But having Entred thus far into the Delectable Study of the Prophecies, he must proceed a little further; and finding all the Prophets as with one Mouth, D[e]claring, what the Protevangelium[139] in the very Head of our Book, has given us the Comfort of; That after a long War between the Messiah and the Serpent, of which War our Earth is the Seat, the Messiah shall be Victorious over the Serpent, and, as in every Victory, the Vanquished must Leave the Field in the Possession of the Conqueror; Finding also, that such a Belief was maintained by All the Orthodox before the first Nicene Council,[140] and the Fathers of that Famous Council also, set their Seal in Strong Terms unto it; And it was not Condemned, until Damasus the Bishop of Rome, towards the End of the Fourth Century, did his best that the Kingdom of CHRIST might be forgotten, as the Kingdom of ANTICHRIST was coming on; (the *Spes Fidelium* was lost, as well as Tertullians Book of such a Title!)[141] he now found himself under a Necessity to become a Sober Chiliast. When he considered, That IMMEDIATELY AFTER the long Tribulation under which the Jewish Nation is now Languishing, THEN the Son of Man comes in the Clouds of Heaven with Power and Great Glory; And That at the Arrival of the Kingdom under the whole Heaven given to the People of the Saints of the most High, at the Expiration of the Fourth Monarchy, THEN the Thrones are Pitched, and the Appointer of Times appears on His Throne, and a Fiery Stream issues from it, and the Judgment is Set, and the Body of the Romish Beast,[142] is given to the Burning Flame; And, That our SAVIOUR is to destroy Antichrist with the Brightness of His COMING; And, That there will be a Resurrection of the Dead, when the Time, and the Times, and the Half-Time, allow'd for the Reign of Antichrist is Expired, or at the End of the Four Monarchies; And, That when the Seventh Trumpet Sounds, which next follows on the ceasing of the Turkish Hostilities upon Europe, there comes on the Time of the Dead, when they shall be Judged, & a Reward shall be given to them; and This is the Time when the Kingdoms of This World shall be the Lords; And, That the First Resurrection foretold in the Holy Oracles can be no other than (what every one owns the Second is) a Literal and a Corporal Resurrection: He saw himself shut up unto the Faith of it, and Compelled unto the Perswasion, That the SECOND COMING of our SAVIOUR will be at the BEGINNING of the Happy State, which is to be Expected for the Church upon the Earth in the latter Days. And about the Year 1668. he wrote in Latin, a Book Entituled by him, *Diatriba de Signo Filii Hominis, et de Secundo Messiae Adventu;*[143] Which was afterwards Published in Holland: wherein he maintains the genuine Doctrine of the Millennium; and had he then so fully studied the Distinction between the New Heavens and the New Earth, as he did afterwards, a Golden Key to Open many of the Things hard to be understood, there had been a bright Addition to his Good Performance. But by Studying the Prophecies, he found, as many Holy Servants of GOD have done, a Communion with the Lord GOD of the Holy Prophets to be Sensibly Assisted & Advanced, And by Meditations on the Paradisian State of Things, which there will be at the Restitution of all Things, he failed so near to the Land of Promise, that he found the Balsamic Breezes of the Heavenly Country upon his mind, which, where they come, usually Refine and Sweeten, and Marvellously Purify the Souls that are Favoured with them.

I find, that on his Days of Prayer about this Time, he mightily look'd up to Heaven for Direction and Assistence, in the Composing of this Book; and in all his Enquiries into the Characters and Approaches of the Holy Kingdom[.] And I take t[h]is Opportunity to Remark it once for all; That still when he had any Book upon the Anvil, his Days of Prayer made it a considerable Article, That the Glorious Lord would be with him in the Writing of that Book, and give it Acceptance among His People, and make it useful to the Purposes for which it was designed. We all saw, how Acceptable the Books generally Proved, and how Serviceable, and with what a Quick Dispersion the Impression went off; and how sensibly the Prayers were Answered.

Article XV.

Chastened Sore, but not Given over to DEATH.

In the Month of April, 1669. His Father, being Moderator of a Cou[n]cil met at Boston, and Lodging at his House, was taken so very Ill, that he was Obliged thereupon to Accompany him in the Conveyance of a Coach to Dorchester; Where the Venerable Old Man, after little more than a Weeks Torture from that Scourge of Students, from which he had hitherto Suffered very little, but now bore a Terrible Assault from it with Incredible, and Incomparable

Patience, (in the Intervals reading Dr. Goodwins little Book, *Of Patience*)[144] resigned his Holy Soul into the Hands of his Redeemer: and there was this odd Circumstance in his Malady, that there did come from him, and were found in him, just as many Stones, as there were Years of his Age, which were Seventy Three. He did with all Filial Affection Attend and Comfort and Strengthen his Afflicted Parent in his Agonies; and received from him those Instructions relating to the State of Religion in the Churches, which afterwards he Published unto them. And then, after the Death of his Father, he gave the People of GOD, a Tast[e] of what he Lived upon, in a Sermon on those Words; Phil. IV. 20. *GOD—our Father.*

Quickly after this; that is, on July 24. he felt a Soul so on the Wing for Heaven, for a Night and a Day together, as he had scarce felt in his Life before; He wrote at the Time, how strangely his Heart was Moved and Melted within him, from the Thoughts of Heaven Working there. On the Third Day after this, Messengers brought him the Heavy Tidings, that at That very Time, the Soul of his Brother Eleazar (above an Hundred Miles off,) which had been strung so much to an Unison with his, Actually took Wing for the Heavenly World.

The Death of his Brother Obliged him in the latter End of the Next Month, to take a Journey unto Northampton, for the Assistence of the Desolate Widow and People there. But there, on the Second of September, a Violent and a Dangerous Fever siezed him; and he became Sick, nigh unto Death: But he Comforted himself, that he was, as the Sick Epaphroditus of Old,[145] a Minister on a Journey, and on his Duty. Being in Extremity of Pain, some of the Godly Brethren there, set apart a Day to Pray for his Deliverance; and while they were yet Praying, he was Delivered. But the Fever continuing, there were on the following Week, no less than Three Days of Prayer kept by the Good People in the Town, for the Preservation of his Precious Life. His Church at Boston also kept a Day of Supplications for it; and sent him likewise a Physician, to use the best means for his Recovery. After Thirteen Days his Fever left him; and assoon as he was able to Write, he Wrote this brief Account of his Inner Man, under the Visitation. "GOD was wonderfully Gracious to me. He did not leave me to Doubts & Fears concerning my Eternal Estate; but caused His Face to Shine upon me. I felt His Love, and saw that Jesus Christ gave Himself, even for me. I could not think of any Sin I had been Guilty of, but my Conscience, and I think the Holy Spirit of GOD with my Conscience, told me, that It, and all my Sins though Many and Great, were Repented of, and done away in the Blood of CHRIST. I found myself very Willing to Dy. When I thought of my Wife and

Children, my Heart gave them up unto GOD, firmly believing, that he would take Care of them. And I had as much Quiet in my Mind, as if I had neither Wife nor Children to Care for. When I thought of that Blessedness, which is to be Enjoy'd in Another World, I longed to be there. Oh! The Presence of GOD! Oh! The Presence of GOD! Oh! The Presence of GOD: It is sweeter than Life it self. My Soul knoweth it!—But when I thought of doing Service for JESUS CHRIST, I became desirous to Live yet a little longer."—

Before Winter came on, he returned unto Boston: But under such Languishments, especially from that Comprehensive Mischief which they call, The Hyprocondriac Affection,[146] that he lay confined all the Winter; and his Recovery to any Service, was by many very much Despaired of. That which added unto his Affliction, was a grievous and little short of Mortal, Molestation from the Ephialtes;[147] which indeed ever now and then Afflicted him, all the rest of his Pilgrimage.

While he lay yet very Low, he Wrote, "Some Considerations, which make me ready to Believe, That GOD will continue me, to do Him Service in the World. 1. Because much Prayer hath been put up in many Places, that my Life might be Spared. 2. GOD hath returned me Home, through Wonderful Hazard and Hardship. He that hath done thus much will do more. 3. When I lay Sick at Northampton, there was a Strong Perswasion on my Spirit, that GOD would Spare my Life; Which I then told my Sister; Desiring her to read, Psal. CXVIII. 17, 18. 4. I am apt to hope, that GOD hath some Special Service for such a Poor Sinful Creature as I am, to do with Reference to the Rising Generation, and the Establishment of these Churches, upon foundations of Truth, Order, and Purity. This I am the more apt to Believe, because of my Fathers Dying Council to me. 5. There is Faith in the Hearts of many of my Christian Friends, concerning this matter. They Believe, That GOD hath more Work for me to do. 6. There is an Alteration on my Spirit since my Sickness, For I am not so Desirous to Dy as I have been, but more Desirous to Live, that I may Glorify GOD in my Lord JESUS CHRIST."

He was after all, *By Faith out of Weakness made Strong.*[148] And Prayer to the Lord our Healer, the Glorious GOD of our Health, had its Efficacy very Conspicuously Signalized in the matter. I will single out one Passage from his Diary to Illustrate it, Written while he was yet under his Confinement.—"I Pleaded with the Lord for my Life and Health, and my Heart was raised in some Measure to Believe, That GOD would Restore me to His Service, and to my former Strength again. The Grounds of my Perswasion, were such as these. 1. I had Considered the Poor, GOD therefore Will Preserve me Alive, and Bless me upon Earth. 2. GOD's Name and Truth is a little

Concerned in my Restauration; For some say, That my Sickness is come upon me, for my being an Apostate from the Truth, and that I shall never Preach again. 3. GOD hath begun Mercy towards me; and His Works are Perfect. 4. GOD hath stirred up the Hearts of His Servants to Pray for me; and my own Heart also to Pray for my Recovery. 5. The Reason why I desire my Health again, is not that so I might Enjoy Honours & Pleasures in this World, but that so His Name might be Glorified by me. Now seeing I have Prayed for Such Ends, and from Such Grounds, My Desires will be fulfilled. 6. My Heart doth Trust in GOD for His Salvation. Therefore He will Save me out of this Distress. 7. Because of His Covenant, and because of the Blood of the Covenant. Zech. IX. 11. And, because I have Humbled myself under the Hand of GOD. 1 Pet. V. 6."

In the Spring of the Year, 1670. he returned unto his Beloved Pulpit: And made his first Sermon on those Words: Psal. XCIV. 12. *Blessed is the Man, whom thou Chastnest, O Lord, and teachest out of thy Law.* But being still under feeble Circumstances, and having a Strong Impression on his Mind, that the Drinking of the Mineral Waters might be of use to him, he took a Lodging at Lyn, where he might repair every Morning, to a Spring there, which was then Famous through the Country. I will Transcribe a Passage or two from his Diary, which he wrote in the Time of his being there.

One is this. "At the Waters, retiring myself under the Trees, I poured out my Soul before the Lord, and there met with Him. I did humbly and believingly (through the Lords Grace towards me) betake myself unto GOD, and unto JESUS CHRIST, for the Healing of my Bodily Distempers. I Believed, Because, though Sin had brought these Distempers on me, yet GOD had accepted the Sacrifice, which CHRIST has offered for my Sin. Because also GOD had formerly heard my Prayers. And because CHRIST has Redeemed my Body as well as my Soul. CHRIST intends to bestow Eternal Glory on my Body as well as on my Soul: And therefore He will not deny unto me so small a matter as Bodily Health, which is nothing in comparison of Eternal Glory. Finally, Because I desire Health, for the Lord's Sake, and not for my own; Even that I may do Service for Him. After Prayer, I went away Inwardly Rejoicing, because, I have Prevailed! I have Prevailed! I have Prevailed for Mercy!"

Another is This. "At the Waters. There again the Lord Enabled me with Tears, and Perswasion of a Gracious Answer, to pour out my Desires before Him, for both Bodily & Spiritual Healing to be vouchsafed unto me. My dear GOD in JESUS CHRIST, will certainly accept of some Service from me; Blessed be His Glorious Name forever and ever! Amen! Amen!"

It was not long before the Lost Jewel was restored unto him. Nevertheless, in the way to it, he met with many grievous Pangs of Overwhelming Melancholy: of which he also says, *I found the Prayer of Faith to be the best Remedy against it.* But of this also, I will from his Diary, only note a Couple of Passages.

One is this; "As I was returning home from Lyn, at the end of the Town, a poor Godly Woman (whose Name is Mansfield) desired those that Rode with me to go forward, for she must needs speak with me. When I stop'd, *O Syr,* (said she, with much affection, and many Tears) *I am troubled at my Condition. I am afraid, that I grieve the Good Spirit of GOD, by not being so cheerful as I ought to be. I am Dejected, and my Soul is Disquieted; and when I meet with Affliction, I lay them too much to Heart; and I doubt, I herein offend so Gracious a Father, as GOD has been unto me; a GOD who has done much for me, and sometimes Manifested Himself unto me.* I was astonished to hear her speak, and see her come thus to me for some Relief in such Temptations. I concluded, that this poor Woman (who little thought so herself) was a Messenger sent from GOD unto me; For she spoke to my very Condition, as if He that knows all things had put Words into her Mouth. Oh! Let the Great Physians [Physician] of Souls (said I then) Look upon me, and let Him Heal me, and give me Power of Grace to be more than a Conqueror over my Special Infirmities."

Another is This. "I was in much Distress and Anguish in my Spirit, lest all my Faith should prove but Phansy and Delusion. In this Distress, I betook myself to CHRIST, and wept before Him, saying, Lord JESUS, let me be Destroyed, if thou canst find in thy Heart to Destroy, a poor Creature, who desires above all things to Glorify thy Name[.] Here I am before Thee; Do to me and with me, what thou wilt, If thou wilt Glorify thyself in my Confusion, thy will be done; I have deserved that it should be so: But, Oh, that thou wouldest pitty me! After I had thus fled & cried unto the Rock that is higher than I, I was revived. But Anxiety returning the next Day, and being hurried with Temptations, I professed before the Lord JESUS, That if the Tempter did fall upon me to destroy me, he should find me at the Feet of CHRIST; and will CHRIST suffer him there to destroy me? I therewith Promised before the Lord, that if He would bring me out of my Distress, I would endeavour in all Respects a better Carriage before Him. After this, I had some Perswasion That GOD heard my Prayers, and beheld my Tears, as He did those of Hezekiah, and the Weeping Jacob."[149]

And so it Proved[.] Health and Peace returned unto him; And though the Labours of the Pulpit now became near Twice as much as they were before, yet he Comfortably went through those & all his other Labours: and Opportunities to do Good, grew upon his hands continually.

By way of Gratitude unto Heaven, and as an Effect and Symptom of a Perfect Recovery, One of the first Things he did was TO WRITE THE LIFE OF HIS FATH[E]R: which as I told you before, was Transcribed into Clark's Collections. He also Published the last Sermons of his Brother Eleazar, who was led from the Dying Words of his Father about care for the Rising Generation just before, to Preach diverse Lords-Days on those Words, I King. VIII. 57. *The Lord our GOD be with us, as He was with our Fathers.* He likewise Prepared for the Press, a very Savoury Book, Entituled, *Some Important Truths about Conversion,*[150] which was then quickly Printed at London, (and fifty Years after, he saw it Reprinted in Boston,) with a Preface of Dr. Owen unto it, who gives the Author something of his Deserved Character; saying among other things, *It is known unto all, to whom he is known, that he is a Person of Singular good Learning, and Reading:* and here—*a Workman that need not be ashamed.*

In fine, from an Heart now more than ever set upon doing for GOD, he now Wrote; Jun. 11. 1670.

"The Threefold Wish of the Chief of Sinners. I Wish! I Wish! I Wish!

"1. That I may do some Special Service for my dear GOD in JESUS CHRIST before I leave this World.

"2. I would fain Leave Something behind me, that may be doing of Good upon Earth, after I shall be in Heaven.

"3. After I have finished my Doing Work, I would fain Suffer for the Sake of my dear GOD, and for JESUS CHRIST."

Article XVI.
What Occur'd in the Approaching and Finishing of the Indian War.

On the Entrance of the Year 1674. Observing the Sins of the Times, and therewith Discerning the Signs of the Times, he had a sad and strong Impression on his mind, and a Spirit that could not rest until he had Publickly Declared it, That a Time of grievous Trouble was quickly coming on the Country; yea, that a Sword should quickly be drawn, which would bring a dark and a dismal Time upon it. Under this Impression, he delivered on a Day of Prayer kept in his own Congregation, What the Learned Mr. Oaks[151] in his Praeface to it, calls *A Solid, Succinct, Comprehensive Discourse,* on Ezek. VII. 7. *The Day of Trouble is near;* Which was by the Ordering of the Divine Providence immediately Published and Scattered through a Country, *Warned thus to flee from the Wrath to come.*[152] The Country was then in all Possible Tranquillity and Security. But the Next Year, was the most Bloody one that ever New-England saw; from the Indians, whom King Philip Seduced into a War, that fill'd the Land from one end unto the other with Desolations.[153]

In the Time when the Sword of the Wilderness was Devouring what it had its Commission to fall upon, he Employ'd the growing Opportunities which were now put into his Hands, especially in Sermons Preached in the Audience of the General Assembly, to bear the most Public Testimon[i]es against the Miscarriages, which he thought had incensed Heaven against the Land; and particular[l]y procure Wholesom Laws against such Provoking Evils, as might properly fall under the C[o]gnisance of the Civil Magistrate. At the same time, there being a Prospect of Poverty coming in like an Armed Man, and very many Poor People driven to extreme Necessities, he did by his Letters, procure a whole Ships load of Provision, fr[o]m the Charity of his Friends in Dublin, and a considerable Sum of Money, and much Clothing, from the like Charity of his Friends in London, to be distributed among the Indigent.

But the Armies of Prayers, with which he did in this Calamitous Time, *Caelum tundere et Misericordiam Extorquere!*[154] The Land had then many true Sons of Jacob in it, who *Wept and made Supplication;*[155] But this Israelite indeed made a bright Figure among them. And the Successes of the Prayers were so very Remarkable, (and the Blessed Calvins cry, *Nunquam irritas fore Preces!*[156]—which occurs an Hundred times over in his Commentaries on the Psalms, was in so strange a manner Verified,) that when the War was over, he made a Collection of them, which he Published under the Title of, *An Historical Discourse Concerning the Prevalency of Prayer.*[157] In this History, there is not the least Notice taken of his own share, in the Prevailing Prayers: But I myself Remember those things, which enable me to say Certainly no Man had a Greater Share. On each of the Articles in the History, he had himself some Remarkable Experience. But I will Single out one Instance, that had something Singular in it. He found his Prayers animated with a Singular Importunity, That King Philip, the First Mover and Grand Actor, in the War, might be reach'd by the stroke of Heaven, that should cut him off. At length, he set apart a Day in a Study often Perfumed with such Days, wherein he noted this down, for one of his Humble and Earnest Requests unto Heaven, That GOD would deliver up Philip, the Principal Enemy of His

People here. In Two or Three Days, less than a Week, after This, the Thing was Accomplished! And there was this also a little Singular. He had for diverse Lords-Days, made the Death of that Miserable King, a Petition which in his Public Prayers he somewhat Enlarged upon. But on one Lords-Day he quite forgot it: for which Forgetfulness I well Remember, that I heard him wondring at, and Blaming of, himself in the Evening. However, he was more Satisfied, when a few Hours after, there came to Town the Tidings, That before That Lords-Day, the Thing was Accomplished. It was a great Maxim with him, *Homine probo Orante nihil Potentius:* A Prayerful Man, is a Potent Man. O mighty Man, What greater Proofs than thy own Prayers, need be Produced for it!

Article XVII.
Strange Impressions and Predictions.

In the Year, 1676. he had a strange Impression on his mind, that caused him, on Nov. 19. to Preach a Sermon on those Words, Zeph. III. 7. *I said, surely thou wilt fear me, thou wilt receive Instruction; So their DWELLING SHOULD NOT BE CUT OFF;* and Conclude the Sermon with a Strange Praediction, That a Fire was a coming, which would make a Deplorable Desolation. After he came home, as he was Walking in his Study, he was Exceedingly moved and melted in such a Soliloquy; *O Lord GOD, I have told this People, that thou art about to cut off their Dwellings; but they will not believe it. Lord, who has believed! Nevertheless, O Lord GOD, I beseech thee to Spare them: If it may Stand with thy Holy Pleasure Spare them, Spare them!* So did he walk Weeping before the Lord! At the same time, he Earnestly urged upon his Consort, a Speedy Change of Habitation; which could not be Accomplished. On the next Lords-Day he Preached, (Not aware of its being so!) a Farwel-Sermon, on those Words, Rev. III. 3. *Remember how thou hast Received and Heard.* And the Conclusion of the Sermon was, *That Praedictions of Evil to come ought to be Remembred;* And, that when the Lord JESUS is about to bring any heavy Judgment upon His People, He is wont to stir up the Heart of some Servant of His, to give Warning of it; which Warning should be Remembred, that so People may be ready to entertain what must come upon them. His last Words were, "People won't Remember, nor Mind these Things. But, as Jehu said unto his Captain, *Remember how the Lord laid this Burden,*[158] so, when the Evil is come, you will Remember what you heard concerning it." The very Night following, a Desolating Fire broke forth in his Neighbourhood. The House in which he with his Flock, had Praised GOD, was Burnt with the Fire. Whole Streets were Consumed in the Devouring Flames, and laid in Ashes. His own House also took a part in the Ruines: But by the Gracious Providence of God, he lost little of his Beloved Library: Not an Hundred Books from above a Thousand; Of those also he had an immediate Recruit, by a Generous Offer which the Honourable Mrs. Bridget Hoar made him, to take what he Pleased from the Library of her Deceased Husband. In less than Two Years also, he became Owner of a Better House; And though his Flock was now Scattered, for several Months, GOD made it an Opportunity for him to Preach every Lords Day, in the other Churches, and Entertain Successively the whole City, with his Enlightening and Awakening Ministry.

I will not here Theologize, much less will I Philosophize upon the Original and Operation of those Praesagious Impressions about Future Events, which are often Produced in Minds, which by Piety and Purity and Contemplation, and a Prayerful and Careful Walk with GOD, are made more Susceptible of them[.] I am only to Observe, that this Holy Man of GOD, was no Stranger to them; and that I may dispatch at once all the Instances, that I think proper to mention until some while hence I foresee I shall be compelled unto some further Notice of them, I only add what in the Order of our Story should be Introduced here. He did no less than three Times as the Year, 1678. was coming on, very Publickly Declare, That he was verily Perswaded, a very Mortal Disease would shortly break in upon the place; and the Slain of the Lord would be many. Some of his Friends were troubled at him, for it. But when the Year[,] 1678. was come on, we saw the Mortal Disease. The Small-Pox broke in, which prov'd a Great Plague unto the Country; and never did Boston see so Fearful a Mortality: The Cry of the City went up to Heaven!

The famous Dr. Henry More, who is not Ordinarily numbred among Fanaticks, has a Passage that may a little Solve some of these Appearances. "Though the Spirit of Prophecy in some sense be ceased, yet GOD hath not hereby Precluded His own Power, nor yet that of His Ministring Spirits from Visiting and Assisting of His Servants as He Pleaseth. And there are some Pious Persons to whom it must not be Denied, that very Unusual Things of one sort or another, have sometimes happened."

Article XVIII.
The Reforming Synod.

The Man, with whom the First Born of his Wishes, was, not for the Great or Sweet Things of This World, but that he might be Employ'd in the Doing of **Special Service** for the Kingdom of GOD in the World; Behold, what the King of Heaven will do for the Man who so Delights to Honour Him, and whom He Delights (as He ever will for Such!) to Honour!

Mr. Mather was one excellently Prepared for Special Service; And GOD made him, all along so Significant and Conspicuous, but by'nd by (and Now) so placed him at the Head, in all Considerable Affairs relating to Religion, in the Country whereof the main concern was Religion, that one can scarce Write the History of his Life without Writing the History of his Times, and it will be the History of his Country for Three-score Years together. But That having been already done, I know not whether This may not be under a Necessity of Suffering some Amputations: They shall be however as few as may be.

I am arrived now to a Stage, & the Year, (1679) wherein a Synod of all the Churches in the Colony, whereof Mr. Mather was esteemed a great part, even that which was called, The Reforming Synod, appears Convened. It is an Awful Observation, which the Excellent Comenius has concerning his famous Bohemian[159] (which were in many things like the New-English) Churches; That they were nearer to the Sanctuary than other Churches, and therefore when some Apostasy was found among them, CHRIST Expressed His Displeasure against them in most Swift and Severe Dispensations. New-England was not become so Degenerate a Country, but that there was yet Preserved in it, far more of Serious Religion, as well as of Blameless Morality, than was Proportionably to be seen in any Country upon the face of the Earth. Nor were they overgrown with the Vices which are Enumerated by Cyprian as Abounding among the Primitive Christians, for which he said, *Vapulamus itaq; ut meremur.*[160] Nevertheless, the Spirit of the World began so far to Operate, that there was a Sensible Decay of Real and Vital PIETY, and the Power of Godliness began sensibly to suffer some Abatements: Watchful, and Fruitful, and Prayerful Christians, and Humble Walkers with GOD, were not so many as they had been, among a People greatly Multiplying; and the Holy GOD might also say, *There are found Wicked Men among my People.*[161] In the Time of the War, there were noble Essays in the Churches, (especially in the way of Renewing their Covenants) to recover out of these Declensions; and the Success of them was Admirable and very Memorable. But the Country saw a Succession of Heavy Judgments: and still upon the Relaxation of Calamity there was an Augmentation of Iniquity: so that Good Men thought it high time to enquire with all possible Solemnity into the Grounds of the Controversy, which it appear'd that the Glorious GOD had with the

Country; and this the rather, because many did not Enquire Wisely concerning the matter. Indeed, as our SAVIOUR has no where Promised a Temporal Prosperity, unto a Life of Piety; but bid us look for the Discipline of the Cross, and has told us, *That through much Tribulation we must enter into the Kingdome of GOD:*[162] So if a whole People were made up of such as led a Life of Piety, yet a Promise of all Temporal Prosperity could not be claimed for them. If every Individual Believer be still Obnoxious to the Things that are not Joyous but Grievous, how can a People consisting of such, look for an Exemption from them? It is true, the Israelites had a Promised Land, wherein they might hope for a Temporal Prosperity, while they kept the Condition of the Covenant by which they held it. But the Christian Church, is got out of that Minority. Nor has our SAVIOUR Promised His Church any Land flowing with Milk and Honey in this Present Evil World. We actually see this, in every Generation; That the most Reformed People of GOD (the Vaudois for That!)[163] have been harassed with Persecutions, as well as they that by Sinking into Criminal Corruptions have Provoked the Holy JESUS to say, *I have Something against thee;* At the same time, they that Work Wickedness, have not wanted for Exaltation. Yea, let us look where we will at this Day; The People among whom the Covenant of the Gospel is most adher'd unto, see much more Temporal Adversity, than many People who pay very little Regard unto it. Nevertheless, it will be the Wisdom of any People under Heavy Judgments of Heaven, to Apprehend Loud calls unto Repentance in them; and Confess and Forsake their Sins, that they may find Mercy with the Lord: They make a very ill use of the Divine Dispensations, and run the Hazard of being dealt withal as the Refractory and Incorrigible, if they do dot [not] so. Yea, they have cause to be Apprehensive, that the Heavy Judgments, may come to manage a Special Controversy, and be Inquisitive, what and where it may be, and be Sollicitous for the Removal of it. Be sure, the Prayers of such a Reforming People, under their Distresses, will be the most likely to be Prevailing ones: GOD has also Wondrous Rewards for the Encouraging of Piety, and Equity, and Sabbatizing and Almsgiving, even in the Life that now is. And good Order Flourishing among any People, has a Natural Tendency to befriend many Points of their Temporal Prosperity; *Righteousness will Exalt a Nation.*[164]

Wherefore upon a Motion of Mr. Mather in Conjunction with others excited by him for it, the General Court called upon the Churches to send their Delegates for a Synod in Boston; To consider, *What are the Evils that have Provoked the Lord to bring His Judgments on New-England.* And, *What is to be done that so those Evils may be Reformed?* The Churches having first kept a General Fast, that a Gracious Direction might be Obtained of GOD in what was now to be done, the Synod met at Boston, Sept. 10. 1679. The Synod also kept a Day of Prayer with Fasting; in which Mr. Mather was chose for one of the Preachers, when the Venerable Old Mr. Cobbet[165] was chose for the other. Several Days were then Spent in free Discourses on the Two Questions; and at last, a Result with a Preface, were agreed unto, which were of Mr. Mathers drawing up. On the Day, when a Committee of the Ministers Presented it unto the General Court, Mr. Mather Preached a very Potent Sermon, on the Danger of not being Reformed by these Things: And the General Court thereupon Commended it unto the Serious Consideration of all the Churches and People in the Jurisdiction.

GOD made this Instrument a Special Service to the cause of PIETY. Especially in that the Faithful Ministers throughout the Country, were Directed and Strengthened, in *Lifting up their Voice like a Trumpet,*[166] against the Provoking Evils. But the most notable Effect was, the Renewal of Covenant, which was attended by many Churches, in Pursuance of the largest Article among the Reforming Expedients, which the Synod had Recommended. The Churches under the Conduct of their Pastors, having on Previous Days of Prayer set apart for that purpose, considered what Heaven Expected from them, were willing Anew to declare their most Explicit Consent unto the Covenant of Grace, and most Explicitly to Recognize their Obligations to those Duties of it, in which the Singular Temptations and Corruptions of the Day called for their Excited Vigilance. When their Praeparatory Church-Meeting had produced a Concurrence in this Resolution, they Publickly Devoted a Day for this Holy Intention; and with Suitable Prayers and Sermons, there was Read their Covenant, whereto their Assent was expressed by the Brethren lifting up their Hands, and the Women only standing up. The Church whereof Mr. Mather was the Pastor, was a Pattern to many others, in this Religious Action; And as there was usually a vast Confluence of People on these Occasions, thus, there were Thousands of Spectators who testified, that they never saw what may be called, A Special Presence of GOD our SAVIOUR, more gloriously Discovered, than in those awful Solemnities.

As a sort of Parenthesis unto these Designs, of PIETY, it may not be amiss here to Observe, that Mr. Mather being a Person Polished with an Erudition beyond what was Ordinary, among other Symptoms and Effects of it, a little after this, he formed a Philosophical Society of Agreeable Gentlemen, who met once a Fortnight for a Conference upon Improvements in Philosophy and Additions to the

Stores of Natural History; From which the Learned Wolferdus Senguerdius a Professor at Leyden had some of the Materials, wherewith his *Philosophia Naturalis* was Enriched;[167] And in part from their Collections also One that had a share in that Combination, and is now a Fellow of the ROYAL SOCIETY in London, afterwards transmitted Communications thither. But the Calamity of the Times, anon gave a fatal and a total Interruption to this Generous Undertaking.

Article XIX.
Another wholesom Fit of Sickness.

The last Parenthesis being so dropt, we may go on, where we left off before it, in our History.

On May. 12. 1680. The Synod had a Second Session at Boston; When Our Confession of Faith was agreed upon. Though there were many Elder, and some Famous, Persons in that Venerable Assembly, yet Mr. Mather was chosen their Moderator. He was then Ill, under the Approaches & Beginnings of a Fever; but so Intense was he on the Business to be done, that he forgot his Illness; and he kept them so close to their Business, that in Two Days they dispatch'd it: and he also Composed the Praeface to the Confession.

On this he immediately took his Bed under a dangerous Fever; which anon left him under an Ague; and this was attended with a Cough, which carried the Symptoms of a Consumption with it; so that he was brought very low, and his Life was much despared of. But GOD stirred up the Hearts of many Godly and Worthy People, to be much in Prayer for him. His own Church expressed their Love to him, in keeping of no less than Three Days of Prayer, that his Life might be Prolonged, and his Health restored. On one of those Days, the Venerable Old Mr. Eliot[168] Preached a Sermon on those Words, Joh. XI. 3. *Lord, Behold, he whom thou Lovest is Sick.* And after the Sermon, that Man of GOD returning to him, said, *Blessed be GOD! Brother, you are ours, we have Obtained you from GOD; you shall yet continue with us.* And Mr. Mather himself also, being asked by some of his Friends, Whether he did himself think, that his Time was now come to Dy? He Replied; *I am not at all Careful about that matter; I have the Satisfaction, that I have endeavoured to Walk before GOD with a Perfect Heart, and to do that which is Well-Pleasing in His Sight. Nevertheless, I do not think, that I shall Dy at this Time; For I have not yet Suffered for my Lord JESUS CHRIST, so much as I have Desired.* He Recovered; and that he might Express the purpose of his Life after his Recovery, his First Sermon upon it, was on Phil. I. 21. *To me to Live is CHRIST.* His Church also did him the Uncommon Honour, of keeping a Day of Public THAN[K]SGIVING to GOD for his being Restored unto them. Soon after which, the Death of his Pamphilus, the Excellent Praesident of Harvard-College, Mr. Urian Oakes, opened a New Field of Special Service for him; Whereof—more hereafter!—I will Remember my Obligations.

I will here take notice only of one point, wherein the Restored Servant of GOD, grew yet m[o]re Abounding in the Work of his Lord. Good Old Mr. Eliot, as long ago, as not long after the Death of Mr. Mitchel, said unto Mr. Mather: *Brother, The Lord has Bless'd you with a Leading Spirit, as he did Mr. Mitchel, who is gone unto Him. Certainly 'tis no little Notice, that is taken by our Holy Lord, of what is done in the Meetings of His Ministers. I pray, Brother, Lead us, in our Meetings: Bring forward as much Good in them as you can.* Accordingly Mr. Mather made it one of his Particular Studies, from this Time, unto the End of his Pilgrimage; to make the Weekly (and other) Meetings of the Ministers Profitable. How much Special Service he did in them, and how many Good Motions, he brought forward, there is no Record kept, except in that *Book of Remembrance,* which our GOD has Written before Him, for them who Think upon His Name.

Article XX.
The Charter appeared for.

But you said, Syr, *Not Suffered so much for my Lord JESUS CHRIST, as I have Desired!* Never doubt; Sufferings will come on fast enough: Satan is not Asleep: His Children and Factors,[169] every where, as of Old, Fill the Country. But then, though the Persecutors will Perfidiously Invent and Pretend other Causes, for the Sufferings which they Inflict upon the Faithful, and will not own, that it is directly for such and such Points of Religion, that they molest them, yet if the True Cause that lies at the Bottom of all the Molestations which their Adversaries give them, really is, Their Godliness and Usefulness, and their Significant Appearance as Witnesses for GOD and CHRIST, and Instruments of his Kingdom, they THEN Suffer for the Lord JESUS CHRIST, in all that is done unto them. Now, Come on, Sufferings; We are Preapred for you!

In the latter end of the Year, 1683. there arrived a Declaration from King Charles II. with a Signification to the Country, That except they would make a full Submission, and entire Resignation of their

Charter to his Pleasure, a *Quo Warranto* against it should be Prosecuted. The Question was offered unto Mr. Mather, whether the Country could without a plain Trespass against Heaven, do what was Demanded of them; and in his Elaborate Answer to it; he Demonstrated, That they would act neither the part of Good Christians, nor of True Englishmen, if by any Act of theirs they should be Accessary to the Plot then manageing to produce a General Shipwreck of Liberties. Communicating his Answer to several of the Magistrates, the Copies thereof came into many Hands; and with so much Efficacy, that the Country was preserved from a Mean Compliance with the Vile Proposal. Great was the Rage of Adversaries on this Occasion; and Mr. Mather was by them called and spited as, The Mahomet of New-England. He felt it; but yet so Satisfied in the Good Work, that when the Freemen of Boston met on Jan. 23. that they might give Instructions to their Deputies for the G[e]neral Court, and the Deputies with others, desired him to be present, and give them his Thoughts on the Case of Conscience before them; he made a short Speech in the Town-House; and This was it, as I find it in his own Copy of it. "As the Question is now Stated, *Whether you will make a full Submission and entire Resignation of your Charter and the Priviledges of it, unto his Majesties Pleasure,* I verily Believe, We shall Sin against the GOD of Heaven if we Vote an Affirmative unto it. The Scripture teacheth us otherwise. We know what Jephthah said, *That which the Lord our GOD has given us, shall we not Possess it!*[170] and though Naboth ran a great Hazard by the Refusal, yet he said, *God forbid that I should give away the Inheritance of my Fathers.*[171] Nor wou[l]d it be Wisdom for us to Comply. We know, David made a Wise Choice, when he chose to fall into the Hands of GOD rather than into the Hands of Men. If we make a full Submission and entire Resignation to Pleasure, we fall into the Hands of Men Immediately. But if we do it not, we still keep ourselves in the Hands of GOD; we trust ourselves with his Providence: and who knows, what GOD may do for us? There are also Examples before our Eyes, the Consideration whereof should be of Weight with us. Our Brethren hard by us; what have [they] gain'd by being so Ready to part with their Liberties, but an Acceleration of their Miseries? And we hear from London, that when it came to, the Loyal Citizens would not make a full Submission and entire Resignation to Pleasure, lest their Posterity should Curse them for it. And shall *We* then do such a Thing? I hope, there is not one Freeman in Boston, that can be guilty of it! However I have Discharged my Conscience, in what I have thus Declared unto you."

Would such a Speech have been made by a Danish or a Swedish

Clergyman?—Upon this pungent Speech, many of the Freemen fell into Tears; and there was a General Acclamation, *We Thank you, Syr! We Thank you, Syr!* The Question was upon the Vote carried in the Negative, *Nemine Contradicente;*[172] And this Act of Boston had a great Influence upon all the Country. But could some Folks have had their Will on Mr. Mather, they would at least have Johnsonized him.[173] However, Sufferings are coming on!

Article XXI.
A Variety of Sufferings.

In the Year, 1684. he was under a Third Visitation brought very nigh unto Death, from a Dangerous Fever; under which there were (as formerly) many Prayers put up to Heaven for him. And he enjoy'd (as formerly) a calm Serenity of a Mind Rejoycing in the Hope of the Glory of GOD. After some Weeks of Confinement, he was Restored unto his Flock; whom, at his first coming abroad (on the Twenty fourth of August,) he Entertain'd with an agreeable Sermon, on Isa. XXXVIII. 18, 19. *The Grave cannot Praise thee,—The Living, The Living, He shall Praise thee, as I do this Day:* Insisting on This; *That the Servants of GOD, whilst Living in this World have many Opportunities and Advantages to Glorify GOD, which the Saints in Heaven have not:* Of which he proposed That as the last Article; *The Servants of GOD, while they are in this World, may Suffer for Him.* And now, we must expect, Syr, that you will Confirm your Doctrine.

I said, Sufferings are coming on. Some Wicked Men, whereof the Principal was one Randolph,[174] the Tool whom the Court sent over with the Demand of the Full Submission and Entire Resignation which we have been Speaking of: Perpetrated an Uncommon Villany, which brought the very Life of Mr. Mather, as the Ahabitic[175] Times then went, into no little Danger. Having in their way, that is to say, Basely, Circumvented some Innocent Letters of his, to an Eminent Person in Amsterdam, which Enabled them to Imitate his Hand in Subscribing of his Name; They forged a large Letter of Three Pages in Folio, full of not only Ridiculous, but also Treasonable Expressions, whereof n[o]t one Sentence was his; and with a Date of, B[o]ston, 10. m. 3. d. 1683. they Subscribed his Name unto it. This Letter was Read before the King and Council, and Motions were made for Mr. Mather, to be fetch'd over, and made a Sacrifice: A Sidney, or a Cornish; or as afterwards they would have done, a Rosewel.[176] The Advice of this, gave no little Trouble to Mr. Mather, and his Friends; and what he wrote upon it was; *That which Troubled me, was, that I was like to Suffer as an Evil-doer, through the Malice and Fals[e]hood of Wicked Men. Might I have Suffered for any Truth, which I had born Witness to, I could have rejoiced in it; But now, GOD was not like to have Glory by my Sufferings. This was a very sad Thought unto me.* Methinks, (if I may say so,) He did not Comfortably enough consider, That his Testimonies to Truth and Right, and the Figure he made in Serving the Churches of GOD, lay at the Bottom of all, and Procured him what he was now Suffering from the Malice and Fals[e]hood of Wicked Men; and their Contrivances to Represent him as an Evil-Doer, were b[u]t Aggravations of the Suffering. But it may be, he will by'nd by, after the Aestuation[177] is a little spent, come to a Just Reflection.—

However much Prayer to GOD on the behalf of His Persecuted Servant, was made not only by his own Flock, but also by many other Pious People up and down the Country. He himself also made his Vows, That if GOD would Save him from the Evil Designed against him, he would (His CHRIST helping of him) endeavour to do yet more for His Glory, than he had yet ever done in his Life before. And at the Bottom, he Wrote; *My GOD hath Saved me.*

A Gracious GOD Over-ruled the Spirits at Whitehall. The Thoughts of giving any further Trouble to Mr. Mather were laid aside, for the Present. Probably the Forgery might appear too plain unto them. They might have a View of a more Effectual way by'nd by to take him off. Randolph miss'd of this Bloody Purpose. Wretch, I shall have a further Occasion to mention thee!

However, that Father of Lies, (as one stiles him) the Infamous Le Strange, did in several of his Execrable *Observators*[178] Publish as much as he thought fit of that Forged Letter, with his wretched Annotations upon it, that so Mr. Mather might have the Honour of Cruel Mockings all over the Nation. And, I Pray, what is there in Death itself more uneasy to a Great Mind, than what he feels in the Indignities under which he must Complain, *They Laugh me to Scorn!*[179] And Sr. Richard Dutten, with the Satisfaction proper to such Spirits, brought a Copy of it unto Barbadoes and scattered it all over the Caribee Islands, that so Mr. Mather might be made the Song of the Drunkard, and have a further share in the Allatrations, which the Bright Witts of those Islands use to treat him with. He Observed, That now the Book of PSALMS, was what he could more feelingly, and with more Application than ever in his Life, Converse withal. Such Passages, as, *Princes have sat and spoke against me.—I am fill'd with the Contempt of them that are at Ease.—The Proud have had me greatly in Derision.—They have forged a Ly against me.—They have digged Pitts for me.—The Wicked have Waited for me to Destroy me.—Deliver me not up to the Will of my Enemies.—False Witnesses have risen up against me, and such as breath out Cruelty.* These and Innumerable other Passages in the Psalms, he now could Read over and Pray over (he said) so as he never could in his Life before. By'nd by, when the Storm was over, he was able to Write this Reflection. "The Lord has had Respect unto all the WISHES, Written down before Him; on Jun. 11. 1670.—Yea, He had so far Gratified my Desires of Suffering for Him, that my Name hath been cast forth as Vile & Wicked Men in England[,] Scotland, Ireland, Barbadoes, & the Leeward Islands, & elsewhere, have been Speaking all manner of Evil of me falsely. And the Ground of these my Sufferings has been, because I have desired to Approve myself Faithful unto the Lord JESUS, and unto His Kingdom and Interest."

But what shall we say, if all these Humiliations of this Great Man, were only to Prepare him for Marvellous Exaltations: and if these Things which thus Mortified him, were only to make way for the Accomplishment of that Word: Zeph. III[.] 19[.] *I will get them Praise and Fame, where they have been put to Shame!*

Article XXII.
Strange Deliverances.

Judgment was entred against the Massachusett-Charter: and the Court was full of Indignation against the Country. The Religion of the Country was enough to render It Obnoxious to the Rage of such a Generation as then carried all before them. The Fidelity of the Country to Legal Constitutions rendred it more Liable to an Exemplary Vengeance. In a very Singular manner, Mr. Mather had nothing but the Roaring of a Lion to look for. To Execute the Tragedies which were intended for New-England, that Cruel, and Horrid, and Hideous Tigre, whose Barbarous Cruelties Committed quickly after in the West, have rendred him Famous to all Succeeding Ages, had a Commission for it, and was coming over, with a Regiment of Myrmidons,[180] in Quality of Governour. Had this Kirk arrived, what Barbarities must this People have Expected; even like those worse than Gallic Immanities,[181] under which their Brethren in Scotland, at this time were Languishing; whereof my most Valued and Learned Brother Mr. Woodrow, has given us an Edifying History? Be sure, Mr. Mather had fared no better, than a Mr. Guthry.[182] In the Time of this Doubtful Expectation, as a Man of Desires, he kept many Days of Prayer;

And at last, on the SIXTH Day of FEBRUARY (as the Year One

Thousand Six Hundred and EIGHTY FIVE was coming on,) which he set apart for Supplications, what a Messenger came unto him? He has noted in his Diary. "THIS DAY, as I was Praying to GOD for the Deliverance of New-England, I was very much Moved and Melted before the Lord, so that for some time, I was not able to speak a Word. But then, I could not but say, GOD will deliver New-England! GOD will deliver New-England! GOD will deliver New-England! So I rose from my knees, with much Comfort and Assurance, that GOD had heard me. These things, I hope, were from the Spirit of GOD. Before I Prayed, I was very sad, and much dejected in my Spirit; but after I had Prayed, I was very Cheerful and Joyful. I will then Wait for the Salvation of GOD!" Thus he wrote on the Sixth of February.—

—And on the Fourteenth of April following there arrived the Tidings, that on THAT VERY DAY, there fell out THAT, which happily diverted and entirely defeated, the coming of Kirk with his Commission for the Government of New-England, and the horrible Slaughters, which the Roaring Lion and Ranging Bear would have made among the Best of the People; and which indeed brought those Quick and Strange Revolutions upon the Nation, that gave such a Man as Mr. Mather, Opportunities to Appear at Whitehall, in Circumstances that could little have been Imagined. New-England never saw a more Astonishing Deliverance!—

Article XXIII.
New Troubles on the Country.

In the Year 1686. New England saw it self delivered into the Hands of Sr. Edmund Andros,[183] whom K. James II. made the Governour of the Country, with as Arbitrary, (and one may say Treasonable) Commission, as ever any part of the English Nation was abused withal, a Commission by which the Governour, with three or four more Unreasonable Men, w[h]ereof none were Chosen by the People, had power to make what Laws they would, and Levy Taxes according to their own Humours upon the People; and he himself had power to send the best Men in the Land more than Ten Thousand Miles out of it, as he Pleased. The Case of poor New-England was now, what Old Wendover tells of the Time, when Strangers domineer'd over Subjects in England; *Judicia committebantur Jujustis, Leges Exlegibus, pax Discordantibus, Justitia Jujuriosis;*[184] and Foxes were made the Administrators of Justice to the Poultry. It would make a Long and Black Story, to tell a Tenth Part of the Vile Things done, by that Scandalous

Cruc [crook] which then did what they would in the Administration of the Government: even Randolph himself who was then their Secretary, Confessed in a Letter of his, which anon came to Light; *They were as Arbitrary as the Great Turk*. But Awakened and Alarmed People in the English Nation, began to take notice in their Public Remonstrances, of what was doing at New-England, as an Essay of the French Government, whereunto England was then hurrying with a Phaetontic Praecipitation.[185] The Administration, was almost entirely a Complication of Shameless and Matchless Villianies. The Honest Gentlemen in the Council were Overlooked and Browbeaten, and rendred Insignificant. Three or Four Finished Villians did what they Pleas'd: There was no Controling of them. Among other Instances of the Vile Things in it, there was This Comprehensive One; The Banditi gave out, that the Charters being lost, all the Title that the People had unto their Lands was lost with them; (for which a small Defect in the Legal and Public Settlements of them, was Pretended:) and therefore they began to Compel the People every where to take Patents for their Lands. Accordingly Writs of Intrusion were Issued out against the Chief Gentlemen in the Territory; by the Terror whereof many were driven to Petition for Patents, that they might Enjoy the Lands, which had been Fifty or Sixty Years in their Possession: But for these Patents there were such Exorbitant Prizes Demanded, that Fifty Pounds could not Purchase for its Owner an Estate not Worth Two Hundred: nor could all the Money and Moveables in the Territory have Defray'd the Charges of Pattenting the Lands at the Hands of these Crocodiles; Besides the Considerable Quitrents for the King. Indeed, the Bruitish Things done by these Wild Beasts of the Earth, are too Many to be Related, and would be too Bruitish to be Believed. Guess what was to be, Expected from a Parcel of Hungry Wretches, who had cast off all Sense and all Face of Honesty, and who Publickly told the Poor People, *They must not think that the Priviledges of Englishmen would follow them to the Ends of the Earth;* and, *They had no more Priviledges left but This, that they were not Bought and Sold for Slaves.* In short, All was done, that might be Expected from a Kirk, Except the Bloody Part[.] But That was coming on. The Lives of the Best Men began to be Practised on. The Learned, Pious, Peaceable Mr. Morton for That![186] And Mr. Mather stood fair, for that from which he thought he had been Delivered.

In this Time, you may be sure, Mr. Mather had not forgot his Old Stroke. I find him still at Prayer as much as ever: And still under the like Impressions! take a Touch or two. As 1687. was coming on, I find him Writing, on one Day, thus. *After I came home from the*

Public Labours of the Lords-Day, as I was alone in my Study Praying for Good Tidings out of England, I was Exceedingly Melted before the Lord. On another Day, thus. *I sought unto GOD in Secret with Tears, that He would send Reviving News out of England: And I could not but Believe that He will do so.* He had them Immediately.

Article XXIV.
Whitehall, after many Obstructions Repair'd unto.

The King in the beginning of that Year, (Just Three Years & an Half, after—) Published his, *Declaration of Indulgence;* which the Protestant Dissenters had abundance of Reason to be Thankful for; inasmuch as it *brought them out of their Graves:*[187] And if it assumed an Illegal Power of Dispensing with Laws, yet in Relation to Them, it only Dispensed with the Execution of such Infamous Laws as were *ipso facto* Null and Void before: Laws contrary to the Laws of GOD, and the Rights and Claims of Humane Nature. Be sure, the New-English Protestants found the Benefit of the Declaration; for it rescued the Maligned Churches of New-England out of a Devourers Talons, when he was just on the point of making many Violent Invasions upon them. The Ministers hereupon at Mr. Mathers motion, made an Address of Thanks to the King, for the Benefit which they enjoy'd by his Declaration; and it Proved a considerable Service to the Country. But then he Moved, that the Churches, as well as their Pastors, might come into such an Action; which also was readily complied withal. The Adversary was enough Enraged at these things; And when the Ministers of Boston agreed with their Congregations upon keeping a Day of Thanksgiving to Heaven, for the Shelter which their Brethren as well as themselves found by the Declaration, Sr. Edmond Andros with many Menaces forbad their Proceedings, and Particularly threatned that he would set Guards or Souldiers on their Church-Doors, if they Attempted what they Pretended to.

The Superiour Gentlemen in the Oppressed Country, thought, that a Well-qualified Person, going ov[e]r with the Addresses of the Churches to the King [James II], might, by the Help of such Protestant Dissenters as the King began upon Political Views to cast a fair Aspect upon, Obtain some Relief to the Growing Distresses of the Country; And Mr. Mather was the Person that was pitch'd upon. Being in Distress about this Important Affair, he did as he use to do. In the Day of Prayer which he kept upon it, he put it upon this Issue; That he might know the Direction of the Glorious GOD, by the Inclinations of the Church he belong'd unto, when the matter of his going for England, should be Proposed unto them. The next Day, the matter was proposed unto the Church; and he said unto them, *If you Say to me, Stay, I will Stay: But if you say to me, Go, I will cast myself on the Providence of GOD, and in His Name I will go. I know not how to discern the Mind of GOD but by your Inclinations.* To his Wond[e]rment, They that at another time would have almost assoon parted with their Eyes as have parted with him now were willing to it; They Unanimously Consented. They Fear'd what w[o]uld quickly be done by Bloody and Crafty Men, if he did not in this Honourable way get unto some Distance from them. And they Hop'd that he might be an Instrument of some Deliverance for a Land like to be Desolate and Overthrown by Strangers. What should be made of the Political Views in the Court at this Time, Who can Say? Upon the Numbring of the People, it was then Reckoned, there were about One and Thirty Hundred Thousand which at Present Professed Adherence to the Established Church: About Eleven Hundred Thousand, Protestant Non-Conformists, of several Denominations; And about Ninety Thousand (if so many) Roman-Catholicks. Though the Non-Conformists might for a while fly to a Tree that gave them some Shelter from their Idumaean[188] Unreasonable Persecutors, yet they were Discrete and Honest enough to have kept their Stops; and it could never enter into the Kings Mind, that they would go so far as to Assist the Roman-Catholicks in gaining the Power, with Forreign Aids, to Devour them all. Nor could it enter into Their Mind, that a King, whose Sword was Steel, his GOD was but a Wafer, and who could not keep in any Terms with the Church whereof he was but a Vassal, if he did not assoon as he could, Order all that would not Worship his Idol to be thrown into the Fiery Furnace could be their Hearty Friend, or could long forbear to Harass them with Perfidious, and Barbarous, and Inhumane Cruelties. Indeed, I know to whom it was, that King James in a Private Conference, Expressed an Horror of the French Kings Horrid Cruelties, and said, *I Wonder what Almighty GOD will do to him!* Nevertheless, was not King James too a Roman Catholic? He was a Son of the Church, and he must Ob[e]y! Or, What better was the State of the Protestants in Ireland, under Him, than that of the Hugonots[189] in France, under his Brother?

But yet, Mr. Mather might hope at least for some Temporary Advantages for his Country, and such as might be worth seeking for, from the present Posture of Affairs.

Let it not be cavilled, That he was now going, *Extra Theologiae Sphaeram.*[190] A Public Distress, a Common Danger, is enough to Legitimate his Listing for the Service. Yea, The Life of Churches was now at Stake. Churches were to be Served.—New England knows how to take its Ministers upon occasion, & use them as Instruments of doing what none else could have done, to serve its Interests. Yea, an Eminent Writer Propounds it, That the Reformed Churches ought always to have some or other of their Ministers, resident in the Courts of Princes, that so their Interests may not Suffer, but be Preserved and Promoted there.

A sort of Panic Terror fell now upon the Adversary. Something must be done to stop the Intended Voyage. Randolph must be the Tool. A Copy of his Forged Letter, being sent over hither, Mr. Mather in a Letter to the Person [t]hat received it, Intimated some Reasons he had for a Suspicion that Randolph (with a Brother of his) might be one Author of the Forgery. Tho' the Villian knew himself to be so, and his Good Fame was not worth half a Farthing; yet he now Arrested Mr. Mather in an Action of Defamation, and Five Hundred Pounds Damage. And it was a thing little short of Miraculous, that considering the Tricks and Frauds, wherewith every thing was then Managed, the Point was not gained. But the Good Old way was taken; much Prayer was made unto the Glorious Lord from whom every Man has his Judgment: and the Day whereon the Court sat, was a Day of Prayer with some Societies of Christians, for a Good Issue of the Perplexing matter. Behold, The whole Jury cleared Mr. Mather, and ordered the Plaintiff to Pay Costs of Court.

Mr. Mather went on with his Praeparations for his Voyage; and had his Mind more and more Irradiated with a Strong Perswasion, That GOD would give him to find Things in England, in such a State, as that he should have an Opportunity to do Special Service for His People here. Yea, he went so far in it, as to Write these Marvellous Words upon it;—*I know, it will be so; For Thou, O Lord GOD, hast told me, that it will be so!* And the Truth is, If he had not had some such Faith as this, to have Inspired him with an uncommon Courage, a Person of his Prudence would never have Exposed himself, as he did on a Thousand Accounts in his present Undertaking.

He Waited on Sr. Edmond Andross, the Governour and Oppressor of New-England; and acquainted him, That he designed a Voyage for London. He also gave the Country notice of his Voyage, in a Sermon at the Great Lecture; on Exod. XXXIII. 15. *If thy Presence go not with us, carry us not up from hence.* Hereupon Randolph again, Assisted by one 'Pothecary Bullivant, a Memorable Justice (and Something else!) Privately sent an Officer to Arrest him once more (Such the Equity of those Times!) upon the former Action of Defamation. But it fell out, that he was just then under the Operation of a more wholesome Physic, than what that 'Pothecary had sent him; and so the Officer was Ignorantly denied Admittance. The 'Pothecary as

Ignorantly reported, That Mr. Mather was Arrested; and the Report flying like Lightening about the Sollicitous Town, it soon reached Mr[.] Mathers Ears; who then kept upon his Guard.

Of Randolph I said a good while ago, That I should have a farther Occasion to mention him. I have now done it; And that I may never mention him any more, I will here take my Eternal Farewell of him, with Relating, That he proved a Blasted Wretch, followed with a sensible Curse of GOD wherever he came; Despised, Abhorred, Unprosperous; Anon he Died in Virginia, and in such Miserable Circumstances, that (as it is said) he had only Two or Three Negro's to carry him unto his Grave.

Mr. Mather withdrew Privately from his House, in a Changed Habit, unto the House of Colonel Philips in Charlstown; In which withdraw, it is Remarkable, That a Wicked Fellow, whose Name was Thurton, and who was placed as an under-Sheriff, to Watch him, and Sieze him, if he stir'd abroad, now saw him and knew him, and yet found himself struck with such an Enfeebling Terror, that he had no power to meddle with him. From thence, he was by certain well-disposed Young Men of his Flock, transported unto Winnesimmet; And from thence, he went aboard a Ketch, which lay ready to assist his Voyage: From which he was on Apr. 7. 1688. gladly received aboard the Ship (called, *The Praesident,*) on which he had at first Shipped himself, and so bore away for England.

After the Ship had made the Land, in a Foggy Day, they narrowly escaped Perishing among the Rocks of Silly. And some very Wicked Fishermen of St. Ives also after That gave them false Advice, on purpose to have Shipwreck[']d 'em; which they again Escaped by Mr. Mathers taking one of the Sharks aside, and hiring him with Four Half Crowns to tell the Truth. But on May 6. a Weymouth Boat coming by the Ship, he (with his Youngest Son whom he carried over with him) went ashore, at Weymouth, which was the last Town he had Lodged in, when he left England, Seven and Twenty Years before; And he had the Satisfaction, which he ha[d] Exceedingly desired, of seeing his old Friends yet Surviving in Dorset-shire, who now received him with the Greatest Joy Imaginable, and even as an Angel of GOD.

Article XXV.
An Admission into the Closet of K. James II.

But Mr. Mather, willing to lose no Time, hastened up to London, where he arrived, May. 25. 1688. And he found Things in such a state, as that he had Opportunity to do Special Service for his People; Even beyond what he could have Imagined. An Eminent Person often at Court, Informed King James, of his coming with Addresses to His Majesty from New-England: And upon May 30[,] which was the Time the King had ordered for it, he attended on his Majesty, in the long Gallery at Whitehall. Offering to kneel, the King forbad that Posture to him: whereupon Presenting the Address, he said, *Syr, Your Majesties most Loyal Subjects in New-England, with all Possible Veneration, Present this Address of Thanks to Your Majesty, for Your most Gracious Declaration of Indulgence unto them and their Brethren.* The King replied, *Read it, Syr;* which he did, and added the Number of the Ministers who had Subscribed it, in the Name of their several Congregations. The King then received it out of his Hand, and said, *I am glad my Subjects in New-England are sensible of any Ease and Benefit by my Declaration: And it shall Continue. I hope, by a Parliament to Obtain a Magna Charta for Liberty of Conscience.* He then Presented an Address to the King from Plymouth; to which His Majesty replied, *I kindly accept of this Address also, and I say again, as I said before; You shall have a Magna Charta for Liberty of Conscience.*

Two Days after this, Mr. Mather was Admitted into the Kings Closet; and there said unto him: *Syr, Your Majesties most Loyal Subjects in New-England, think, they can never be Sufficiently Thankful to GOD, and to Your Majesty, for the Benefit they have received by Your most Gracious Declaration of Indulgence.* The King Replied, *I am sure, they that are truly Conscientious, are Pleased with my Declaration; As for those that are not Satisfied with it, they are Men that have little Designs of their own; and their Tricks are well kn[o]wn to the World. I was for Liberty of Conscience before I was King: And I Thank GOD, that since I was King I have been able in that matter to give some ease unto my Subjects.* He then said unto the King; *Syr, Your Subjects in N[e]w-England are a People that were Persecuted thither on the meer Account of Religion. Inasmuch as Your Majesty has Delivered them from the Fear of a future Persecution, they are Transported with Joy; and there are great Numbers, Desirous that I should report their Dutiful Affection unto your Majesty.* The King thereupon asked him, whether Sr. Edmond Andros gave good Satisfaction to his Subjects there.

The Dialogue went on in these Terms.

Mather. *Syr, If he would but duely attend to Your Majesties Declaration, the People there would be better Satisfied.*

King. *Does he not do That?*

Mather. *There have been some of Your Subjects Fined and Im-*

prisoned, because from a Tenderness of Consc[i]ence they Scrupled, Swearing by the Book. I brought an Address of Thanks to Your Majesty, from a Number of our Congregations. I believe all the Congregations in the Country would have Concurr'd in the Address, had not the Ministers been Discouraged by Sr. Edmond Andros, who in a menacing way, bid them, have a Care what they did; And One of the Council with him there told us, we should make no Addresses to the King without their Leave. The Ministers of Boston proposed unto their Congregations, that they might keep a Day of Thanksgiving, to Bless GOD for what they have enjoy'd by Your Majesties Declaration. But he sent for them, and bid them keep the Day at their Peril, and assured them, that if they did, he would clap a Guard on their Persons and their Churches too; so that the intended Thanksgiving was Diverted.

King. *I wonder at it; For in other Plantations, the Governours themselves have sent me Thanks for my Declaration.*

Mather. *All the Hope under GOD, that your Subjects in New-England have, is in Your Majesty. They cannot but hope, that the Great GOD in whose Hand is the Heart of Kings, will incline Your Royal Heart to relieve them, when once you shall truly and fully be Informed how it is with them.*

King. (who seem'd Pleas'd,) *No Man shall be more ready to relieve them than I will be. Do you therefore bring to me in Writing, the things which Trouble you.*

Upon this, Mr. Mather kneeled, and the King Offering his hand unto him, he Kissed it; and for this Time took his Leave.

Mr. Mather Immediately got ready, not only a Memorial of the Grievances which filled his Country with the Cry of the Oppressed, but also a Petition for a Redress of them, in several Proposed Instances. Indeed, he could not now propose the Restoration of the Condemned & Vacated Charter; But he did Propose (what the King himself had Instructed him to call) a MAGNA CHARTA, for an Everlasting Liberty of Conscience to the Churches, to the Religion whereof no less than an utter Extinction was intended and eagerly pursued by the Sons of Strangers who now Lorded it over them. He did therewithal Propose, a Confirmation of the Peoples Title to their Lands, which had been brought under such an Abominable Contestation. He did also Propose, a Liberty for an Assembly. But he had nothing more at Heart than the Interest of the College; whereof he was now the Rector: (and his appearing in that Quality was no little Advantage to him in his Present Agency:) but the Ruin whereof was evidently in the View of the Persecutors. Having prepared the way for it, by Private Applications, to the Lords of the Kings Privy Council, and the Chief Ministers, he again Waited on His Majesty, (July 2.) and was Admitted into his Closet; where he Presented kneeling his Memorial and Petition. The King put forth his Hand to take him up, and said, *You shall not kneel, Syr:* and therewithal received the Papers out of his Hand; saying, *I suppose these Papers concern New-England, and are about the same things, which you had some Discourse with me, not long since upon:* And then putting them into his Pocket he said, He would take care about it. Mr. Mather was accompanied with Two Gentlemen whom the King treated, (not to say, Cheated[191]) as his Favourites: Both of whom Declared unto his Majesty, That if he shewed Favour to New-England it would have a Good Influence on the whole B[o]dy of Dissenters in England; Whereto the King Replied, *I believe so, and it shall be done!* And Mr. Mather then added, *That his poor Subjects in New[-]England, very much Desired, he should be Acquainted with their Condition.* But he said, *The Obligation will be beyond Expression great, if Your Majesty, will Please to grant them a Charter for their College* [Harvard]. *Certainly, Syr, they may think it hard that the College built by Non-Conformists, should be taken from them, & put into the Hands of Conformists.* The King Replied, *It is Unreasonable, & it shall not be!*

On Sept. 26. Mr. Mather again waited on the King in his Closet; and there said unto him; *Syr, I count it my Duty, most Humbly to Thank Your Majesty, in that you were Pleased some time since to give Assurance, that you would Confirm to your Subjects in New-England, their Liberties and Properties, and the Benefit of your Gracious Declaration.* The King Replied, *I will take the same Care of New-England, as of England; And you may be sure, they shall have what I have Promised.* Mr. Mather went on, *I Humbly Pray, Syr, that the matter may be Expedited. Your Majesties Affairs here may feel some Advantage from it.* The Kings Answer was; *Trouble yourself no farther; I will take Care, that the thing shall be done with Expedition.*

But,—*Quid Verba audiam quum facta non Videam?*[192]—There was nothing Effectually Performed at all that had been Promised.

Mr. Mather made as many Friends as he could: And it was Remarkable to him, That not only the Lord-Proprietor of Pensylvania, (then a Great Man at Court) treated him with much Civility, but even the Goggle-Ey'd Monster[193] too who used no other Man so, treated him with some Humanity, and the Roman-Catholicks themselves used him very Courteously. It often made him think on that Word, *They shall take up Serpents, and it shall not hurt them:*[194] The Serpents were so far from Hurting him, that they Extremely Caressed and Flattered him. He had something better than a Staff of Laurel for his Preservative![195] When he was in the midst of these Dangerous People.

Among these, Nevil Pain[196] told him, That Father Peters would gladly Speak with him, and was willing, (Pray, Master Apella,[197] can even you Believe a Word of this?) to do Good Offices for New-England. But Mr. Mather did not see cause to trust him; nor did he ever Exchange Ten Words with him; though Reports were spread by some Spiteful Persons of his maintaining an Intimacy with him; and he was once in Eminent hazard of losing his Life, by a Mob, which from some Resemblance of Stature and Habit mistook him for the most contrary Thing in the World. Some that were Friends to New-England strongly advised him to seek an Acquaintance with that Gentleman, and use his Interest with the King; but he always declined it and said, *It was next to going to the Devil for Help, and he could never find in his Heart to do it.* Some others, he did more freely Apply to; and especially, the Lord-Praesident, and the Earl of Melfort; who both still Promised Fair. He also hoped, That the Distress and Terror of the Impending Revolution, would compel the Doing of Something: And for this purpose, he attended on the King, once again in his Closet, on Oct. 16. who then Positively told him, That Liberties, and Properties, and the College, and all that he had Promised, should be Immediately Confirmed: And it seem'd indeed on the point of being Executed. But upon the false Rumour of a Diversion given to the Prince of Orange's Expedition,[198] there was a Demur put upon it; Whereupon Mr. Mather said, in his own Mind[,] *I will see thy Face again no more.* He thought he had heard Good Words enough; and saw, They were All he was like to be put off withal. And indeed, what were the Dark Purposes of the Court about poor New-England at that Critical time of Isaac on the Alter;[199] whether not something little short of a Total Extirpation for Colonies that were so Distinguished for the Reformed Religion in the greatest Purity of it!—Unriddle me, those Two Things. The one; That in the Account of the State of the Protestants in Ireland, which no Protestants make any Question of, One Article of the Suggestions made by the Irish Catholicks to King James, was, *That if any of the Irish cannot have their Lands in Specie, but Money in Lieu, some of them may transport themselves into America, particularly near New-England, to check the growing Independents of that Country.* The other; That in a letter sent from King James to his Holy Father at Rome, the Published Copy of which every Body looks upon as Genuine that Intoxicated Prince, declares his full purpose to set up the Roman-Catholic Religion in the English Plantations of America. However, *Blessed be the Lord, who has not given us as a Prey to their Teeth; Our Soul is Escaped as a Bird out of the Snare of the Fowlers; the Snare is broken, we are Escaped.*[200]

Article XXVI.
The History of the NEW CHARTER.

Let my Reader, I beseech him, now be armed with abundance of Patience. I am entring into a Story, which I wish I could manage with the Dispatch of the He-Goat in the Visions of Daniel.[201] But it is a Story that should and must be told: and I foresee, it will prove a long Chapter, let me do what I can. Of the Poets, whereof tis Remark'd, the one knew what to Say, the other knew what Not to Say, I am Confident, even the latter, (and he who has made his *Eneids,*[202] as we now have them, twenty times as short as they were in the first Composing of them) could not give it much more Concisely than what shall now be endeavoured.

But, Reader, if thou are not in a Time or a Frame, for the Reading of Civil matters, Turn over a few Leaves, and Skip the Chapter.

Perhaps, the Partitioning of the Story into Sections may give the Reader some necessary Breathing-Spaces.

1. England made and saw an Happy REVOLUTION. And New-England upon, (and almost before) the Advice of it, made as Just and Fair an One, in Conformity to it; and not Resisting an Ordinance of GOD, but Restraining a Cursed Violation of His Ordinance, Imprisoned Sr. Edmond Andros, and his Accomplices.

In the mean time, the Prince of Orange Arriving in London, and he with the Princess, being soon after, Chosen and Crowned, KING and QUEEN, of the British Empire, Mr. Mather had a New Field, and a Large one, for special Service offered him.

The Prince of Orange, having declared, the Restoration of Charters to be one Intention of his Expedition into England, Mr. Mather immediately used his most Vigorous Endeavours, That the Charters of New-England might be Restored as well as those of England. The good Old Lord Wharton, whose Memory ought forever to be Precious unto New-England, went with Mr. Mather, to Wait on the Prince of Orange, at St. James's; and on Jan. 9. then Presented the Petition for it unto His Highness. That noble Person, with a great Zeal told his Highness, That if he were sure to Dy the next Day, he would as he now did this Day, appear on behalf of New-England, and Sollicit His Favour to that Religious Country. He said, *That they were a Godly Conscientious People, and there were Proportionably more Good Men in New-England, than in any part of the World.* He said, *They did not Petition for Money, nor for Souldiers, nor any other Succours under their heavy Difficulties; but for their Ancient Privileges.* His Highness replied, *That His Purpose was, to take the Best care he could about it; and He would give order to His S[e]cretary Mr. Jephson! concerning it.* My Lord then carrying Mr. Mather to Mr. Jephson, said, *Cousin,* (for such he was) *Observe this Gentleman; and whenever he comes to you, Receive him, as if I came myself.*

And Mr. Mather soon had something to do with Mr. Jephson! For by the Procurement of some old Courtiers and Jacobites, a Circular Letter was drawn up unto all the Plantations, and unto New[-]England among the rest, Confirming all their Old Governours until further Order. Mr. Mathers Vigilance, got the Knowledge of this Letter, from the Secretary: But what a concern did it give him! Had this Letter come to New-England, and the Pounded Rulers taken the Advantage of it, as they would have done, to have resumed the Government, Boston would have been a Shambles. Mr. Mather Effectually Remonstrated it unto the Secretary, who carried his Remonstrance unto the Prince; and he then gave Order that the Letter to New-England should be stop'd; but the rest proceed. This one Special Service was well worth his Voyage to England for it!

2. It is Commemorated among the Memorable Things in the *Prudentia Veteris Ecclesiae;*[203] That the People at Antioch having by some rash doings, exceedingly Incensed the Emperour Theodosius,[204] and Fearing his Vengeance upon them, Composed very Mournful Hymns, which they sang in their Publick Devotions. Upon which they also sent their Pastor, even the most Eminent Minister in the City, as an Agent for them, to the Imperial Court, who Prevailed with the Young Men that were Singers at the Emperours Table, to Sing those Mournful Songs: At the hearing whereof the Emperour when he understood the Original & Intention of them, was Dissolved into Relenting Tears, and shewed Mercy to the City.

New-England had not so far Incurred the Royal Displeasure; though some Displeasing Things had been Unwisely done in the Country. Mr[.] Mather being in an Agency for them, like his Predecessor Flavian,[205] thought it no Imprudence to let the King hear something of what passed in the Public Devotions of the People for which he was concerned.

On March 14. 1689. The Lord Wharton introduced him to King WILLIAM; and Mr. Mather knowing that the King desired none but very short Speeches, only said, *I Congratulate your Majesties happy Accession to the Crown, and I Humbly Implore Your Favour to New-England.*

King. *You may rest Assured, that I will shew them all the Favour which it is in my Power to do.*

Mather. *I may Humbley and Freely Speak it; The very Prayers of that People, will be of Some Service to Your Majesty. They are a Good and a Praying People.*

King. *I Believe, they are a Good People; But I doubt, there have been Irregularities in their Government.*

Mather. *I durst Engage, that they shall at the first Word Reform any Irregularities they shall be Advised of.*

Lord Wharton. *And I'l be their Guarantee, and here is Mr. Mather the Rector of the College there, shall be the other. We Two will stand bound for New-England, that they shall act Regularly for the Future.*

King. *I will forthwith give Order, that Sr. Edmond Andros shall be removed from the Government of New-England, and be called unto an Account for his Male-Administration. And I will direct, that the Present King and Queen shall be Proclaimed by their former Magistrates.*

Mather. *Syr, They will do it with the Joyfullest Hearts in the World.*

3. This true New-England-Man considering how Wonderfully New-England had Prospered under the Old Charter, and how Desirous the People for whom he was now concerned, were to have it Restored; he Advised with the Wisest Friends he could find, about this Momentous Affair. Their Concurrent Judgment was, That the best course would be to Endeavour for a Reversion of the Judgment against the Massachuset-Charter by an Act of Parlaiment; and afterwards Petition to the King for the Additional Privileges, without which the Old Charter would not answer the Occasions, and Necessities of the People. Mr. Mather hereupon made most Indefatigable Applications unto the Principal Men in that Convention Parliament; The Effect of which was, That in the House of Commons the Charters of New-England were expressly put into the Charter-Bill: It was Voted, That the taking of them away, was a Grievance, and that they should be Restored. And a great Interest was also made in the House of Lords, that when the Bill should come up to them, for their Concurrence, New-England might be there also Favoured. At the same time, (July 4. 1689.) Mr. Mather was again Introduced by the Lord Wharton unto the King at Hampton Court: and said,

Mather. *I Presume Your Majesty has been Informed, of the Great Service, which Your Subjects of New-England, have done for Your Majesty, and for this Nation, and for the Protestant Interest, in Securing that Territory for King WILLIAM.*

King. *I have seen some Letters that Speak of it, and I Kindly accept of what they have done.*

Mather. *If Your Majesty would Please to Command that Your kind Acceptance of what they have done shall be Signified unto them, it will be a great Encouragement.*

King. *I will give order to the Secretary of State, that a Letter be Written to them, to let them understand, that what they have done is Acceptable to me.*

Mather. *Your Majesty may, by the Assistence of New[-]England, whenever You Please, become the Emperour of America. I durst engage, that Your Subjects there, will readily Venture their Lives and Estates in Your Service. All that is Humbly Desired on their behalf, is only that they may Enjoy their Ancient Rights and Priviledges.*

King. *I do assure you, I will do all that it is in my Power to do, that it may be so.*

Mr. Mead being with him, told the King, that he could not possibly do any thing more grateful to his Dissenting Subjects in England, than in being kind unto New-England in the Restoring of their former Privileges. The King bad them rest Satisfied, *That it should be done.*

But behold, while the Charter bill was Depending, the Convention-Parliament was Unexpectedly Prorogued,[206] and then Dissolved; and Mr. Mather found the Sisyphaean Labour[207] of a whole Year come to nothing.

4. The Disposition of the next Parliament soon appeared such, that nothing in the Favour of New-England was to be Expected there. Mr. Mather then made some Essays, to see if by a Writ of Error in Judgment, the case relating to the Massachuset-Colony might be brought out of Chancery into the Kings Bench; but this Attempt also was Defeated by so Surprizing a Providence, that Mr. Mather Declared upon it; *Never did I see a more Signal Hand of Heaven in any matter, than in Disappointing all H[o]pes, for the Obtaining the so much Desired full Restitution of all our Charter Privileges, by a Reversion of the Judgment Entred against them.*

All Hopes of Obtaining the Restoration of the Old Charter being at an End, there was no way left, but a Flight unto the Royal Favour; For though it was not in the Kings Power to Reverse the Judgment against the Old Charter, yet His Majesty had power to Re-incorporate his good Subjects there, and grant them a NEW CHARTER, that should contain all the Old, with the New and more Ample Privileges; Without which, the Old would not have been Sufficient.

Mr. Mather, with Two other Agents, which the Massachuset Colony had then joined with him, now Signed a Petition to the KING, for such a NEW CHARTER: which Petition the Right Honourable Earl of Monmouth Condescended so far, as to deliver with his own truly Noble Hand. Whereupon Mr. Mather Obtained the Intercession of a great Personage, which Prevailed with the King to refer the Affair of New-England unto the Consideration of the Two Lord Chief Justices, with His Majesties Attorney and Sollicitor-General: All of whom had by Mr. Mathers Powerful and Assiduous Applications been brought into the New[-]English Interests. They met Three or Four Times, and kindly gave him leave to be Present with them at all their Consultations. The Heads of the Massachuset OLD CHARTER, and Sr. Ferdinando Gorges, were Presented in Writing, together with such Additional Privileges, as were then Pray'd for: And they all judged, there was nothing Unreasonable, or Prejudicial to the Kings Interest in what was Proposed. They were Presented unto the King, by the Lord Chief Justice Holt; and the King Ordered him to Present them unto the Conncil [Council]; who did accordingly; and from thence they were transferred unto the Lords of the Committee for Trade and Plantations.

5. Immediately upon this, the King took his Voyage for Holland: and before his Return, there was no more to be done. But still Mr. Mather would be doing of something for the good of his Country. He Published, *Reasons for the Confirmation of Charter-Privileges, granted to the Massachuset-Colony,* which he Dispersed among the Lords of His Majesties most Honourable Privy-Council; and Personally Addressed himself unto the most of them, humbly Praying their Lordships Favour to New-England, in a matter that appeared so Equal. His Maxim was, *That in all Affairs, a Few did All;*[208] and his Method was, To find out the most Potent Leaders in all Affairs, and make sure of them. If he knew any N. C. [Non-Conformist] Minister, who had an Interest in any Person of Quality, he would engage that Minister to Employ his Interest on the behalf of New-England; One way of engaging him, was by Preaching for him: And, This also Introduced him into the same Acquaintance. There were several Noblemen, who likewise, brought him into the Knowlege and Favour of others. But none did more for him that way, than that Cordial and Constant Lover of all good Men, the Aged Lord Wharton, who was the last Surviving Member of that Famous Assembly of Divines at Westminister. Among those Eminent Persons, who Admitted him to be Familiar with them, I will particularly mention Two that were of an Ecclesiastical Character, for the sake of the Good that was done to New-England by his Acquaintance with them. The one was Dr. Tilotson, the Arch-Bishop of Canterbury: who did at his Desire, often concern himself to do kind Offices for the Country, and Pray, both the King and Queen to put Marks of their Favour on their Faithful Subjects there; and once he went so far as to tell the King, *It would by no means do well for him to take away any of those Privileges from the People of New-England which K. Charles I. had granted them.* And indeed Mr. Mather o[f]ten spoke of the Catholic Spirit, with which the Arch[-]Bishop of Canterbury blamed the Conduct of his Predecessor Land,[209] in his Discourses with him. The other was, Dr. Burnet, the Bishop of Salisbury: who besides many

Real and Weighty Expressions of his kindness for the Country, told him, That he would on the first Opportunity declare Openly in the House of Lords, *That there was a greater Sacredness in the Charter of New-England, than in those of the Corporations in England; Because those were only Acts of Grace, whereas the Charter of New-England was a Contract between the King & the first Patentees: They Promised the King to Enlarge his Dominions, on their own Charges, Provided, that they and their Posterity might enjoy such and such Privileges: They had Performed their part; Now for the King to Deprive their Posterity of the Privileges therein Granted unto them, would carry a Face of Injustice in it.* A Lord great in the Court, then told Mr. Mather, That his having Engaged the Bishop of Salisbury to appear for New-England, was the best Jobb he had done these Seven Years.

6. But a Greater than any of these, must not be left Unsollicited. Mr. Mather was by Madam Lockart Introduced unto the QUEEN, on Apr. 9. 1691. and she left him alone with her Majesty, that he might the more freely represent the case of New-England unto her.

The Discourse was, as followeth,

Mather. *I do most Humbly pray Your Majesties Favour to your Good Subjects in New-England. There are none in the World more in Your Interest than they; nor any that do with greater Devotion Pray for Your Long and Happy Reign. They have indeed been Exposed unto great Troubles on the account of their Loyalty unto your Majesty. For the French at Canada, who have invaded them, and have Destroyed several of their Plantations, gave that as the Reason of what they did; Because the People there have Declared for King William and Queen Mary. They now only Pray, that they may be Resettled in the Enjoyment of those Privileges, which they were Possessed of, until the last Year of King Charles II.*

Queen. *That matter has been a Long Time before the Council. I would have that which is Just done by them; and not only so, but that something of Favour should be shown to them.*

Mather. *I most Humbly Thank Your Majesty, for the Kind Words which Your Majesty was Pleased to Speak to my Lady Southerland about New-England.*

Queen. *Mr. Mather, I have had a great Character of you, from my Lady Southerland. I have spoken to the King on the behalf of New-England. He told me, the matter was before the Council.*

Mather. *It has been referr'd unto the Two Lord Chief Justices, with the Attorney and Sollicitor-General; we only Pray, that the Articles Approved by them, may be Allowed and Confirmed to us.*

Queen. *That seems Reasonable; and I doubt not, but it will be done for you.*

Mather. *I Humbly beg, That your Majesty will Please to Speak so Kind a Word unto the King upon his Return. You will thereby bring the Blessing of the Prayers of a Good People on Your Royal Person and Government.*

Queen. *I shall be willing to do all I can for them.*

Mather. *I have Reason to Believe, that Your Good Subjects there have been Misrepresented unto Your Majesty. Some that bear them Ill Will, have Printed many Reflections on them.*

Queen. *I have not seen all the Pamphlets.*

Mather. *Sr. William Phips*[210] *has with many of Your Majesties Subjects, endeavoured to enlarge Your Majesties Dominions; and they are willing again to expose themselves in your Majesties Service.*

Queen. *Are they Able to do it? I hear they are but in a Bad Condition.*

Mather. *They are in a Bad Condition. But One great Reason of it is, because their Government yet remains Unsettled.*

Queen. *That I Believe; It must needs be so!*

Mather. *If by your Majesties Favour, they shall be Restored unto their former Privileges, they will Revive, & become able to Serve Your Majesties Interest.*

Queen. *I doubt, there have been Differences There, as well as Here, about Church Government.*

Mather. *In New-England they are generally those that are Called Non-Conformists: But they carry it with all due Respect unto others: We Judge some of them to be better Men than ourselves. This Nation has cause to Bless GOD, for the KING, and for Your Majesty, in regard of that Act of Indulgence, and the Liberty of Conscience, which through Your Majesties Favour we now enjoy.*

Queen. *Tis what I am for. It is not in the Power of Men to Believe what they Please; and therefore I think, they should not be forced in matters of Religion, contrary to their Perswasions and their Consciences. I WISH ALL GOOD MEN WERE OF ONE MIND; HOWEVER IN THE MEAN TIME, I WOULD HAVE THEM LIVE PEACEABLY, AND LOVE ONE ANOTHER.*

O mentis Aureae Verba bracteata![211] My Ink, Too Vile a Liquor art thou, to Write so Divine a Sentence!

7. Before the Month was out, the King returned from Holland; And though he staid but a Fortnight in England, Mr. Mather twice had the Honour of waiting on Him. The first time he only Presented an Address from the General Court at Boston, with a Petition from a considerable Number of Merchants in London, Praying that Charter-Privileges might be Restored unto New-England. But Mr. Mather was desirous once more to Plead with him for Favour to his Country:

and therefore by the Mediation of the Duke of Devonshire, he was, on Apr. 28. Admitted a second time, and it was now into the Kings Bed-Chamber: Where what then Passed was, as followeth.

Mather. *I most Humbly Thank Your Majesty, in that you were Graciously Pleased to Signify unto my Lord Devonshire, that I might have leave to wait on your Majesty on the behalf of New-England. None of Your Subjects are or can be more in Your Interests than They; None Pray more Heartily for Your Long Life, and your Happy Reign, and the Success of Your Arms.*

King. *Syr, What do you Desire, that I should do for them!*

Mather. *May it Please Your Majesty, That they may be Restored unto their Ancient Privileges; and that their Settlement may be Expedited. They have an Humble Confidence, that through Your Majesties Goodness, they shall be made Happy, in having their Ancient Privileges Restored unto them; which will Oblige Your Subjects there to be Your Servants forever. Your Majesty has been Graciously Pleased to refer the Consideration of this Affair to the Two Lord-Chief-Justices, with the Attorney and Sollicitor[-]General. We only Pray Humbly that what they have thought Reasonable for us to Desire, may be Granted by Your Majesty.*

King. *I Expect within two or three Days, to have a Report from the Lords of the Committee for Trade and Plantations; and then shall see what may be done.*

Mather. *Your Majesties Subjects have been willing to Venture their Lives that they may enlarge Your Dominions: And are willing to do the like again, if Your Majesty Encourage them. Will Your Majesty Please, in Your Great Wisdom, to consider the Circumstances of that People; as in Your Wisdom you have considered the Circumstances of England and of Scotland. In New-England they differ from other Plantations; They are such as are called Congregational and Presbyterian. So that such a Governour will not suit with the People of New[-]England, as may be very Proper for the other English Plantations.*

Having so spoken, he bowed unto the King; who then retired into his Closet.

Two Days after this, the Lords of the Committee Proposed unto the KING, whether he would have the People of New-England, make what Laws, and Appoint what Officers They Pleased? Or, Whether He would not Appoint a Governour of His own, that should have a Negative Voice on all Acts of Government? The King was very Inquisitive to know, whether he might without any Breach of Law, set a Governour over that Colony? Diverse Lords of the Council, and some of the Judges, answered, That whatever might be the Merit of the Cause, inasmuch as the Charter of the Massachuset-Colony stood Vacated by a Judgment against it, it was in his Power to put them under what Form of Government he should think best for them. The King then said, That he was Desirous to Promote the Welfare of New-England as well as of England; and that he Believed it would be for the Advantage of the Subjects in that Colony to be under a Governour appointed by himself: but that he would have the Agents of New-England Nominate a Person that should be Agreable to the Inclinations of the People there: And that notwithstanding This, he would have Charter-Privileges Restored and Confirmed unto them.

8. The next Day, the King began his Voyage to Holland: but an Order of Council was drawn up, (Who can tell, How, or Why?) for a Charter to be Prepared, with something in it, very Disagreable to Mr. Mather; who immediately waited upon Four or Five Lords of His Majesties most Honourable Privy-Council with his Remonstrances; Every one of which Declared, that in their Opinion, it was not worded according to His Majesties Intentions. He also caused a Copy of the Order to be transmitted unto One of his Majesties Principal Secretaries of State then with Him in Flanders; Praying, That if the Order were not according to the Kings Mind, His Majesty would Graciously Please to Signify His Disapprobation thereof: But no such Signification ever came. In the mean time, the Attorney General, Prepared a Draught of a Charter according to what he took to be the Kings Mind, as Expressed when His Majesty was last in Council. In this Draught, the Freemen (and not all Free-holders) had Power to choose the Deputy-Governour, and the other General Officers; And the Kings Governour had not a Negative Voice in any case allow'd unto him. The Draught being presented at the Council-Board, it was by some Objected, That by such a Charter as this, the Kings Governour would be made a Governour of Clouts: And Order was given for other Minutes to be Inserted, which Deprived the Massachuset-Colony of some very Considerable Privileges in their former Charter. The Secretary gave Mr. Mather a Copy of them, with an Order from their Lordships, That if the Agents for the Massachuset-Colony were not Satisfied, they should bring in their Objections to Mr. Attorney-General. Mr. Mather on this occasion Expressed his Dissatisfaction, to the Attorney-General, with a Pathos, that upon Reflection he thought might be too Extraordinary: Earnestly Protesting That he would sooner part with his Life than Consent unto such Minutes, or unto any thing that might Infringe any Liberty or Privilege that justly belong'd unto his Country. The like Declaration he made unto several of the Chief Ministers; who all replied, That no body Expected or

Desired his Consent: for they did not look on the Agents from New-England, as Plenipotentiaries from another Sovereign State; But that if they Declared, they would not Submit unto the Kings Pleasure, His Majesty would settle the Country as He Pleased, and They were to take what would follow. However, Mr. Mather drew up Reasons against the Minutes Proposed; and particularly urged, That Charter-Privileges might with as much (if not more) of Justice, be witheld from the Corporations in England, which were never legally Restored, as from New-England: with several other Arguments. These Reasons he Delivered in Writing to the Kings Attorney-General, who Presented them unto the Lords at the Council-Board; and he also caused a Copy of them to be sent unto the King in Flanders; Procuring some Great Persons at the same time, to sollicit by Letters, the Ministers of State with the King, that they would use their Interest with His Majesty, to prevent any thing that might be grievous to His Good Subjects in New-England. Some thought, that if the King were in England, there might be more likelihood of Stopping the Disagreable and Undesireable Minutes; and the Queen was therefore Prevailed withal, to Write unto the King, requesting him, That He would Graciously Command, that the Charter should pass as the Attorney-General had prepared it, or else that it should be deferr'd until His Majesties coming over. Mr. Mather taking it for granted, That he might get some Liesure to recover his Health, which had been greatly impaired, by his Neglect both of Rest and Food in his close Attendance to the Service of his Country, made a short Recess unto the Waters. But he was quickly surprized, with Notice, That the King had signified His Approbation of the Minutes, and His Royal Pleasure, that the Charter should be accordingly forthwith proceeded in. His Majesties Principal Secretary of State shewed Mr. Mather the Letter, wherein the King also Declared, That he did by no means Approve of the Objections, which had been offered. When there could no more Good be done, what remain'd was to stave off Harm as far as might be; and in Pursuance of This, he Presented a Petition, That no Property belonging to the Colony, or to any therein, might by the New Charter be taken from them, nor any Privileges which they had a Right to; That the Province of Main might be confirmed, and Nova Scotia added unto the Massachusetts: (Both of which were obtain'd against much Opposition:) And, That Hampshire might be under that Government: (But This was refused, because it was declared, That the People there had expressed a great Aversion for it.) Just at this Time, he received Letters from the General Court of Plymouth-Colony, which Thanked him for his Preventing their being annexed unto New-York, which had been above a Year before if he had been out of the way; and Pray'd, That if they might not be confirmed as a Distinct Government among themselves, he would, for the Lords Sake, endeavour to get them annexed unto Boston; And This was accomplished. When the New Charter was finished, and had been Read before the Lords, he pray'd, that he might see it; because there might be some Clauses in it, which their Lordships might upon a Suggestion of Reasons for it, think proper to alter; and perhaps there might be something Added for the Good of the People, which their Lordships might also be Pleased withal; which Request was granted, with a Limitation of Three Days for the Return of the Copy Upon his motion, the Phrase of Corporal Oath was altered, that so no Snare might be laid for any who might Scruple Swearing on the Book. A clause was added, Confirming al[l] Grants made by the General Court notwithstanding any Defect that might attend the Form of Conveyance; that so mens Titles to their Lands mig[h]t not be Invalidated, only for that the Laws which gave them their Right, had not passed under the Public Seal in the Time of the former Government. Some other Alterations he pray'd [f]or; but could not Obtain them. Thus was the New Charter Finished!

9. NOW came on a Strange Question: Whether the Agents for the Country should Submit unto this NEW CHARTER? Or, in hopes of Obtaining at some time or other a Reversion of the Judgment against the OLD CHARTER, Signify to the Ministers of State, that they had rather have NO CHARTER at all, than such an one as was now Proposed!

On this occasion, Mr. Mather advised with as many Unprejudiced and Judicious Persons as he could; with Noblemen, Gentlemen, Divines, and Lawyers; and with the Best Friends New-England had in the World. They ALL agreed, That it was a Duty, to accep[t] of the Offered CHARTER; And some greatly wondered at them that should make any Question of it: and were almost ready to say of them, as Plato in his *Philebus* does of some who made Question of another matter; *Let them be Committed unto the Care of some Learned Physician, who by wholesome Physic may restore their Heads unto a better Temper.*

A Peremptory Refusal, would have brought a Fatal Ruin on the Country; and the Blame would have been laid on those, who when they could not Obtain all they would have, would Refuse what they might have had.

The Lawyers declared, That a passive Submission here, had nothing of a Surrender in it; for here was nothing of Hand and Seal in the Case. Besides, Judgment was already Entred and Recorded against the Old Charter. And a taking up with the New Charter, did not render the Colony uncapable of recovering their Old Privileges if there should be a favourable Opportunity to Sollicit for it.

At present, there was no Possibility of getting a Reversion of the Judgment against the Old Charter.

Yea, and it was considered, That the Old Charter was on more Accounts than One, so very Defective, that without a Grant of Additional Privileges, it would have left the Colony under Insupportable Infaelicities.

By it, the Massachuset-Government had no more power than the Ordinary Corporations have in England; But those Corporations have no power in Capital Cases. Though Corporations have Power given them in Criminal, yet they have not in Capital Cases, except it be Expressly Declared; which it was not here.

The Old Charter directed not an House of Deputies, or Assembly of Representatives.

Nor did it give Power unto the Governour and Company to Impose Taxes on any but the Free-men.

And it knew not Courts of Admiralty; So that if the New Charter have them not, it is not the Loss of the Old One that has Lost them. Yea, The Deficiencies were so many, That the Kings Attorney[-]General declared, the Two Lord-Chief-Justices and Sollicitor[-]General Concurring with him; That Supposing the Judgment against the Massachuset-Charter to be Reversed, yet, if the Government should exert such Powers as before the *Quo Warranto* against the Charter they tho't it necessary to do, there would now be a Writ of *Scire facias* issued out against them in Westminister Hall, and their Charter-Privileges would undoubtedly be taken from them.

It was moreover Considered, That if the Judgment against the Old Charter had been fully Reversed by Act of Parliament, (which Mr. Mather had so much Laboured for,) the Massachuset-Colony would, for all that, have been reduced into Miserable Circumstances.

The Province of Main, as to the Government, would have been taken from them. Hampshire and Plymouth would have been put under a Governour sent from England. This Governour would have had the Power of the Militia, as well as the Courts of Admiralty, in the Massachuset-Colony.

How much of its Trade had Boston Lost? What an insignificant Atom had the Colony been Squeez'd into! If they had Exerted Powers, without which they could not have Comfortably or Tolerably Subsisted, Perpetual Complaints would have been made against them. Its probable They would have been at more Charge every Year, to answer Complaints, than they would have been to Support their

Governour. And how long must they have lain under their Impotency, Saying, *Syr, I have no Man to help me!*

Besides all this; If the Agents of the Colony, had signified unto the Ministers of State, that they had rather have No Charter at all, than This which the K[i]ng had now granted, Who would have been Immedia[t]ely made the Governour? Who the Lieutenant-Governour? Who the most of the Counsellers? And the Governour would have had Power, as in the other Plantations, to Appoint General Officers. What the Consequence of This at that Angry Time? *Dicat Neo-Eboracum!*[212]

There were also Persons, who were seeking Patents for all the Mines, and Gums, and some other Valuables, in the Country; whose Expectations, nothing but the New Charter gave a De[f]eat unto.

But, Let us come to the NEW CHARTER, THIS grants Great Privileges to the People of New-England; and some Greater than what they formerly Enjoy'd.

They have all English Liberties Restored unto them. They can have no Laws Imposed, not Taxes Levied on them, without their own Consent, by Representatives chosen by themselves.

Religion is forever Secured; A Righteous and Generous Liberty of Conscience Established. And the General Assembly may by their Acts, give a Distinguishing Encouragement unto that Religion, which is the General Profession of the Inhabitants.

They may still have their Judges as at the first, and their Counsellours as at the Beginning, if the Fault be not their own. As long as their Principal Majestrates, and Justices, favour and express Piety, and abhor and punish Wickedness, tis to be hoped, Religion will be kept in Heart. And if they have not such, the Fault will not be in the New-Charter, but in Themselves. Behold, a wall of Defence about the Vineyard!

Now the Massachuset-Colony is made a Province, the General Assembly hath, with the Kings Approbation, a Power in New-England, like what the King and Parliament have in England; and may do abundance of Important Things, which could not be done by vertue of the Former Charter: And the Country may also look for more Protection and Assistance from England, than under That.—

Suppose a Stork should get a Commission for the Government; What can such a Governour do? He cannot, without the Consent of the Council chosen by the Representatives of the People, appoint Sheriffs to pack Juries for him, or Judges that will Displease GOD rather than him. He can't give any Man any Disturbance for his Religion, without Violating the Magna Charta of New-England. He can't exert any of the Violences, under which there were heard, The Groans of the Plantations in the Days if K. James II. When, the People of New[-]England would have given, who can say, how many Thousands of Pounds, for such a Charter as they now have before them?

The Kings Governour has indeed a Negative in all Acts of Government; (And indeed all Government forever implies a Negative:) which renders the Government of New-England, less Democratical than once it was. Nevertheless, the People have a Negative upon him: In which respect, New-England is by the NEW CHARTER more Privileged, than Ireland, or than any other English Plantation, or than even England itself.

Appeals to England are allow'd in the New-Charter, but only in Personal, (not at all in Real or Mixed) Actions, where the matter of Difference, is of above Three Hundred Pound Sterling in Value: So that as to Titles of Land, there cannot be any Appeals to England: They have a Final Determination in Courts of Judicature among themselves.

The Laws Enacted by the General Court, are, tis true, to be transmitted unto the King for His Royal Approbation: But those Laws, when made, are in Force, assoon as they are made; and until such Time as they are Disallow'd by the King: And if within the space of Three Years the Kings Disapprobation be not Signified, the Laws are Perpetual until the General Court shall Repeal them. Now by the Old Charter, the Governour and Company might not make any Laws Repugnant unto the Laws of England; and the Laws which have Reason and Justice in them, under the New Charter, need not fear losing the Royal Allowance, if the People be not Egregiously wanting to themselves.

Upon the whole, The Persons of the most Consummate Wisdom that Mr. Mather could consult withal, agreed in This; *Take your NEW CHARTER and be Thankful for it!* The most sensible Men added, That as Poor a Charter as wanton and froward Minds might think it, if any People of Sway in the Country should be so under the Sting of an Hornet as to do those Rash and Mad Things, which may procure the Loss of the Privileges which it brings unto them, the rest of the People will certainly have little Honour for the Memory of the Unhappy Men, who have been the Instruments of bringing such Mischeifs upon them. Among the rest, that Sagacious and Ingenious Person, Praesident Bond of Barbadoes (then at London) said unto him: *What would not we in our Islands give for such a Charter as yours[.]* And the famous Mr. Matthew Mead then wrote unto the Person who is now Writing about the Faithful Agent, *If Men Reward not his Great Work, and Labour of Love, I am sure, GOD will. What he has done has not been without the Counsel and Advice of the Best Friends New-England has: Parliament-men, Lawyers and Ministers.*

10. Wherefore, not only on Oct[.] 23. upon the Kings Return to England, the Earl of Notingham introduced him, only to kiss the Kings Hand, & bid him, Welcome to England again: when the King at the first sight of him, smiled on him, & steping aside unto him, said, *I am very glad to see you, Syr!* But also on Nov. 4. the same Noble Person Introduced him again to His Majesty, the Earls of Devon and Portland, being also Present. He then said, *I do on the behalf of New-England most humbly thank your Majesty, in that you have been Pleased by a CHARTER to Restore English Liberties unto them; To Confirm them in their Properties; and, To grant them some singular Privileges. I doubt not, but that your Subjects there will demean themselves with such a Dutiful Affection and Loyalty towards your Majesty, as that You will see cause to enlarge Your Royal Favours towards them. And I do most humby Thank your Majesty in that You have been Pleased to give leave unto those that are concerned for New-England, to Nominate their Governour. Sr. William Phips has been accordingly Nominated by us at the Council-Board: Who has done a Good Service for the Crown by enlarging Your Dominions, and reducing of Nova Scotia to Your Obedience. I know, that he will Faithfully Serve Your Majesty to the utmost of his Capacity; And if Your Majesty shall think fit to confirm him, in that Place, it will be a further Obligation on Your Subjects there.* The KING replied, *I shall take that Colony under my Protection, and I shall do what is in me for their Encouragement, and I shall take what concerns the Government there into my Consideration.*

11. And now, Mr. Mathers Agency for his Country in the Court of England is drawing towards its Period, it will be time to enquire, whether his being so Plunged into a Conversation with Great Men, and with all Sorts of Men, and his Overwhelming Sollicitude about Civil Interests (*In Ordine ad Spiritualia; For, The Care of the Churches,* was what lay at the Bottom of all!) did not Interrupt those Interviews with Heaven, which he had formerly been used unto; and Incommode that course of Real, Vital, Watchful PIETY, which he had formerly Maintained? Far from it! But above all, that Breath of PIETY, his Old strokes [stroke] of Incessant PRAYER, was kept in its Unintermitted Respirations with him.

It is a little Observable That though Homer, by first Introducing the Gods as having the same Vicious Characters, and Actions with miserable Mortals, Proved one of the Greatest Apostles the Devil ever had in the World; yet the Testimonies born to many Points of Morality in his Famous and Wondrous Epic Poem, are numberless. But there is nothing more worthy of Observation in the *Iliad*, than This; That he will Recommend Prayer to Heaven as a most necessary Preface unto all Important Enterprizes: and he never Speaks of any Prayer, but he brings in a Gracious Answer to it. I have seen the Quill of an High-flyer[213] Scoffing at Homer for this, as making his Hero's to be of the same Religion with the Dissenters in our Nation. And yet, what has Homer done, but Justified the Wisdom in the Maxims of our Holy REDEEMER, with a Confession from that Natural Conscience, which such Scoffers of the Last Days have Silenced? Let them Scoff on, if they Please; while I go on to relate, That I find Mr[.] Mather still in his Good old way, of Setting apart whole Days for Secret Supplications to the Glorious GOD; Especially, when Critical Hours for our Affairs were coming on. In these Days, I find him sometimes under those Afflations from Heaven, which assured him, That he should Return to New-England, with *Good Tidings for the People there.*[214] When he saw his Designs Crost, and his Labours Lost, in his pursuit of the Old Charter, it greatly Perplexed him to see what look'd unto him, as if his Prayer and Faith were Baffled. But GOD was Graciously doing better than he Imagined, for him, and for his People, whom the Old Charter, (as it was) would not have near so well Accommodated (as things go) as what is now Obtained for them. Nor was he without his whole Days for Secret Thanksgivings, when GOD had Remarkably smiled upon him. And he would sometimes (after a well-known Pattern in the Bible,) prevail with his Friends to meet, and Fast and Pray, when he was to go in unto the King: Or when our Affairs had any dark Obstructions upon them. Yea, such was the Sanctity and Purity of his Good Conversation in CHRIST, that wherever he Lodged, the Families felt Piety Practically and Powerfully Commended unto them. Among other Instances of this; The Young Gentlewoman that waited on him, at Mr. Whitings in Copt-hall Court, was by what she saw in him, and heard from him so brought home to GOD, that afterwards, when she was Married, she gave the World a lasting Testimony of her Gratitude, in the Remembrance of the Good which her Converted Soul had received from him. He likewise rarely Omitted Preaching on the Lords-Days: for which, in Honour to his Country he would accept of no Gratuities; but Obliged the Ministers to do Good Offices for his Country. Once a month, he Preached with Dr. Bates, at Hackney: who though he were a Person of so Catholic a Spirit, had one of the Smallest and Purest Churches about the City; with which he chose to have his more Constant Communion at the Holy Table: And the Doctor told his People, *That if Mr. Mather might be detained in England, he had rather have him joined with him in the Pastoral Charge, than any man in the World.*

12. But, shall we go on to enquire, whether the People of New-England, were the only People, that were served by him? No, There was a Special Service, of a greater extent, wherein His Glorious Lord Employed and Honoured him. There was an Happy UNION accomplished between those Two Religious Parties, which go under the Names of Presbyterian, and Congregational; and which had through Devices of the Great Adversary, kept at more of a Needless Distance from each other, than they should have done. Dr. Annesley and Mr. Vincent and others, often Declared, That this Union would never have been Effected, if Mr. Mather had not been among them; and they often therefore Blessed GOD, for bringing him to England, and keeping him there. He had Thanks from the Country, as well as the City on that Account: And among the rest, a General Assembly of Ministers in Devon, sent up to London this Instrument.

"Junij 23. 1691. Agreed, That the Reverend Mr. John Flavel, Moderator of this Assembly send unto the Reverend Mr. Matthew Mead, Mr. John How, and Mr. Increase Mather, and give Them, and such Others as have been Eminently Instrumental in Promoting the Union, the Thanks of this Assembly, for the great Pains they have taken therein."

And since it is Proper to be mention'd somewhere, why may I not bring in the mention of it Here? While Mr. Mather was in London, he Cultivated a singular Friendship and Freedom, with that very Great Man, Mr. Baxter, who treated him with a Deference, which he paid unto few other Men. In this Acquaintance, Mr. Baxter not only made this Generous Request unto Mr. Mather, *Syr, If you find any Errors in any of my Writings, I request you to Confute them, after I am Dead;* But also made unto him a very Respectful Dedication of a Book, which he Published a little before he Died. I find in Dr. Bates's Funeral Sermon for Mr. Baxter, a mention of the Visit which he with Mr. Mather made unto Mr. Baxter the Day, before his Expiration, (which was, Dec. 8. 1691.) when the last Words of Mr. Baxter to Mr. Mather were, *I Bless GOD, that you have Accomplisht your Business; The LORD Prolong your Life!*

13. The Business being so Accomplished, there yet remains One Enquiry more; How was he Subsisted for the Expences of his Agency.

In the Year, 1691. while he was yet in London, he wrote these Words, in a brief Account of his Negotiation, which he sent over to the Government.

"Besides what was sent to me out of New-England, I Expended

upwards of Two Hundred Pounds of my own Personal Estate, out of Love to that People. And I did for their sakes, borrow of a Merchant in London, above Three Hundred Pounds more, which it was Two Years before Care was taken for the Repayment of it. The last Year, some who were hearty Well-wishers to New-England, wrote thither, That they must consider, how much depended on a suitable Supply; yet for more than a Twelve-month, not one Penny was returned; so that I was necessitated, either to suffer a Ruin to come upon the Country, or else must borrow Money again to Serve them; which I did, and engaged all the Estate I have in the World, for the Repayment thereof."

Some time after this, there was Published a Venemous and Malicious Libel, by a mean Hand, instigated in part from the Invisible World, and well worthy to be Recommended unto the Rebuke of the Lord, which was Entituled, *More Wonders of the Invisible World.*[215] The Conscience of Duty to the Ninth Commandment of my GOD, as well as the Fifth, obliges me to Declare, (which I hope, I may do without any Railing Accusation,) That the Book is full of Gross, Base, Notorious LYES; and has been Unanswerably Convicted of being so; and they who take their Accounts of New-England from it, follow but an *Ignis fatuus.*[216] On the occasion of the Slanders uttered in that foolish Book, Mr. Mather gave under his Hand unto some Honest Men, who Published a Victorious Answer to them, an Instrument, which had these among other Passages.

"I am also told, that his great Friends Complain, That I spent the Country a great deal of Money, during my Agency in their behalf. These little Men know not what it is, to attend in the Courts of Kings for Four Years together: if they did, they would not make that Objection. And sure I am, that when I did, at the desire of many Principal Persons in the Country, undertake a Voyage for England, in April. 1688. People in this Province would have given Ten times more than what I Expended in their Service, on condition they might have Restored and Confirmed unto them, what they now Enjoy; yea, if it had been but in One Article of it. But besides this, I may truly affirm, that in Effect I served the Country on Free cost. For I never demanded the least Farthing as a Recompence for the Time I spent in attending on their Affairs; but instead thereof, I procured in Donations for the public (besides the Privileges of the Charter itself, which, though not so great as I would have had, and as I would gladly have parted with all I have in this World for to have purchased, are greater than what any other Plantations besides New-England enjoys: I say, Besides these Things I procured in Donations to the Province and the College) at least Nine Hundred Pounds more than all the Expences of my Agency came to. This being plain Matter of Fact, which the whole

General Assembly once had before them, I suppose, all Reasonable men will own, That Reproaches cast on me, for my Expensiveness in the Public Service are most Ungrateful and Unworthy."

But here, this Long Chapter shall have a Period; and, I hope, a Pardon. Only it seems I must again ask a Pardon also for the Agent, whose Actions I have been telling of. Some who have been vexed at good Things done by Ministers of the Gospel, have made mighty Clamours against Ministers having any thing to do in Secular Affairs. But the Scripture which forbids Ministers to Entangle themselves with the Affairs of this Life, or be so taken up with them, as to neglect the Duties of their Ministry, does belong to other Vocations as well as to that of Ministers. A Physician, an Husbandman, a Merchant, may not so meddle with State-Affairs, as to neglect the Personal Business which GOD has call'd them to. We may as well forbid Ministers, to Write any Books, but those of Pure Divinity, as forbid them all Cognisance of Secular Affairs on some Great and Just Occasions. A Speech of an Eminent Person once in the House of Lords observed, That no Reformed Church in the World, held that Ministers may not Intermeddle in Secular Affairs. He particularly mention'd Calvin and Beza, whose Influences very much governed the Council of State at Geneva: Brentius and Scultet, and Du moulin, and Rivet; and others who were Privy-Counsellors to Princes.[217] Tis true, Ministers usually have enough to do, in attending to their Pastoral Charge; and the Ordaining of them to That, is a Filling of their Hand. They must Watch for Souls as those that must give an Account. But when without Injury to That, they do upon Public and Pressing Emergencies, apply their Superior Talents to some things of a Secular Importance, they do but what Honest Men ought to do. Opportunities to do good, not only Legitimate the Application of their Capacities to do it, but also Oblige them and Require them to do it.

Hence it is among the sayings of the great Seldon:[218] *Tis a foolish Thing to say, A Minister must not meddle with Secular matters, because his own Profession will take up his whole man: May he not Eat, or Drink, or Walk, or Learn to Sing? The meaning is only, That he must Seriously attend his Calling.* This Mr. Mather did, even in the midst of his greatest Avocations.

Article XXVII.
The Returning Dove.

It is now high Time to be Looking Homewards.

As far backwards as the Year, 1689. Things were in such an hopeful tendency towards an Happy Settlement of the Country, that Mr.

Mather, in his Chamber at London, (in Copthall Court, Throgmorton Street) set apart several whole Days, to Acknowlege the Favours of GOD Hitherto Assisting and Succeeding of him. So, having obtained a Letter from the KING (Dated, Aug[.] 12. 1689) unto those who were now in the Government here, Signifying His Approbation of what had been done by them in Re-assuming of the Government, and encouraging them to go on until an Orderly Settlement for His Service and their Satisfaction, should be Accomplished; And the Bill for the Restoring of Charters, and particularly those of New-England, having passed in the House of Commons; and there not being then any apparent Hazard, but that it would be carried on unto Perfection; he thought he might Return to New[-]England with Comfortable Tidings. He took his leave of his Friends at London; and on Aug. 20. went as far as Graves-End; and the next Day to Deal, where the Ship lay on Board of which he took his Passage. Here he lay Windbound, until Sept. 3. when his Youngest Son, then with him, was taken so Dangerously Sick of the Small Pox, that it was Impossible to leave him in that Condition. The Ship went away without him; and he (with his Restored Son) returned unto London, in the Beginning of October; where it was not long before he found such a Turn of Affairs, as fulfill'd what his Friends told him, when they welcomed him upon his Return, *That the Gracious GOD had stop'd his Voyage in great Mercy to his Country.* We have now seen the Great Mercy intended in it: And all things being finished, which concerned the Settlement of the Country, the Earl of Nottingham introduced him once more to the KING at Whitehall, Jan. 3. 1691, 2. in the Evening. After he had Kissed the KINGS hand, His Majesty said to him, *Are you going to New-England?* He answered, *With Your Majesties Leave, I am so. If in any thing I may Serve Your Majesties Interest there, I shall count myself Happy, that Your Majesty will Please to lay Your Commands upon me.* The KING replied, *Syr, I Thank you; I Wish you a Good Voyage.* He then said, *There is one thing, which I would humbly put Your Majesty in mind of. We have in New-England a COLLEGE, where many an Excellent Protestant Divine has had his Education.* The KING said, *I know it!* He thereupon added, *If Your Majesty will cast a favourable Aspect on that Society, it will yet Flourish more than ever.* The KING returned, *I shall willingly do it.*—And so Ended the Final Conference.

Mr. Mather, upon a Review of his Agency, was now able to use those Words, "As Day and Night have seen it; so I can and do Appeal to Heaven and Earth, that I have Served the People of my Country, with all Fidelity, and unto the Very utmost of my Capacity." And so, with an easy mind in himself, but great Expressions of Affection in his

Friends at his taking his *ultimum Vale* of them,[219] he left London, on Mr. 7. 1692. and Sr[.] William Phips, then having received the Royal Commission for the Government of New-England fetch'd him in a Yacht from Southampton, to Cowes in the Isle of Wight, where the Ship lay in which he was to take his Passage. There he Preached both parts of the Day; which he afterwards had Opportunity to do in Dartmouth, and in Plymouth.

On Mar. 29. 1692. he with the Companions of his Voyage, left Plymouth; and had a Comfortable Passage for New-England, under the Convoy of the None-Such Frigat. Instead of their falling into the Hands of their Foes, which was much feared by their Friends, a French prize fell into their Hands. And they had also a notable Deliverance from what they commonly call, A Tartar: For spying some Ships which they took for French Merchant-men, their Convoy made away for them; until contrary Winds compelled them to leave the chase. But on the Day following, a French Vessel which they took, informed them, That they were Four French Men of War, which were bound home for France, from the Island of Martinico.

On May 14. he arrived safe to his House and Flock, at Boston. And soon after the first Great and General Assembly of the Province was Convened; unto whom he repaired, and Reading over the Instructions he had received from the Government, he upon each of them Demonstrated unto the Satisfaction of the whole Assembly, that he had unto the utmost of his Power Punctually observed them. After some Days, and upon the most mature Examination and Deliberation, the Speaker in the Name of the whole House of Representatives, returned him Thanks for his Faithful, Painful, Indefatigable Endeavours to serve the Country; and added, That they were willing to Reward his Meritorious Endeavours; but by reason of the Expensive War under which they were Labouring, they were at present unable to do any thing Proportionable to his Merits: To which Mr. Mather answered, That he Sought not Theirs but Them, in all that he had Endeavoured, and for his Recompence, he was willing to expect it in Another World. However, he had in This World, so much as This comes to; That the Great and General Assembly, appointed a Day of Solemn THANKSGIVING to Almighty GOD, through the Province, for Granting a Safe Return to His Excellency our Governour, and the Reverend Mr. Increase Mather, who (as the order expressed it) have industriously endeavoured the Service of this People, and brought over with them a Settlement of Government, in which their Majesties have Graciously given us Distinguishing Marks of their Royal Favour and Goodness.

He was fortified with diverse Letters from Eminent Persons, Testifying and Celebrating his Indefatigable endeavours for the Good of the Country, and adding, *While Some with you may perhaps Wonder, that he has Obtained no more, we here, who have the Advantage of a better Prospect, wonder that he has done so much.* But I shall Supersede all Citations from them, with only Producing a Copy of a Letter, Prepar'd by the Venerable Dr. Bates, and Signed by Twelve more; all of them Eminent Ministers in London; and such as the Doctor chose for that purpose. This was a Thing, which Mr. Mather, had never Desir'd or Propos'd, but that Great Man did it, and had the Names of Ten Ministers to it, before ever Mr. Mather spoke one Word unto any of them about it: nor could any Two of them ever be Prevailed withal to suspect any overdoing in any one expression of it.

The Letter is worth Preserving, if it were only for the Excellent Hand that Composed it; For, *Caelum est Quicquid tam Docta Manus condidit.*[220] This it is.

"To the Much Honoured General Court Assembled at Boston in New-England.

"Much Honoured Gentlemen.

"The Restoring of your Charter, upon which the Security and Public Good of Your Colony Depends, We Congratulate with as Joyful Affections, as with Tender Resentments, We Condoled the Deprivation of it. When Your and Our State was in Appearance Desolate beyond Humane Power and Councel to redress, Then Deliverance came from above: And in our Deep Darkness, the Day Spring from on High visited us. We must humbly Admire and Adore the Glorious Author of that Blessed Work: And we cannot but Pay our Grateful Respects, and Dutiful Subjection to His chosen Servant, our Sovereign, the Happy Instrument of it. All the Colours of Language are not Lively and Grateful enough to express His Benefits to us. He has the Honour of Establishing our Religion at Home, and gives us Hopes of Restoring it abroad, in places from whence it has been Unrighteously and Cruelly expelled.

"Some among You may Wonder, there has been so long Delay before Your Charter was finisht, but if you consider the Torrent of Affairs in Court after the Late Revolution, it will Lessen the Wonder.

"The Truth is, Your Affairs were so Difficult, & Thorny, that the Rare Union of the Wisdom of the Serpent, & the Innocence of the Dove, was requisite in the Commissioners manageing of it. A Peremptory Refusal of any Charter, but of an Uniform Tenor with the First, had been like too Strong a Medicine, that Exasperates the Disease instead of Curing it. In Affairs of great Importance, tis Wisdom Maturely to Deliberate, and consider Conditional Events, and by the foresight of Inconveniences that will otherwise follow, to accept of such things as are Best with respect to their Circumstances. We must therefore give this True Testimony of our much Esteemed and Beloved Brother, Mr. Increase Mather, That with Inviolate Integrity, excellent Prudence, and Unfainting Diligence, he hath Managed the great Business Committed to His Trust. As he is Instructed in the School of Heaven, to Minister in the Affairs of the Soul, so he is furnished with a Talent to Transact Affairs of State. His Proceedings have been with that Caution and Circumspection, as is Correspondent to the Weight of his Commission; He with Courage and Constancy has Pursued the Noble Scope of his Employment, and understanding the True Moment of Things, has preferred the Public Good to the Vain Conceits of some, that more might have been Obtained if Peremptorily Insisted on. Considering open Opposition and Secret Arts, that have been used to frustrate the best endeavours for the Interest of New-England, the Happy Issue of these things is Superior to our Expectations. Your Present Charter secures Liberty and Property the fairest Flowers of the Civil State: And which is Incomparably more valuable, it secures the Enjoyment of the Blessed Gospel in its Purity and Freedom. Altho' there is a Restraint of your Power in some things that were granted in the Former Charter, yet there are more Ample Privileges in other things, that may be of Perpetual Advantage to the Colony.

"We doubt not but Your Faithful Agent will receive a Gracious Reward above: And we hope his Successful Service will be Welcomed with your entire Approbation, and Grateful Acceptance. We now with ardent Affections recommend our Dear Brother to the Divine Mercy, that thro' such Dangerous Seas he may safely arrive at his desired Place. And We earnestly Pray, that the Blessings of Heaven may be always upon Your Colony; that by the Light and Power of the Gospel, the Prince of Darkness may be Expelled from his Ancient Dominions; and the Kingdom of our Saviour, may be Established and Enlarged, by the Accession of the American Heathen to be His Inheritance. Much Honoured Gentlemen,

We are,

Your very Humble and Faithful Servants,

LONDON
Oct. 17. 1691.

William Bates.	Thomas Woodcock.
Matthew Mead.	John James.
Matthew Barker.	Samuel Annesly.
Richard Stretton.	George Griffith.
Vincent Alsop.	Richard Mayo.

John How. Isaac Chancy.
John Quick."

There needs no more.

—Except I should now add, That I have at this Moment before me, a Letter from Dr. Bates to this his Friend, which has these Expressions in it; "I am truly sensible of the Ungrateful Returns of Some in your Country for all your Prudent Conduct, your Unwearied Patience, and Happy Success, in the Management of their Affairs. But as your Aims were above their Poor Acknowledgments, so your Reward will be in the Acceptance of Him who Judges Righteously.

Article XXVIII.
Troubles from the Invisible World.

One born to do Special Service for his People, arrived unto them, at a Time, when Scores of poor People had fallen under a Prodigious Possession of Devils, which it was then generally thought, had been Introduced by Witchcrafts, or the Arts and Acts of such as had made Compacts with Daemons, to annoy their Neighbours. The Devils, who had perhaps by the little & foolish Sorceries, or Magical Tricks, of too many rash People, plaid withal, were Permitted now by the Irritated Vengeance of Heaven to break in upon the Country, with *an Horrible Tempest.*[221] Some Scores of People, first about Salem, and then in several other Places, were Arrested with many Preternatural Vexations upon their Bodies, and a Variety of Tortures, which were Indisputably Inflicted from the Daemons of the Invisible World. The People that were Infected and Infested with such Daemons, in a few Days, arrived unto a Sight, wherein they Imagined that they saw their Tormentors: a Devil of a little Stature and a Tawny Colour, attended still with Spectres that appeared in more Humane Circumstances. These Tormentors tendred unto the Afflicted, a Book, requiring them to Sign it, or to Touch it at least, in token of their Consenting to be listed in the Service of the Devil; which they refusing to do, the Spectres under the Command of the Black Man, as they called him, would apply themselves to Torture them with Unaccountable Molestations. They would be Pinch'd Black and Blue; Pins would be run into their Flesh; They would be kept Fasting for whole Weeks together; and not to mention a Thousand other Things which would be Incredible unto others, but are not so to us, who saw them, and are Infallibly sure that we were not Impos'd upon[.] I'l mention but one more, that—*Crimine ab uno,*[222]—the rest may be Judged of. The

Miserables (some of them) Exclaimed, of Branding Irons heating at the Fire on the Hearth to mark them. Now though we the Standers by could see no Irons, yet we could see Distinctly the Print of them in the Ashes, and smell them too as they were carried by the Unseen Agents, unto the poor Creatures for whom they were intended; And these poor Creatures were thereupon so Stigmatized with them, that they will bear the Marks of them to their Dying Day. These Afflicted people, vehemently Cried out upon several Persons in several Places; that the Spectres which Afflicted them did exactly Resemble Them; until the Importunity of the outcries, with the Calamity of the Accusers, compelled the Magistrates to Examine them. When the Accused came upon their Examination, it was found, that the Daemons had unto the Afflicted People, exactly Represented them, and it was found, that the Accused but casting their Eye on the Afflicted, the Afflicted though their Faces were never so much another way, would fall down, and ly in a sort of a Swoon, wherein they would continue, whatever Hands were laid upon them, until the Hands of the Accused came to touch them, and then they would revive Immediately. And it was found that Various kinds of Natural Actions, done by the Accused in or to their own Bodies, as, Leaning, Bending, Turning awry [away], or Squeezing their Hands, or the like, were presently attended with the like Things Preternaturally done on the Bodies of the Afflicted, though they were so far asunder, that they could not Possibly Observe one another. It was also found, that the Flesh of the Afflicted was often bitten at such a rate, not that only [that not only] the Print of Teeth would be left on their Flesh, but the very Slaver of Spittle too: And there would appear just such a Set of Teeth, as was in the Accused, even such as might be clearly distinguished from other Peoples. And usually the Afflicted went thorough [through] a deal of seeming Difficulties from the Tormenting Spectres, and must be long waited on, before they could get a Breathing-Space, from their Torments to give in their Testimonies.

Now many Good Men took up an Opinion, That the Providence of GOD would not Permit an Innocent Person to come under such a Spectral Representation; and that a Concurrence of so many Circumstances would prove an Accused Person to be in a Confederacy with the Daemons thus Afflicting of the Neighbours. Diverse of the Accused People were brought upon their Trial, while this Opinion was yet Prevailing in the Minds of the Judges and the Juries; and though against many of the Tried, there was brought in some other Evidence, yet several were Executed mainly upon This, which was called The Spectre-Evidence. And it happened, that some of the Accused coming to Confess themselves Guilty, their Shapes were no more seen by any of the Afflicted, though the Confession of the former had been kept so Secret that the latter knew nothing of it: But instead thereof, these Accused ones fell under the same Vexations with the Afflicted; This Confirmed many in their Opinion. The Apparitions of Ghosts, which Declared themselves Murdered by the Accused, (and were some of them also seen by some Others besides the Afflicted,) and some of the Murders thereupon Confessed by some of the Accused; These also added unto the Zeal of the Proceedings. And Wiser Men, than those Flashy and Fleering[223] Witlings, who at a Distance think a Scornful Scoff to be a Sufficient Solution for these things, had they been on the spot, could not but have been extremely Puzzled with them. On the other part, there were many very Wise Men, who from the Beginning, were very much Dissatisfied at what was adoing; and feared that in the Extraordinary Descent of Wicked Spirits from their High-Places upon the Country, such Principles, and so such Practices, might be taken up, as would cause the Righteous to Perish with the Wicked. It Affected them to see that the more the Afflicted were Hearkened to, the more the Number of the Accused was Increased; until at last, many Unquestionably very Good People were Cried out upon. The Neighbouring Ministers of the Province, exhibited unto the Government, an Instrument Composed by the same Hand, that under a Desire to have a stop given unto Legal Prosecutions, in a case too hard for us who dwell in Houses of Clay, and only the Methods of Religion and of Devotion kept unto, offered, that if the Afflicted might be Separated, he would singly Provide for the Accommodation of six or seven of them, that the Success of Extraordinary Prayer with Fasting might be on this Occasion waited for. In that Instrument, there was a Disswasive against Credulity for Things only received on the Devils Authority; and against using any Test for the Trial of the Suspected, the Lawfulness whereof may be doubted among the People of GOD: and against Convicting any upon such Feeble Evidence, as the Representation of the Accused unto the Afflicted; Inasmuch as it is an Undoubted and Notorious Thing, that a Daemon may by GOD's Permission, appear even unto Ill purposes in the shape of an Innocent, yea, and a Vertuous Man; Nor can Alterations made in the Sufferers by a Look or Touch of the Accused, be an Infallible Token of Guilt, but frequently Liable to be abused by the Legerdemains of the Devil. It concluded so; "We know not, whether some Remarkable Affronts given to the Devils, by our Disbelieving of those Testimonies, whose whole Force and Strength is from Them alone, may not put a Period unto the Progress of a direful Calamity begun upon us, by the Accusation of so many Persons, whereof, we hope, some are yet clear from the Great Transgression laid unto their Charge."

Mr. Mather Concurred unto this Instrument, But what gave the most Illumination to the Country, and a Turn to the Tide, was the Special Service which he did, in Composing and Publishing his very Learned, *Cases of Conscience concerning Witchcraft:*[224] In which Treatise he did with Incomparable Reason and Reading, Demonstrate, That a Devil may Appear in the Shape of an Innocent and a Vertuous Person, to Afflict those who Suffer by Diabolical Molestations, and that the Ordeal of the Sight and the Touch is not a Conviction of a Covenant with the Devil, but liable to great Exceptions against the Lawfulness as well as the Evidence of it. Upon this, the Governour Pardoned such as had been Condemned; and the Spirit of the Country ran Violently upon Acquitting all the Accused. The Confessors came also as out of a Dream wherein they had been Fascinated: And the Afflicted grew many of them Easy. It was likewise a very strange Occurrence, That some of the most Fierce Assertors of the Opinion, *That the Devils could not Afflict in the shape of a Good Man,* were terribly Confuted, by having their own Shapes, and the Shapes of their most intimate and valued Friends thus Abused. Upon which it is my Duty to Remark, That an Insinuation which I have somewhere seen, that a Godly and Gracious Relative of Mr. Mathers was at last one of the Accused, and some occasion to the stop of Prosecutions, has not one syllable of Truth in it. The first Publisher (the Lover, & it is probable, the Maker) of that LYE, was a Quaker, who did not so hearken to his Conscience as he should have done; And surely, such Scribblers do not afford fit Materials for an Historian to rely upon.

I would willingly write this History with a due Regard unto the Admonition, with which Master Richard of Abkond begun every Paragraph, *Sic sine Felle pius.*[225] But yet what is done by one Dr. Hutchinson, in what he calls, *An Historical Essay concerning Witchcraft,*[226] requires to have some Notice taken of it. The Gentleman might have served the good Cause, (as Mather the elder d[i]d) of rescuing the Lives of Innocent People from such Ungrounded Prosecutions for Witchcraft, as the World has too often run into, without such a Weak, and Rash, & Unfair Way of Representing Things, as he has used in this mean Performance. He had also shown himself a Better Christian, if he had Recommended (what Mather the Younger still insisted on) the Methods of PIETY, which are the True and Best, and oftentimes the Only Ones, to be taken under the Diabolical Obsessions which often pass for Witchcraft: but he appears rather disposed for the Ridiculing of these. Had he been upon the Spot, and Seen the Things which he has Written of, as We have done, he had been better Qualified for a Writer of them; he would not have treated some things as He has done, and thought a few Doggrel Rhimes of his Precious and Beloved Hudibras,[227] enough to make a Dead Weight against Ocular Demonstration: or imagined, that the most Incontestible Histories, are Sufficiently Answered, and Arguments refuted, by Nibbling here and there at the Edges of a few Pages, and leaving a few Excrements upon them. The *Nouvelles de La Republique des Lettres,* mentions a Terrible sort of Logician, who denied a plain matter of Fact, after this manner, *I have Undeniable Reason against it, and it is more Probable that the Eyes are mistaken than the Reason.* Such an Unreasonable Man is Dr. Hutchinson. And after all, for him to make Mr. Baxter and the Two Mr. Mathers, the Causes of the Troubles which the Country Suffered from the Invisble World;—it is a piece of Baseness, to be expected no where, but in a party, which he belongs unto. He Observes, what every Doctor of Theology would not have expressed so, That St. James has *taught us to Speak with more Guard* than St. Paul has done; about the Doctrine of Justification; And I will Observe, that one who Writes not with more Guard than He, will be in danger of such Works as cannot themselves be Justified; and therefore, I am sure, will not Justify the Doer of them. In the mean time, the Cain and Abel stroke with which he treats the Persons & Prayers of the Dissenters, and his Abominable Exhibition of The Surey [Surrey] Daemoniac, would make one wonder what sort of Dissenters they should be, that can applaud a Book, so liable to be by them at least Complained of. These few Strictures are what a just Regard unto the Ashes of a Wronged Parent have Compell'd me to. And I will make so bold with the Gentleman who has given the occasion for them, as to take my Farewel of him, in the Words of Jerom; *Imperitiam tuam neno Potest fortius accusare, quam Tu ipse dum Scribas.*[228]

Article XXIX.
A Good President.

I Remember my Obligations. It was as long ago, as the Year, 1681. that I began to mention the Care of HARVARD-COLLEGE Devolved upon Mr. Mather, and the Opportunities for Special Service, with which His Glorious Master therein favoured him.

He Discharged his Trust, with a Diligence, and a Discretion, and a Fidelity, in his Weekly Visits to the Society, which found a General Acceptance; and the Commencements he also Managed, as became a decent Orator and a Learned Moderator. His Commencement-Performances, were always indeed very much Admired! His Church refusing to Relinquish the Right they had in him, he Declined for a while, to do the part of a Praesident, and got another chosen; upon whose Death in the Year, 1684. the Overseers, with the Fellows of the College again Devolved his former Care upon him; Desiring him to act as, *Praeses pro Tempore*,[229] till a further Settlement could be Procured.

In that Station he was found, when the Charter of the Colony was Destroy'd; but they into whose Hands the Government of the Territory fell, Changing his Title from that of Praesident into that of Rector, continued him in the Government of the College; where he set himself to Prevent all Disorders, and Encourage Piety, and Industry, and Erudition.

When he went over to England, he carried his Care of his beloved College with him. Among other Expressions of it (whereof some have been related,) he Procured some valuable Donations to it. Yea, it was His Acquaintance with, and His Proposal to, That Good-Spirited Man, and Lover of all Good Men, Mr. THOMAS HOLLIS,[230] that Introduced his Benefactions unto that College; to which his Incomparable Bounty has anon flow'd unto such a Degree, as to render him the Greatest Benefactor it ever had in the World.

Upon his Return to New-England, one of the first Things he did, was to Obtain from the General Assembly of the Province, (what he was in England advis'd unto, when he began there to move towards Obtaining a Charter from the King for that purpose) An Act for the Incorporation of the College, upon a larger Foundation than the Former Settlement. By this Act, The College was enabled among other Things, to Confer Degrees, which could not by its former Charter be pretended to; and Particularly, to Create Batchelours, and Doctors of Theology. At this Time, and while that Act was yet in Force, this University (as now it was) thought it their Duty to Present unto their Praesident, a Diploma for a Doctorate, under their Seal, with the Hands of the Fellows annexed; which being the First and the Sole Instance of such a Thing done in the whole English America.

I shall here Transcribe it.

Quum Gradus Academcos tam in Theologia quam in Philosophia pro more Academiarum in Anglia Conferendi potestas, ab Amplissimo Gubernatore, et a Summa Massachusettensis Curia, Secundum Serenissimi Regis ac Reginae Gulielmi et Mariae illis Concessum Diploma, sit nobis Commissa; Et quoniam Vir Clarissimus D. CRESCENTIUS MATHERUS Collegij Harvardini in Nova Anglia Praeses Reverendus, Libros quam Plurimos tam Anglice quam Latine edidit, Omnigena Literatura resertos, Multisque Praeterea Modis non Solum in Linguis et in Artibus Liberalibus peritissimum, verum etiam in S. S.

Scriptures, et in Theologia se Ostendit Versatissimum; atq; per Studia et Merita vere extraordinaria, non tantum apud Americanos [Americanas], sed et Europaeanas Ecclesias Commendatissimum se reddidit; propterea dictum D. CRESCENTIUM MATHERUM. Doctorali Cathedra dignum judicamus; Eumq; pro Authoritate nobis Commissia [Commissa], S. S. Theologiae DOCTOREM, nominamus ac renunciamus. In cujus Rei Testimonium Academiae Sigillum hisce Literis affiximus; Nos quorum hic sunt Subscripta Nomina. Datum Cantabrigiae Nov-Anglorum, Die Novembris Septimo; Annoq; Domini Millesimo, Sexcentesimo, Nonagesimoq; Secundo.[231]

The fate of the College after this, belongs not unto our Story. The Care which the Doctor took of it will. He required a Conforming to the Statutes of the College, with a Stedy Government, and Faithful Discipline. He gave the Students his Directions about their Studies! He advised them what Books they should chiefly Converse withal, and caution'd them against such as might Poison their Young Minds, and give them a Taint which they must Sweat out if ever the Churches of GOD had any Real Service from them. He kept alive the Disputations of the Batchelours, in which he Moderated; and assigned them especially such Questions as led them to an Establishment in the Truths which the Temptations of the Day rendred most needful to be Defended. He usually Preached unto the Scholars every Week, Sermons on such Subjects as he thought most useful for them, and in a manner, Calculated for the Instruction of such as would of him Learn to be True Preachers of the Gospel. And sometimes he Illuminated the College-Hall with Elaborate Expositions. It was also a frequent Custom with him, and how worthy of Imitation!—to send for the Scholars one by one into the Library, and there confer with them about their Interiour State, and Quicken their Flight unto their SAVIOUR, and invite them into the Dispositions and Resolutions of Serious PIETY; and lay the Solemn Charges of GOD upon them to Turn and Live unto Him; and sometimes bestow Pious Treatises upon them. Some of them will Bless GOD all their Days, for these Admonitions; and will never forget the Words that Quickened them. Thus Dr. Mather did continually! Doubtless it was needful, and much for the Welfare and Honour of the College, to take it out of the Hands of such a Praesident!

There were some Disaffected Men who for some Reasons, (God knows, what they were,) were willing to have the College taken out of Dr. Mathers hands. To accomplish it, they Obtain'd a Vote of the General Assembly, which appear'd of a Plausible Aspect; *That no Man should act as Praesident of the College, who did not reside at Cambridge.* The leaders in this Vote, knew very well, That the

Doctor, would not remove his Habitation from a Loving People at Boston, to reside in Cambridge, while the College was,—as then it was. But yet his Abdication was after all brought about, I will but Softly say, Not so fairly as it should have been. I think, there are Thanks due to me, for my forbearing to Tell the Story. This was in 1701. Twenty Years after his beginning to serve that Society in Quality of a PRAESIDENT. And I think, It will do no Hurt for me, to mention a Passage which he wrote on this Occasion; *I have received more Discouragements in the Work of GOD from those whom I have laid under the greatest Obligations, than by all the World besides. Let not my Children put too much Confidence in Men. It may be, such as they have laid under the greatest Obligations of Gratitude, will prove the most unkind unto them. I have often had Experience of it.*

Article XXX.
Good Advice to Ministers.

When the Doctor was upon the Resignation of his Charge, which was in general much to the Dissatisfaction of the Country, he Preached Jun. 29. 1701. unto the Scholars, a Farewel-Sermon on Col. III. 11. *CHRIST is ALL.* And in the Conclusion Addressed this EXHORTATION to them: This Adlocution.

"Unto YOU that are Students in the College, and especially unto such of You as are (what most of you are) Designed for the Work of the Ministry; the ADVICE which I now Leave, is This.

"First, Let the Glorifying of the Lord JESUS CHRIST, and not any Worldly Considerations, induce you to Devote yourselves unto the Evangelical Ministry which you have before you. 'Tis true, Tis an Honourable Calling which you are Entring upon. To be Embassadors of CHRIST who is the King of Kings, is to be in an Honourable Station. The greatest Persons on Earth, have not thought it Beneath them, to Preach the Word of the GOD of Heaven. The King in Jerusalem, and as Great a King as ever they had, is called, The Preacher. Ecclesiastical Writers Affirm, Titus to have been one of a Noble Extraction among the Cretians. And since the Reformation, what was George the Prince of Anhalt? What was the Lord of Chandieu, who goes under the Hebrew Name of Sadeel? What was John Alasco?[232] Yea, and greatly Enriched is that Man, whose Business it is, To Preach the Unsearchable Riches of CHRIST! But you must not propose the Honours of This World, in what you undertake. No, but expect rather to be Despised and Rejected of Men; rather to have all manner of Indignities heaped upon you. As little may you Propose the Riches of This World. The low and mean Intention of, Getting a Living, must not be the Chief Thing in your Eye. You may, no doubt, gain much more Wealth, by betaking yourselves to some other Employments. Yea, Poverty, Narrow and Humbling Circumstances, and Grievous Defraudations from an Unthankful People; are what you must look for. You must count it Honour enough, and Riches enough, if CHRIST may have Service from you. Your Special Advantages to Serve CHRIST, which Ministers have above other men; Here let there be the Honour and the Riches, that your Hearts will be mainly set upon.

"Secondly. Let your Sermons be as full of a CHRIST as may be. Sermons full of Self; and made for the Ostentation of your own Learning; Are these the Sacrifices, that GOD will be well-pleased withal? The Sermons of the Apostles were not such! No, They could say, *We Preach not our Selves but CHRIST JESUS the Lord.*[233] What were the Pauline Sermons! We read, *He Preached those things, which concern the Lord JESUS CHRIST.* Alas, There are Preachers in the World, who have little of a CHRIST in their Sermons; A Morality without the Gospel of CHRIST, is all that is to be found in their Sermons: Nothing higher than what is to be mett withal in a Cicero, a Seneca, an Epictetus, or a Plutarch,[234] is to be found in their Sermons. *Nomen CHRISTI non est ibi!*[235] Nay, They count it a Disparagement unto their Sermons, to have the Name of CHRIST often mention'd in them. How unlike are such, unto that Servant of the Lord, who has the Name of CHRIST, no less than Ten Times in the Ten first Verses of his first Epistle to the Corinthians?[236] CHRIST! How Copious the Subject! How Sublime! There is matter enough in it for your Meditation all the Days of your Lives. Do not Neglect by any means to Preach on the Glories, the Person, the Offices, the Actions, and the Benefits of CHRIST; and the Interest which He indeed has in Every Article of our Holy Religion. Know the Truth as it is in JESUS! Wherefore,

"Thirdly, Have an Eye still on a CHRIST, even when you are Preaching on other Subjects. We may not think, that if a Man Preaches on Subjects wherein CHRIST is not Immediately referr'd unto, CHRIST & the Gospel is not Preached in them: But This I will say unto you. Other Subjects are to be Preached on; and yet still in all, a CHRIST is to be Repaired unto. The Evil of Sin is to be Preached upon; The Misery of Man fallen by Sin, is to be Preached upon. But it must be to Lead the Hearers unto the CHRIST, who is the Mighty and Only SAVIOUR of Sinners. The Moral Law is to be Preached upon as the Rule of our Obedience to GOD. The Duties of

Piety, and Equity, and Charity are to be Preached upon. But the Example of a CHRIST Observing the Law, and a Manuduction[237] to Him for our Assistence and Acceptance in all we do, is always to Accompany it. Remember, The Life of your Preaching will be according to what there is of a CHRIST, who is, The Life, shining in it.

"If you do thus Glorify CHRIST, GOD, even His Eternal FATHER, will take it kindly from you. For there is nothing so Dear to HIM, as that Son of His Love. His CHRIST is Dearer to Him than all the Men on Earth; Dearer to Him than all the Angels in Heaven; Dearer to Him, than all the Worlds, which are the Works of His Hands; yea, tis for HIM that He has made them all. He Delights exceedingly to see His CHRIST Glorified; and if this be what your Hearts are set upon, He will Reward you Wonderfully! You will have this Glorious Reward among the rest; That you will have His Holy SPIRIT Powerfully and Marvellously Breathing in your Ministry. An Eminent Scotch Divine, hearing a Young Minister Preach an Elaborate Sermon; when he Commended the Sermon, yet Complained of it; *I wanted one Thing; I wanted the SPIRIT of GOD, that was not so sensible and apparent in it.* You will take an Excellent way, (Behold, I shew unto you an Excellent way!) to escape this Complaint upon your Services. *The SPIRIT of Truth will Glorify me,* Saith our SAVIOUR.[238] That Holy SPIRIT will sadly withdraw from the Ministry that has not a CHRIST animating of it. No doubt, This may be the very cause, why an Unsuccessful Ministry is become so generally a matter of Observation and of Lamentation.

"And now, My Children, what shall I say more unto you? I hope, that as to many of you, (Oh! That it might be All of you!) I shall meet you with Joy, at the Right Hand of CHRIST, in the Great Day of His Appearing and His Kingdom, when both you and I shall Rejo[i]ce, that ever He brought and placed me among you. But, if any of you, who are the Students in the College, prove so Miserable, as to Dy in your Sins, and in a Christless Condition, I earnestly Protest unto you this Day, that I shall Testify against you before the Lord JESUS CHRIST in That Day, that I have called upon you both Publickly and Privately, to make sure of an Interest in Him. I am now Pure from the Blood of your Souls; If any of you (which Mercy Prevent!) shall Dy in your Sins, your Blood will be upon your own Unhappy Heads. I have done the part of a Faithful Father to you!"

It were to be wished, that such Words might be Translated into as many Languages, as Grotius's Book, *De Veritate*. But—

The Words of Dr. Mather, acting as the Praesident of Harvard-College, are Ended.

—I will ask the Leave to Clench them, with some Symphonizing

Words, of my excellent Bro[ther] Mr. Isaac Watts,[239] lately Published. "Let us Ministers consider how little has been our Success, in Comparison of the Multitudes Converted by our Fathers in the Day of their Ministry. Now it is worth our Enquiry, whether it may not be Ascribed unto the Abscence of CHRIST in our Sermons. And what Reason indeed can we have, to expect the Presence and Influence of the SPIRIT of CHRIST, if we leave His Person, His Offices, His Grace, and His Gospel out of our Discourses, or give but a slight and casual Hint at these Glorious Subjects, which ought to be our daily Theme!"

And that I may, yet Repeat the stroke, and make it yet more Thorough, and Cogent, and Effectual, I will Transcribe the Words which Dr. Mather himself has in his Preface to a Book be Published about Three or Four Years before he Died. "I often think of, (and I wish Young Preachers would think of it!) the Advice of the Famous Dr. Sibs to Young Thomas Goodwin,[240] (who afterwards proved a no less famous Doctor than the other,), *Young Man,* (said he,) *If ever you would do Good, you must Preach CHRIST, and Free Grace.*"

Article XXXI.
The Latter-Days.

The Doctor still had many Opportunities for Special Service continued unto him, and he approved himself a Prudent and Faithful Steward of his Talents.[241] He grew in the Exercises of Repentance and of Patience, and of all PIETY, and Communion with GOD; and in the Painful Discharge of his Ministry; and Watchfully laid hold on all Opportunities to bear Testimonies for the Cause of GOD, and of His People, as the matter might Require. But if I cut the Chapter into little Sections, it may add something to the Relish of it.

1. His Purpose and manner of Life, is Exactly Described, in a Book about Holiness, which was Written by him, Twenty Years before he Died. In that Book he offers Admirable Rules for Growth towards a Perfection of Holiness in the Fear of GOD: which he Introduces with saying, *I shall not set before you Directions impossible to be followed, or heavy Burdens which I would be lothe myself to touch.* No, we saw his Rules Livelily Exemplified. But his Daily Course may be enquired after. Besides his Patient Continuance, in that stroke of Well-doing, which lay in his course of setting apart whole Days for the Religion of the Closet, and which he continued until the last Year of his Life was coming on: His Daily Course was This: And what a Grateful Spectacle to Angels in it!

In the Morning repairing to his Study, (where his Custom was to sit up very late, even until Midnight, and perhaps after it) he deliberately Read a Chapter, and made a Prayer, and then plied what of Reading and Writing he had before him. At Nine a Clock he came down, and Read a Chapter and made a Prayer, with his Family. He then returned unto the Work of the Study. Coming down to Dinner, he quickly went up again, and begun the Afternoon with another Prayer. There he went on with the Work of the Study till the Evening. Then with another Prayer he again went unto his Father; after which he did more at the Work of the Study. At Nine a Clock he came down to his Family-Sacrifices. Then he went up again to the Work of the Study; which anon he Concluded with another Prayer; And so be betook himself unto his Repose.

In the Prayers of the Day, what there fell short of the Number, in the Hundred and Sixty fourth Verse of the Hundred and Nineteenth Psalm, was doubtless made up with Numberless Ejaculations.—Of such Ejaculatory Prayers, no doubt, is to be understood, what Antiquity reports of the Apostle Bartholomew, That he Pray'd one Hundred Times in a Day; and of one Paulus, That he did it Three Hundred Times. I can't say, That this our Eusebius[242] had so many Ejaculatory Prayers as the[e]se come to; But he was the Happy Man, that had his Quiver full of them!

He commonly spent Sixteen Hours of the Four and Twenty, in his Laborious Hive! Being very much of Thomas Akempis his Mind, *Nusquam Requiem invenio nisi in Libro et in claustro.*[243] He was There, some thought even to a Fault. More of his Pastoral Visits were wished for.

2. Unto a Good Man there once came that Message from Heaven; *Thy Prayers and thy Alms are come up for a Memorial before GOD.*[244] This Good Mans did so! His Devotions towards GOD, were accompanied with his Benignities towards Men; And these Two, filled his Life with Sacrifices; and assured him a share in the Royal Priesthood. It was the Doctors Perswasion, That though our GOD is to have our All used for Him, there was a Special Portion of his Revenues, which was more Immediately and more Explicitly to be Devoted unto Pious Uses: A Special Portion to be so set apart for GOD, and be so the Lords, that it would be Sacriledge to Spend it in any other than those which may be called, Pious Uses. Concerning this Portion of GOD, it was his Perswasion, That a Tenth Part of his Revenues, was the least, that could go for the Portion. He thought, That since there is a Part which is the Lords, it is but proper, that the Determination of what part it shall be, should be left unto the Lord. It was his Opinion, That our own Carnal Heart, is no Competent

Judge, to Determine What and When the Revenues which our GOD has given us, are to do for Him. Now, if GOD ever did fix any part, it was plain to him, that nothing lower than a Tenth was ever fixed by Him. As with our Time, it was not left unto our Arbitrary Fancy, to take our own Time for the Worship of our GOD, but He Himself Determined, *I will have a Seventh Part of your Time Entirely mine;* So tis with our Wealth: It is not left unto our own Humour, to say, How much He shall have. He has Determined, *A Tenth Part of the Wealth flowing in upon you shall be mine.* It seems, the Good GOD, who with a Seventh Day will be owned as the Creator, will with a Tenth Part be own'd as the Possessor, of all things. He was aware, That even the Light of Nature taught the Ancient Pagans to Decimate for Pious Uses. He could levy a whole Army of Authors, to carry this cause; *Decima quaeque Veteres Diis Suis Offerebant.*[245] And he thought it strange for Christians to do less for our GOD, than Pagans did for theirs. They built upon This; A Tenth is the least part in any Division of Numbers: The lowest is that of Unites; and less than a Tenth is less than what all Nations make the least. And he thought, shall not our GOD have so much as the Least of the Revenues, whereof we owe so much unto Him? The Light of Scripture was that which further and fully Satisfied him. *Our Father Jacob said, The Lord shall be my GOD, and of all that thou shalt give me, I will give the Tenth unto Thee.*[246] He thought, one way of his owning the Lord for his GOD, & approving himself an Israelite indeed, would be, *To give the Tenth unto Him.* Yea, when he considered, That our Father Abraham did pay unto Melchizedek, the Tenth of all; And that our Lord JESUS is a Priest forever after the Order of Melchizedek; he felt the Force of this Argument upon it. The Rights of Melchizedek, belong to our Blessed JESUS, the Royal High-Priest concern'd in the Heavens for us: The Tenths were the Rights of Melchizedek; Therefore the Tenths belong to our JESUS. I have heard the Doctor say, *That he look'd upon this as an Argument that could not be answered!* Accordingly, he Consciencіously and Constantly Devoted a Tenth Part of his Income to Pious Uses. But this was the least: He often did much more than so. I find in one Paper of his Accounts, (For he kept unto the Maxim, *Noli Decimas dare per Conjecturas:*)[247] That in One Year, he laid out upon Pious Uses, no less than Twenty four Pounds above the Tenth Part of his whole Income that Year, taking in Donations as well as his more Stated Salary. Besides which, the Generous Things which he often did for the Widows and Orphans of Ministers, by ordering them to be the Receivers of the Gratuities, which the Bereaved Churches on whom he bestow'd his Labours would have Presented him withal, times that cannot be numbred; and by Remitting what was owing to him from such, when the College allow'd him some of their Debts, for a Recompence of his Labours there; These are Things that never came into his Reckoning. He knew, whos[e] they would one Day come into! He had a Bountiful Eye, a Liberal Soul, a Tender Compassion for the Miserable. A Noble Demonstration did he give, That they who do Good Works BECAUSE they are already Justified, will not come short of those who do Good Works THAT THEY MAY be Justified;[248] and, That they who Renounce all Pretence to Merit by their Good Works, will more abound in Good Works than the greatest Merit-Mongers in the World.

3. It is Required of a Bishop, That he be, *A Man of Good Behaviour.*[249] Our Dr. Goodwin thinks, part of the meaning may be, that a Minister must not be Slovenly, nor of such an Unmannerly Carriage as may bring his calling into Contempt. He must avoid all the Rudeness, that uses [used] to flow from Ill Nature, or Ill Nurture; but be of such a Modest, Comely Pleasing Behaviour, as to render him fit for the Company of any Gentlemen. Indeed, he should not be too Complemental, or affect the Gesticulations of the Dancing School; or any Airs, that shall trespass upon Gravity:[250] But yet his Behaviour should have no Incivilities committed in it.—Our Dr. Mather, was one so Distinguished, for his Answering this Character; and it was a Remark which I have heard so often made upon him; that I could not well avoid just a Touch upon it; That he was one of a very Gentlemanly Behaviour; full of Gravity, with all the Handsom Carriage, as well as Neatness, of a Gentleman; and though his Conversation lay sometimes with Persons of the First Quality, he was never Charged with an Indecency. He was at the same time a great Enemy to, and Censurer of, Loquacity. His Words were Few, as Wise Mens use to be; and much on the Guard, *(Bis prius ad Limam quam semel ad Linguam;)*[251] Pertinent, and Ponderous, and Forcible. It may be, I am upon too small a matter, and so my Words also shall be but Few upon it.

4. But what? Am I Describing one of them whose Dwelling is not with Flesh? I don't pretend unto it. Sr. Henry Wotton,[252] when he mention'd his Father commonly did it in those Terms, *That Best of Men my Father.* None Faulted him. And yet I durst not come up to those Terms. Let us then hear of all his Humane Frailties. Nay, No occasion for That neither! But some tell me, That a Life which only flourishes on the Vertues and Praises of the Person Written of, and shows only the Bright side of the Object, is not so Edifying, or so Acceptable, or so Comfortable, as a more Impartial Story, and a fair Confession of Infirmities. Well, Then, you shall have something of it, and as much as tis fit for me to give you of it. An Hundred witty

Speeches of our Celebrated Ward, who called himself, The Simple Cobler of Agawam, (and over whose Mantle-piece in his House, by the way, I have seen those three Words Engraved, SOBRIE, JUSTE, PIE, and a Fourth added, which was, LAETE:) have been reported;[253] But he had one Godly Speech, that was worth 'em all: which was, *I have only Two Comforts to Live upon; The one is, in, The Perfections of CHRIST; The other is in The Imperfections of all CHRISTIANS.* And verily, There is Abundance in the latter as well as in the Former Article. If then it will be at all Comfortable to you, I will tell you; Dr. Mather had his Imperfections. But must I Exhibit them, and Represent them, and Amplify upon them? Suppose, I did not see them, as another might. Or, If I did, am not I very finely Circumstanced for the Relation of them? I Pray, which among the Sons of Noah, would afford me a Name, if I should Proceed unto it? And yet, that other Servants of GOD, Mourning under their Deficiencies and their Miscarriages, may be Comforted, you shall be Informed, That I find this Good Man in his Diaries, often taxing himself, as Guilty of Indiscretion; and of sad Mispence of Time; and of not keeping his Heart under such a Government as he should have done. And when his Days of Humilation arrived, he constantly noted with his Pen, *Grounds of Humiliation* before the Lord. Here, he still deeply Charges himself with, *Remaining Iniquities.* Among these he still Bewails, *Great Unfruitfulness.* It Occurs Times without Number. Sometimes tis [this]; *How Unfruitful am I; Alas, How do I even Cumber the Ground?* He often Laments Pride, and Vain Glory, and Selfishness, and Sensuality, and, Earthly Mindedness, and Ungoverned Passions. To these he adds Lamentations over, *Grievous Defects in Gifts as well as Graces;* and, *Much Unfitness for Service to the Kingdom of GOD;* and, *Misbehaviours in all Relations.* These *Remainders of Indwelling Sin,* were such a Constant Sorrow and Burden to him, that they Exceedingly Reconciled him to the Dying Hour; which he always mentioned, with a Sensib[l]e Transport, when that Advantage of it came to be mentioned, *Never SIN any more!*— The Hour upon which he was Particularly Pleas'd with Dying Dr. Goodwins way of Expressing it! *My Corruptions, I shall now shake them off! Those Croaking Toads, I shall never any more be Infested with them!*

Know it, O Soul pressing after a Perfection of Holiness in the Fear of GOD, and with Unutterable Groans Complaining under the Want of it; There are Saints now in the Paradise of GOD, (and one, whose Life is now before thee,) whose Lives were all along filled with the same Complaints, with which thine is now Embittered.

From one more Quoted than he deserves to be, I will yet now

make one Quotation: *Da mihi quemcunque vis Magni Nominis Virum, dicam quid illi aetas sua ignoverit.*[254]

5. Whether it will be thought any Retainer to the former Paragraph, I know not: But I have a Paragraph before me, about which I have a Thousand Struggles in my mind, whether I shall proceed in it, or no. If I do, it will be an Effectual Demonstration of the Impartiality, the Fidelity, the Integrity, with which our History is carried on. But That which finally Determines me to do it, is The Regard which I Owe, and which, I hope, I shall ever Pay, to that more Substantial PIETY, which we are forever to insist upon.

What, what is the meaning of that Particular Faith, about Future Events, with which the Prayerful Servants of GOD, sometimes find their Minds Irradiated, and Marvellously perswaded and Comforted, in their Prayers before Him? There is a Praying in Faith, which is the Duty of every Christian in all his Prayers; An entire Satisfaction in the Power, and Wisdom, and Goodness, and Faithfulness of the Glorious GOD, and in the Mediation of the Blessed JESUS; and so an Hopeful Expectation of such Blessings, as our Advocate in the Heavens will please to Procure and Order for us. But then, there is a Particular Faith, which is not so much the Duty, as the Comfort of them, that have it; and which is Granted, but here and there, but now and then, unto those whom a Sovereign GOD shall Please to Favour with it. The Devout Believer cannot cause himself to Believe What and When he will; but under the Energy of some Superior Cause, when he is on his knees, (or Perhaps, Prostrate in the Dust,) before the Lord, there is a Strong Impression made upon his mind, which Dissolves him in a Flood of Tears, and Assures him, *Thou shalt have the Petition which thou Desirest of thy GOD.* The Impression is born in upon his mind, with as clear a Light, and as full a Force, as if it were from Heaven Angelically, and even Articulately declared unto him; *The Lord has given thee, thy Petition which thou hast asked of Him.*[255] Upon the Voice of the Weeping which he finds himself melted into, he cannot but say, *The Lord hath heard my Supplication; the Lord will receive my Prayer.* It may be, he was of a Sorrowful Spirit before, and full of Anxiety about the matter, but now he is no more sad. The Impression at the same time fills him with all Holy Dispositions, and Holy Resolutions, and Produces an Heavenly Temper, and leaves him with the Lustre of an Excellent Spirit upon him. (Reader, I am only carrying on the History now on the Anvil, in all of this!) It were perhaps as easy for me to give unto a Man born Blind, an Idaea of Light, and of the Colours made by it, as for me to Describe in Words unto the Understanding of a Stranger—How it is! But you may have some Illustration of it in what our Martyrology has related concerning that Blessed Martyr, Mr. Holland. "After Sentence was Read against him, he said,—*And now I tell you, that GOD hath heard the Prayer of His Servants, which hath been Poured forth with Tears, for His Afflicted Saints, which you daily Persecute. This I dare be bold in GOD to Speak; and I am by His Spirit moved to say it: That GOD will shorten your Hand of Cruelty: For after this Day in this place, there shall be no more put unto the Trial of Fire and Faggot.* Which accordingly came to pass; He was the last that was Burnt in Smithfield. You may see it a little further Illustrated in the Strange Afflations, which have Enabled and Impelled many Confessors of CHRIST in the Renoumed [renowned] Church of Scotland, sometimes to break forth into Passages that might be Expected from none but such as have Illapses[256] of the Prophetic Spirit upon them.

—I Enquire, (But not of Thee, O Natural Man; For, thou art no Competent Judge of the matter!) what is the Meaning of this Operation? Whence comes it? Who gives it? How far is it akin to the Faith of Miracles? or, is it all a meer Delusion?

Verily, It looks very like an Operation of the HOLY SPIRIT, wherein His ANGELS may be His Ministers and His Instruments. However, it may Remonstrate, *The Proud have greatly had me in Derision.*[257]

But then, what shall we say, about the Disappointments, that (as they say) have sometimes made this Particular Faith to appear no other, than an Over-heated Fancy, and left the Subjects of it, in Distresses and Confusions that must needs be very uneasy Ones? I make no doubt, that there have been Relations of such Disappointments, which have had little Foundation for them. I know very well, That when a Person has been Praying for a Complication of Blessings, and in the Ardours of Supplication, there have dropt from him only some Words of this Importance, *Our GOD has graciously heard us, and will surely do us Good;* and the Unwary (and it may be, some of them worse than meerly Unwary) Hearers have run away with a Notion, and made a very Formal and Punctual Story upon it; That the Person Declared himself Assured of having Obtained *All and Each of the Blessings* that have been asked; and one of them failing, all the whole Particular Faith remains only to be Laugh'd at. This was doubtless the very case, in a Formal and Punctual Story, which some of our English Histories employ their Banter and Burlesque upon. Yea, I am ready to think, That sometimes the Supplicants themselves have procured some Distresses and Confusions to themselves by not Attending well to the Terms of the Impression made upon their Minds, and carrying the Interpretation beyond what they should have done, or what was Necessary.

It is now Time for me to Observe, That the Instances of a Particular

Faith wherewith Dr. Mather was Distinguished, were very Various and Wondrous. Of these I have told Some in the foregoing History; (and if I had not, the caution of this Paragraph, had not been so Needful to be Introduced:) And I could insert Many more, if it were Proper to treat the Public, with such Personal or Domestic Matters: And, All Accomplished!—

—But One;—And that was This. After his last Return to New-England, he had a Strange Impression on his Mind, That he *should yet have an Opportunity to do Special Service for CHRIST in England.* The Impression was many times very strongly made upon him, for diverse Months together; And even at such times as one would suppose least Obnoxious to Satanic Illusions. But yet,—He never saw England any more. Now, what shall we make of This? Will it be enough to say, That he Misinterpreted his own Impression, when he thought it must needs imply, his own going in Person to the other side of the Atlantic? But that this very Book may sufficiently Accomplish the Praediction? Or, shall we say, what he himself wrote upon it; "As for the Impression, I have had concerning my Doing Service for GOD in England; I know not what to think of it. Such Things are often from Angels: And I sometimes think, that Angels may be Ignorant of some Future Events; but may cause Motions on the Spirits of Men, according to what will in Probability come to pass. I am Desirous to Dy where I am. No quaestion but Jacob thought, that he should return again to the Land of Canaan; and that Joseph should outlive him there. (Gen. XLVI. 4.) Whereas, the Promise was made Good, when his Body was Buried in that Land, and his Posterity returned thither. However it shall be as to myself, I hope, my Son Samuel will do Service for the Name of CHRIST in England; which is in some sort as if I did so; And Books of mine Published there, will be Serviceable to the Kingdom of GOD." One thing which a little Emboldened, that stroke about the Angels, was, that about the Time, when the Impression was in its Liveliest Operation, (October 1694.) there was among some in his Neighbourhood, a strange Descent of Shining Spirits, that had upon them great marks of their being such Angels as they Declared themselves to be. (What they were, GOD knows!) And from these there was that Message (and, no more!) directed unto him; *He is much Exercised in his Mind about his going for England; but he need not and should not be so; For GOD will bring to pass That which will be most for His Glory and Service; And the Angels of GOD will attend him, wheresoever His Providence may dispose of him.* I might say This more upon it. No less than Thrice Seven Years after this Impression, and after a long Sentence of Death had been Written upon it (as there generally is for a while, upon every Thing that a Particular Faith has laid hold upon) he had an Opportunity to Return for England, and there to do Special Service for CHRIST, Surprizingly thrown into his Hands. The Ministers of the Province, by their Delegates met at Boston, (April. 1715.) and Unanimously desired him, to take a Voyage for England, with an Address from them, to our Lawful and Rightful King GEORGE, whose Accession to the Throne gave an Universal Joy to a Country Proportionably fuller of Subjects well-affected unto Him; than any part of His Dominions; as also to Establish and Cultivate a Good Correspondence between the Churches of this Country, and the United Brethren on the other side of the Great and Wide Sea, And there was a Provision made, for the Expences of the Voyage. But, he himself now Declined it.

After all, I will freely Confess what I most of all chuse to say. There might be Danger, lest some Inconsiderate Christians, when they Read the Life of Dr. Mather, might be, as many have been, when they Read the Life of Dr. Winter, unawares led into, and Indiscrete Affectation of Extraordinaries, and Singularities, in the Course of their Devotions. This is a Thing that may have Perillous Consequences! Whereas now, if they find such a Man as Dr. Mather, once Plunged into such Difficulties and Perplexities, in the Affair of a Particular Faith, as left him very much in the Dark about it, and Compell'd him to say, *I know not what to think of it:* This Affectation will be so Discouraged in them, that they will suffer no Danger from it.

If I may be thought Worthy to offer my Advice upon the whole, I would humbly say; Christians, Reproach not a Particular Faith as if there never were a Gracious Work of Heaven in it. But yet he Caution'd against laying too much stress upon it, lest you find yourselves incautiously Plunged into an Hope that will make ashamed. A Particular Faith may be a Work of God; But the Counterfeits of this Jewel are so very fine, that it will require a Judgment, almost more than Humane to Discern them. It is best not being too fond of Enthusiasms, that may carry you beyond the Dispensation of the Day. It is best that you should be Content with the Ordinary Satisfaction of Praying and so Waiting for the Blessings of GOD in such Pious Resignations to His Will and Annihilations of your own, as an Uncertainty about Issues would most properly lead you to.

Article XXXII.
The Period of the Pilgrimage.

Omnes, Nescio quo Desiderio, ad Suprema horum qui Virtute aliqua Excelluerunt, trahimur aut properamus. Heins:[258]

And now the Time draws nigh, in which Dr. Mather is to Dy.

He grows Old, yet what a Green Olive-Tree in the Preseucha [Proseucha] of his GOD!—*nec tarda Senectus Debilitat vires Animi, mutatve Vigorem.*[259]

Old Age came on. But what an one? How Bright! How Wise! How Strong! And in what an Uncommon Measure Serviceable! He had been an Old Man while he was yet a Young Man; I can quote a Rabby for it, *Sapiens appellatur Senex, Etiamsi Diebus sit Exiguus.*[260] And now he was an Old Man, his Public Performances had a Vigour in them, which tis a rare thing to see a Young Man have any thing aequal to.

How did the good People far and near, Discover even a growth of their Appetite, for the Enjoyment of as much as might be Obtained from him! The Churches would not permit an Ordination to be carried on without him, as long as he was able to Travel in a Coach unto them.

Though in the Praefaces of the useful Books which he now Published, he Repeated an Ungrantable Request unto his Friends, *No longer to Pray for his Life;* They only Pray'd the more for it. When he had finished Forty nine years of his Public Ministry, he Preached a Sermon full of Rare and Rich Thoughts upon, *A Jubille* [Jubilee]; And he requested for a Dismission from any further Public Labours. His Flock Prized them too much, to hear of That: But anon, when they saw the Proper Time, for it, that they might render his Old Age as easy as might be to him, they Wisely and Kindly Voted it, That *the Labours of the Pulpit should be expected from him, only when he should find himself able and inclin'd for them.*—It would be no strange thing, if while he wanted yet some Years to reach Fourscore, there should be found some little thing that might carry something of Senile Weakness in it. But, he held it unto Fourscore in a Wonderful Exercise of his Intellectual Powers, and with public Ministrations to very Great Congregations, which his Ministry continued still to give the greatest Satisfaction to. A Treatise, which he Published about this Time, concerning *An Hoary Head found in the Way of Righteousness,*[261] notably Described what he was himself, and as notably Declared, what he was yet able to do. He continued Preaching to vast Assemblies; and such well-composed Sermons, that the Notes taken by some Ready Writers after him, when Communicated unto the Public by the way of the Press found their Acceptance in the Churches. Among which Ready Writers, we owe our particular Thanks to a Vertuous Gentlewoman, whose Exquisite Pen help'd several of his Treatises into the World: in some sort as the Excellent Lady Rich did the most Valuable and Admirable Book of Mr. Strong, on, *The Covenant.*[262] Yea, and even After Fourscore the old Prophetic Strain had not forsaken him.

In September 1720. he Preached an awful[263] Sermon (from Amos III. 7.) on this Doctrine; *When GOD has an Holy purpose to Visit His People with Great Judgments, He uses to give them Notice and Warning of it before Hand.* In the Conclusion he expressly foretold, First, *That an heavy Judgment was Impending over Boston, that would Speedily be Executed.* And then, *That the Churches of the Country were near to some shaking Dispensations.* He added; *My Brethren, I take no Pleasure in Testifying unto you of Evil Days. But when the Word of the Lord is like a Fire in a Mans Bones, there must be something said, that may Awaken you out of your Security.* Now, within a few Months after this, the Small-Pox was brought into Boston, and within as few Months more the Besome of Destruction swept away near a Thousand People.[264] And how Strangely was way made for the Destroying Angel to do his Execution!

But let me not Anticipate. I am saying, That until Fourscore the Doctor held it unto Admiration! And on the Day of his Attaining to Fourscore, he Preached a Sermon full of Light and Life, on those Words, Ezek. XVI. 5. *The Day when thou wast Born.* They that wrote after him, have Printed it. The, *Mens et Ratio et Consilium,*[265] which are by Cicero mention'd as the Praerogatives of Old Age, were found in him to an uncommon Degree. On very many Accounts he might have said, as old Georgias did, *Nihil habeo propter quod Senectutem meam accusem;*[266] Yea, as a Better Man, Old Drusius did, *Senectus mihi melior quam ipsa Juventus.*[267] But that which most of all gave him a Comfortable Old Age, was what Calvin who did not Live to Old Age, well pitches on, as the chiefest Comfort of Old Age: *Tenendum est, praecipuam partem Bonae Senectutis, in bona Conscientia, Animoq; sereno ac Tranquillo consistere:*[268] A Good Heart, fill'd with the Love and Peace of GOD, and the Soul of an Abraham.

In consideration of this *ΕΥΓΗΡΙΑ,*[269] it was not amiss for a Grandson, upon the Birth[-]Day on which he entred Fourscore, thus to Complement him.

"To my most Honoured GRAND-FATHER, on the Day of his entring the Eightieth Year of his Age.

To my GRAND-FATHER in all Good so Great,
His Nephew does his Age Congratulate.
Tis not enough, Syr, that you Live to see
Such Years; We hope, you'l our True Nester be.
We wish the Years in which you Live & Preach,
To those of a Methuselah may reach.[270]

Tis true, in common Reckoning we suppose
You want Eight Hundred Eighty Six of those.
But measuring Life by Works and not by Years,
Your age Nine Hundred Sixty Nine appears.
Methuselah had a Bright father too;
A Walker with his GOD; Syr, such as YOU.
If You and We must have a Parting Day,
Death, strike not!—Let him go in Enochs way.
And, Syr, if Prophets mayn't forever Live,
May you in Grandsons left by You Survive."

But it is now time for me to tell, that after Fourscore the Report of Moses did no longer want Confirmation with him; he BEGAN to be more sensible of those Decays, which not only caused him to recite the Verse of the Roman Satyrist;

O Quam continuis, et quantis plena Senectus Longa Malis!—[271]

but also caused him several times to say to me, *Be sure, you don't pray, that you may Live beyond Fourscore!* Yet Now, he Preach'd nobly on, An Old Disciple: as well as many other Subjects.

And NOW, He that had wished for, *Sufferings FOR the Lord,* must be content with, *Sufferings FROM the Lord.* Even These born with the Faith and Patience of the Saints have a sort of Martyrdom in them, and will add unto the far more exceeding and Eternal Weight of Glory.

On Sept. 25. [1720] he did with an Excellent and Pathetic Prayer, in a mighty Auditory, Conclude a Day of Prayer kept by his Church, to obtain a Good Success of the Gospel, and the growth of Real and Vital PIETY, with Plentiful Effusions of the Good SPIRIT, especially upon the Rising Generation. Within Two Days after This, he fell into an Apoplectic sort of Deliquium;[272] (very much occasion'd, as it was thought, by too extreme a concern of his Mind on some late Occurrences at New-Haven:) out of which he Recovered in a few Minutes; but it so enfeebled him, that he never went abroad any more.

However, His Wisdom yet remained with him. And while it was yet in its unexceptionable Displays, there were a few Questions put unto him, whereto his Answers were immediately written down; and shall be now Produced. Homer ascribes to a Dying Man, . . . *A Prudent and a Pungent Speech on something of the Last Importance.*

Reader, Let such a Speech now have thy Best Attention.

It was asked; "What he thought about the Controversy agitated between our United Brethren in England?"

He answered; *I wish they would agree upon some effectual Method, that the Regards of Brethren in CHRIST, may be withdrawn from them who deny the GODHEAD of the Lord that bought us; Lest they unawares Betray the most Glorious CAUSE in the World. They will but Assert and Preserve the Sacred Scriptures, and keep close to them in making a Reasonable Provision to Reject the Hereticks, who under the Colour of Scripture Terms, hold and broach Damnable Haeresies.*

It was asked; "What he thought about the Country, and the Condition it might come to?"

He answered; *The Country has yet such a number of Godly People in it, that GOD will not yet utterly cast off this People. CHRIST has an Interest here that shall not yet be lost.*

It was asked; "What he thought about Boston, and the things that are impending over it?"

He answered; *There is yet a number of Godly People in the Town; They may be brought low, But the Town shall be yet Preserved. If the MINISTERS continue Faithful, and carry on the Work and Cause of GOD well together, the Town will yet have Things go well in it.*

It was asked; "What he thought of them among us whose late Renouncing of their own Ministry, and that of almost all the Protestant Churches in the World, was an extreme Trouble to him?"

He answered; *It is a very Evil and Grievous Thing, which they have been guilty of. But GOD may so Over rule their Folly & Impiety, that the cause of Truth may anon be a Gainer by it.*

It was asked; "What he thought of the Times in General?"

He answered; *There will be not settled Good Times, I suppose, till the second coming of the Lord. I suppose, His coming will be at the Beginning of the Good Times Promised by the Mouth of all the Prophets. His Kingdom takes not place, nor is the Israelitish Nation restored, until His Appearing.*

It was in this Time, that among other Acts of Special Service which he continued still to do for the Churches of GOD, he signed with much wise Deliberation upon them, several Instruments of Consequence, which were to be transmitted unto London; whereof one was an Address from the United Ministers of Boston, unto our Lawful and Rightful Sovereign King GEORGE, expressing the Just Abhorrence in Them, and All their People, for the Conspiracy then lately Discovered.

But that which his Heart was most of all set upon, was, To bear his Part, with A Faithful Testimony to the CAUSE and WORK of GOD, in the Churches of New-England; Left by the Memorable Mitchel, the Venerable Higginson, and the Honourable Stoughton; and now Published under the Title of, *Elijahs Mantle.*[273] Dr. Mather having

Perused and Pondered the Testimony of those Three Worthies, did with much Alacrity direct the Addition of his own unto it: And Express a deep concern upon his Mind, at the Attempts to introduce, A Lifeless Religion, and an Irreligious Life, into a Country that had been once famous for Better Things. It shall be here inserted; *In perpetuam Rei Memoriam.*[274]

"I am now in the Eighty-fourth Year of my Age, and under a Feebleness in *The Valley of the Shadow of Death,* wherein the Lord is yet a light unto me, and makes it but a Shadow of Death; and I am every Hour waiting and longing for my Dismission to a Better World.

"In these very singular Circumstances, I am willing to add my TESTIMONY; and I do Declare, That the PRINCIPAL DESIGN upon which these Colonies were at first Planted, was to Profess and Practise, and Enjoy, with Undisturbed Liberty the Holy RELIGION of GOD our SAVIOUR, Exhibited in the Sacred Scriptures, and Rescued from the Inventions and Abuses which the Man of Sin has introduced; And, more particularly, To Set up CHURCHES, (even of the Aboriginal Natives, as well as of English Christians,) for our Lord JESUS CHRIST, that shall keep themselves Loyal to Him, their Glorious KING, in His Word giving Law unto them; and faithful to the Religion of the SECOND COMMANDMENT; and free from those Offensive Things, from which our UNITED BRETHREN, of the Presbyterian and Congregational Denomination in the English Nation have withdrawn themselves; and which our Honoured and Beloved BRETHREN in the Renowned Church of Scotland, have abolished and abandoned.

"It was aequally designed by those Followers of the Lord into the Wilderness, when it was a *Land not Sown,*[275] That the Pure and Undefiled Religion delivered unto us in the Sacred Scriptures, (and exhibited afterwards in our Confession of Faith,) should be continually Preached, and our Doctrines of Grace particularly asserted; by MINISTERS of Good Abilities, and exemplary Godliness and Watchfulness, freely and fairly Chosen by the Churches whereof they are to be the Pastors.

"And it also belongs unto the Glory of these Churches, to be so Constituted, as Livelily to exhibit the Kingdom of Heaven unto the World; Both Debarring from their Communion, such Ignorant and Scandalous Persons (who can't or won't Examine themselves) as are to be shut out from the City of GOD; And Admitting of all those (tho' in different Perswasions about lesser points) of whom it may be Judged, That CHRIST has received them to the Glory of GOD. Our Foundation is in these Holy Mountains!

"It is now the DYING WISH, of one that has been about Threescore and Six Years, after a poor manner, but, I hope, with some Sincerity, Serving the Best of Masters, in the Blessed Work of the Gospel; That the CHURCHES may stand fast in the Faith and Order of the Gospel, and hold fast what they have received, and Let no man take away their Crown: And, That the PASTORS would more distinctly from time, and with proper Inculcations, acquaint the Churches with their True Interest, and those Things which will be their Beauty and their Safety.

"And considering the Relation which I have heretofore sustained, as a Praesident, for Twenty Years, it is highly proper for me to leave it as also my more particular Desire, that the Tutors in our COLLEGES, from whence the Churches expect their Supplies, would see to have the Students well informed in the Points, which they must Know and Serve, that so the WORK of GOD among us may not be marr'd by falling into Unskilful and Unfaithful Hands.

"Indeed, I cannot but go away Rejoicing in it, That the means which are indefatigably used, for the drawing of Unwary Poople [People] into the Things that will not Profit them, have had so little Success; and that the Body of the more Sober People throughout the Country (so far as I understand) generally continue to discover such a Conspicuous Aversion to the Things, from the Face whereof their Fathers fled into the Wilderness: though at the same time, too general a Decay of REAL and VITAL Godliness, which is to be the MAIN INTENTION of all, is greatly to be bewailed. But there may be danger of Another Generation arising, which will not Know the Lord, not the Works done by Him, and for Him, among His People here.

"And therefore from the Suburbs of that Glorious World, into which I am now entring, I earnestly Testify unto the Rising Generation, That if they Sinfully Forsake the GOD, and the Hope, and the Religious Ways of their Pious Ancestors, the Glorious LORD will severely Punish their Apostasy, and be Terrible from His Holy Places upon them.

"NOW, The Lord our GOD be with you, as He was with your Fathers; Let Him not leave you nor forsake you. LORD, Let thy Work appear unto thy Servants, and thy Glory unto their Children.

Increase Mather.

Nov. 10. 1722."

In the Biography that has Embalmed Ramus and Calvin, and some other Great Men, for the View of Posterity, something of their last Will and Testament has been inserted. We have as good as done this for Dr. Mather, in our offering of this Instrument. NEW-ENGLAND, Behold and Receive thy Legacy!

The Sovereign Disposer of all things, would not allow us now to say, *Sortitus est facilem exitum, et qualem semper Optaverat.*[276] However, I will not proceed now with such Punctual Relations, of the Doctors last Sickness, as the Funeral Orations on the Professors beyond Sea, use to be stuff'd withal. But for the sake of what follows, I will Relate this: It was not long after this, that among other Infirmities, he was extremely tortured and enfeebled, with an obstinate Hicket,[277] which would sometimes hold him a Week or perhaps a Fortnight, without Intermission, and then Intermit a little while, but Return with the former Violence, to such a Degree that it was at last found, His Diaphragm Suffered a Corrosion from it. Under the Uneasy and Incessant Malady, and the Vapours which produced it, and were produced by it, he grew at sometimes very Forgetful, and even Delirious: And in the Minutes of the Darkness wherein he lay thus feeble and sore broken, he sometimes let fall expressions of some Fear lest he might after all be Deceived in his Hope of the Future Blessedness. His Holy Ministry having very much insisted on that Point, That no care could be too much to prevent our being Deceived in that Important Matter; tis no wonder, that as the Dark Vapours which assaulted and fettered his Intellectual Powers, broke in upon him, his Head should run much upon the Horror of being Deceived at the last. Yea, had there not been any thing at all of a Natural Debilitation and Obnubilation[278] in it, yet it were a very Supposeable thing, and not at all to be wondred at, if the Serpent be let loose to vex a Servant of GOD in the Heel of his Life; and if the Powers of Darkness, knowing the Time to be Short, fall with Great Wrath on the Great Opposers of their Kingdom, and make a very Dark Time for them just before the Break of the Eternal Day upon them. And how justly might it awaken the rest of us to Work out our own Salvation with Fear and Trembling, When we see such a Man as Dr. Mather, concerned with so much Fear and Trembling, lest he should be Deceived at the last? But in the midst of his greatest Obtenebrations,[279] he still discovered such an Holy Sollicitude, that he might not in any thing Dishonour the Glorious GOD, nor lose his Hold of the Blessed JESUS, and such an Holy Resolution to stand by the Choice which he had made Seventy Years before, and which above all things he did now with unspeakable Consolation look back upon; as were indeed Preferrible to those Joys of Impulse that some are Transported withal. The best Judges of Things have agreed in this Judgment; That going to Heaven in the way of Repentance, is much safer and surer than going in the way of Extasy. After all, tis to be declared, That the Doctor often saw the Scattering of these Accidental Clouds, and we saw him Rejoicing in the Hope of that Glory of GOD, which they were to Praepare him for. He not only very often said, *The Infinite Mercy in GOD, and the Infinite Merit in CHRIST, keeps me above all Discouragement:* but he kept continually feeding, on those Words of our SAVIOUR, *Where I am, there shall my Servant be:*[280] upon which he would add, *CHRIST is in Heaven; and if I am a Servant of His (which I am sure I am,) then I shall be There!* In this Time, his Complaints, That he was laid by, and now did no good, were more Frequent and more Grievous, than any that we heard from him about any of his Complicated Maladies: And he would say, *For what Sin is the Holy One thus Chastising me! I have Examined myself, and I can't find what it is!* Yea, in a deep Abyss of Humility, there was utterly Absorb'd with him all Sense of his ever having done any good at all in the World. He chose to Forget all, to Renounce all, and cry out, as he did numberless Times, *Lord JESUS, I will make mention of thy Righteousness, even of thine only.* And he would often have the Seventy First PSALM read unto him. He still express'd his Delight in Prayer, and would call for much of it: scarce let me Leave him without something of it. If he were asked what he would have us Pray for, he often Answered, *That I may do Good while I Live, & that I may Honour CHRIST in my Death.* One Day telling him, that his Excellent Friend Mr. Thomas Hollis in his Letters to me, was Inquisitive whether he were yet in the Land of the Living; He replied, *No, Tell him, I am going to it; This Poor World is the Land of the Dying; Tis Heaven that is the true Land of the Living!*

At last, he began to fall into the Torments of *the Wheel broken at the Cistern:*[281] Which yet became not Intolerable, and forced no Ej[ac]ulations from him, till about Three Weeks before he Died. Under these, about Three Days before his Expiration, coming out of a Dark Minute, he said, *It is now Revealed from Heaven to me, That I shall quickly, quickly, quickly be fetch'd away to Heaven, and that I shall Dy in the Arms of my Son.* After this, he kept very much calling for me; till Friday, the Twenty Third of August, 1723. in the Morning perceiving the Last Agonies now come upon him, I did what I could after my poor manner, that he might be Strengthened by such Quickening Words as the Lively Oracles of our GOD have provided for such Occasions. As it grew towards Noon, I said unto him, *Syr, The Messenger is now come to tell you; This Day thou shalt be in Paradise. Do you Believe it, Syr, and Rejoice in the Views and Hopes of it?* He Replied, *I do! I do! I do!*— And upon those Words, he Dyed in my Arms.—

—But when the Physicians came to the Evisceration of the Dead Body, how astonished were they to find, what cause there had been for the Complaints of the last Three Weeks before he died; and it added unto all our Astonishment that they were no Earlier! They found, besides a Polypus[282] on his Bladder, no less than Six Large Stones in it, of several uneven Shapes, and some of them above an Inch Diameter, the least of which was big enough to have made a Giant roar. Some of the Stones being broken, were found Collections of loose pieces of Gravel, which had a thin shell grown over them— *Animus meminisse horret Luctuque refugit.*[283]

I have said, It was on the Twenty Third of August; A Day so neer to the Black Day, of which it may be said, *There never had been a Day in any Nation under Heaven, wherein so many such Lamps of Heaven were at once extinguished;* that it puts me in mind of Observing, That, I suppose, Dr. Mather now brought up the Rear in that Illustrious Army of Confessors, who go by the Name of The ejected Ministers; and on whose Ill usage, I am sorry the Writers of Mr. Doolittel's Life, have newly seen sad cause to make this Reflection; *Such an Invasion upon the Kingly Office of CHRIST—was an Act that calls for greater Signs of Repentance than have yet appeared, Or than the Present Generation shows any Disposition to.*

But the Storm that is to Shake Sandy Foundations is coming on; And men will then see their Errors.

On the Seventh Day after this, he was laid in the Cave of the Treasure, and GOD Honoured him with a Greater Funeral, than had ever been seen for any Divine, in these (and some Travellers at it, said, in any other) parts of the World. The Honourable, William Dummer, Esq; who was then Lieutenant Governour and Commander in Chief; and his Honourable, Ancient, Cordial Friend, Samuel Sewall, Esq; the Chief Judge, of the Province;[284] with the Praesident of the College, and Three of the Principal Ministers, were they that held the Pall; Before which, One Hundred and Threescore Scholars of the College, whereof he had once been the Praesident, walked in Order; And there were Followers of every Rank, (among which about Fifty Ministers) and Spectators that could not be numbred: All with an Uncommon Sadness in their Countenance, and a most Serious Aspect: concurring to the fulfillment of the Text, on which ONE whom he greatly Loved, and in the Prospect of whose proving a very Faithful and Useful Instrument of Good in the Churches he greatly rejoiced; (Mr. Thomas Foxcroft)[285] on that Day entertained a great Auditory with a very acceptable Sermon: (2 Chron. XXIV. 15, 16.) *He was full of Days when he died; and they Buried him—Honourably,—because he had done Good in Israel.* Indeed he might on many Accounts be called, the JEHOJADA of New-England![286]

And now, at the End of the Story, according to my Engagement, I am to tell; His Church with a noble Gratitude bore the Expences of his Funeral. GOD Reward them!

Immediately after this, the Pulpits throughout the Country were filled with Funeral Sermons on him. The other United Ministers of Boston also Succesively for Nine or Ten Weeks together, with excellent Sermons in his own Pulpit, after a most Agreable and Acceptable manner express'd their Condolence with his own Flock on the sad Occasion.

And indeed, as those Valuable Servants of GOD concurr'd in their Veneration for the Father now taken from their Head; and he had the Faelicity of the Old Man Celebrated by Callimachus,[287] whom . . . *The Young Men Love, and Prize, and help as a Father to them;* So he left them with a Joy Unspeakable upon it, that the Glorious Lord has betrusted His Churches here, with such Pious, Painful, and every way Desireable hands. He saw a set of Young Ministers happily Introduced into the City, whom he Esteemed as more Precious than so many *Golden Wedges of Ophir;*[288] and the Reverse of the Ancient Calamity, which Substituted shields of Brass when the shield[s] of Gold were carried off.

When he saw given to the Churches of the City, a Sewall, a Prince, a Webb, a Cooper, a Foxcroft,[289] all singularly endeared unto him, and saw others of an hopeful Character coming on after them, (of whom the last ordained by him, was a Waldron) it is inexpressible with what Joy, he saw these as his *Children Walking in the Truth,*[290] and Pleading for it: but he express'd a little of it, in his Praeface to their Lectures of Early Piety, in which the Voice of the Lord Remarkably Cried unto the City, just before the Destroying Angel broke in with a Besom of Destruction wherein some Hundreds of our Young People were carried off.

Article XXXIII.
The Preacher; How and What he Preach'd.

We can't part with such an Able Minister of the New-Testament as Dr. Mather so; but we must look back upon the Performances of His Holy Ministry. Though the Preacher, have been, what *all Flesh* is, as *Grass;* and the Glory wherein he shone, prove *like the Flower of the Field;*[291] yet what he brought, and his way of bringing, the Living Word of GOD, may and should Abide with us.

Though I never knew a more Candid Hearer, yet Thousands and Thousands have concurr'd in saying, They never knew a more Compleat Preacher. He was indeed the Rabbi Hadarsan[292] of New-England! and one of whom very Competent Judges would say, *He never Preached a Sermon but what was worthy of the Press.*—And there was nothing more Common then for People, when they would give the Highest Applause unto a Preacher, to say, *He Preaches like Dr. Mather.* A very Accomplished Person, Dedicating to him a Disputation full of Erudition, *De CHRISTI Descensu ad Inferos,* Printed in Holland, 1702. very justly Saluted him, as *Theologorum et Philosophorum omnium, per totam, qua late patet, Nov-Angliam, facile Princeps.*[293] Being such a Prince of Preachers, The Manner and the Matter of his Preaching, will certainly deserve to have some Notice taken of it.

He much despised what they call Quaintness, but affected a Plain and therefore a Short sort of a Style. Though he were such a Scholar, yet his Learning hindred not his Condescension to the Lowest and Meanest Capacity: aiming to shoot not over the Heads, but into the Hearts, of the Hearers. He was very careful to be understood, and concealed every other Art, that he might Pursue and Practise that one Art of Being Intelligible. With Luther, he said, he counted him, the Best Preacher, *Qui Simplicissime docet.*[294] A Simple Diet, he counted the most Wholsom Diet.

It was his perpetual endeavour therewithal to Preach very Scripturally, and like an Hildersham,[295] to back every thing he spoke, with some agreeable Sentence of the Sacred Scriptures Confirming of it. His Judgment was, That the Word of GOD is the Food of Souls; and the more there is of That pertinently Produced, the Better Fed are the Flocks under our Feeding. He judged also, That in the Word of GOD, there is that Voice of the Lord, that is Powerful and full of Majesty. Nor did he think, that any Language could aequal it, for the Beauty of it. I am sure, I ought never to Forget a Passage he had in the Sermon he Preached at my Ordination; (On, Act XIII. 2.) "Since the SPIRIT of GOD is concerned so much in the Separation of Persons to the Work of the Ministry, how much does it concern them, to be very Spiritual in their Ministry! Let it be their Care to Live Spiritually, and be Spiritually-minded Men, and not Grieve the Holy Spirit of GOD by an Irregularities. But let them also Preach Spiritually; and therefore Preach Scripturally. The Word of GOD is the Sword of the Spirit; and they must Have and Quote much of That in their Sermons, if they would have the SPIRIT of GOD breathing in them." It may be added, That he had a notable way now and then, to bring in a Pertinent Passage of Church-History, which mightily Awakened the Attention of the Auditory, and made his Words the more Pungent Goads unto them.

His Delivery had something Singular in it. He spoke with a Grave and Wise Deliberation: But on some Subjects, his Voice would rise for the more Emphatical Clauses, as the Discourse went on: and anon come on with such a Tonitruous[296] Cogency, that the Hearers would be struck with an Awe, like what would be Produced on the Fall of Thunderbolts: He was our Farel, than whom, *Nemo tonuit fortius!*[297]

He used no Notes in his Preaching to the very Last. Though in Committing to his Memory, the Sermons which he wrote in Quarto-Volumns, he would write an Octavo-Page or two, of Texts, and of Words, which he carried in the Beginning of his Bible, to help him in case he were at a loss, yet he never look'd upon it. Once in his Old Age he did; but presently wrote a Remark upon it, as a Symptom of a Decay, which told him, he was to Dy immediately. He was indeed a Friend unto the Using of Notes in Preaching: (The Roman Orator himself did sometimes, *De Scripto recitare:*)[298] But he Distinguished That from the Reading of Notes. He wished, there were more Speaking, and less Reading, in our Sermons: and would have had the Preacher to be more of a Speaker; even so much, that the Necessary Vigour and Address, of proper Preaching, might not be lost, with any that were at all Capable of Preserving it.

I may not pass it over, That his Ministry was carried on, with continual Supplications over it. On his Days of Prayer, a common Article of Petition with him, was, *Direction what Subjects to Preach upon.* He perpetually went from his Knees unto the Pulpit, and before his going forth to Preach a Sermon, the last Thing with him, was, A Secret Prayer for a Gracious Presence of GOD with him, in the Work before him. And when he came home, the First Thing with him was, A Secret Prayer, to give Thanks for the Help he had enjoy'd, and ask a Blessing on the Truths Delivered. I find him sometimes Importunate in these Prayers. Once particularly when he was a very Young Preacher, I find this Passage in his Diary; *After I came home, in my Study I was much affected and carried out, in Prayer for the Conversion of some of those Young Merchants that usually hear me.*

And with what Leadings of Heaven granted unto it, would a Ministry so filled with Visits to Heaven, be likely to be befriended!

Let one Instance instead of many Illustrate it. The Doctor felt once upon his mind, a strong Impression, to Preach a Sermon about the Crime of Self-Murder; but he resisted, he declined, he laid it aside.

He then wrote in his Diary. "This Day my former Thoughts about Preaching on the Evil of Self-Murder, returning upon me again; I look'd up to GOD, and as I was lifting up my Heart to him, then walking in my Garden, I was most strangely moved and melted. I could not speak a word for some time. Tears gushed from my Eyes.

And it seemed as if it were said to me, *Preach on that Subject, and thou shalt Save Bodies and Souls from Death. The Lion is among thy Flock; Resist him with the Sword of the Spirit, and the Sheep Committed unto thy Charge shall be rescued out of his Bloody Hands.* What the meaning of this is, I know not; but wonder at it. There may be something of Heaven in it, more than I am aware of."

The next Lords-Day, he Preached the Sermon (On, Act. XVI. 27, 28.)[.] And Behold, soon after it, there came such to him, as informed him, That at that very Time, the Temptations to Self-Murder were impelling of them with an Horrible Violence. But GOD had Blessed that Happy Sermon for their Deliverance! They afterwards joined to his Church.

But that the Account of Dr. Mathers Ministry, may be given in the most Affectuous as well as the most Expressive way, We will here insert what was given of it; in a Sermon to his Flock, a few Days after his Expiration.

On Sep. 8. 1723. there was a Sermon Preached unto the Old North-Church; whereof the Beginning was This.

"My Design this Day is, to preach over some Thousands of Sermons; and yet I design but one Short Sermon for you. My Design this Day is, to Preach over the Sermons of another Man; and yet the Sermon shall be honestly and entirely my own. My Design is, if it be possible, to give a little Pungency unto a Ministry, whereof our GOD has now deprived us; and apply over again the Goads, which the late Master of our Assemblies had used upon us, or to clench the Golden Nails, which he has for more than Threescore Years together been driving into us. I remember, the Ingenious Rosenbergius, in his *Rhodologia*,[299] mentioning that Quality of the Rose, That it soon withers, and feels the Blast of Death upon it; and being thereby led unto Thoughts on that Epigram.

> *(Humanum in Terris nihil est quod non sit humandum;*
> *Avolat hinc Animus, Caetera Sorbet humus:)*[300]

"He cannot forbear a long Digression, by way of Parentation for his Deceased Father; On which he employs near Thirty Pages of Lamentation. As the Reverse of This, having in the Decease of mine, beheld, *That all Flesh is Grass, and all the Glory of Man, as the Flower of the Field;* I would no more insist on That; but fly away to think on, *The Word of the Lord which endureth forever;*[301] and particularly endeavour, that the Word of the Gospel, as he Preached it unto you, may, endure for ever in your Affectionate Remembrance of it; yea, and be Remembred, yet further than so, by being in the Hands of your Children after you. The Advice given to the Church of Sardis, may be a very proper Introduction to my Undertaking;

Rev. III. 3.

Remember, how thou hast received and heard.

This Doctrine, That People ought to Remember What they have heard in the Gospel Preached unto them, and Remember How they have Received it;"

Having been then spoken to; the Conclusion of the Sermon was this.

"I hasten to transfer the Admonition into what the Congregation has Heard; and particularly call upon this Assembly of Zion, to Remember how they have Received and Heard, in the bright Ministry of the Gospel, which GOD has now brought unto a Period.

"It is a Memorable Passage, I Thes. II. 19. *What is our Hope, or Joy, or Crown of Rejoicing? Are not even ye in the Presence of our Lord JESUS CHRIST at His coming?* It is here Sufficiently insinuated, That people who have been by their Pastors brought home unto GOD, will afford a marvellous & mutual Satisfaction to one another, in the World to come; when it shall be enquired, How we have Received and Heard the Gospel which has been Preached unto us? Our Deceased Father, and Pastor, and Patriarch, we shall see him again in the World to Come: And it will then be Remembred, How we have Received, what we have Heard, from him. If we have Received it as becomes the Oracles of GOD, we shall Rejoice together, and our Joy in one another, and in the Lord will be Wonderful. If we have Refus'd and Rebell'd, we shall give up our Account with Grief and not with Joy: Yea, we shall be Destroy'd; The Mouth of the Lord hath Spoken it.

"The Pastor, who This Day Sixty Two Years ago, Preached his First Sermon to the North-Church in Boston, has of latter Years, ever spoken of you, as a Loving People. The Expressions of your Love to him, were Notable, and were Numberless, and were such as greatly Comforted him. What you express'd in the Last Years of his Life, and especially after he became an Emerited Souldier, and singularly at his Departure, is what I know not that any Church has ever aequalled. In a very Public manner I now do, and in a more public manner, I hope, I AGAIN SHALL render you the Thanks, which are to be expected on the occasion. But I am now to tell you, That the most Significant way of Expressing your Love, will be, To Remember how you have Received and Heard, in the Ministry of that Burning and Shining Light, wherein ye Rejoiced for so long a Season.

"It is pressed, Heb. XIII. 7. *Remember them who have Spoken to you the Word of GOD.* But then surely, we should Remember what they have spoken to us from the Word of GOD; Remember how we have Received and Heard; Yea, Remember it, after we have seen the end of their conversation. Ecclesiastical History mentions one, who having word brought him, That his Father was Dead, made this Answer, *Desine Blasphemias loqui, Pater meus est Immortalis.*[302] No, Syr, *My Father is one who never can Dy.* Upon the Death of him who was the Father of my Flesh, I desire to take the Great Consolations of GOD, that I have in Him who is my Immortal Father, and with whom the Fatherless find Mercy. But at the same time you will allow me to do what I can, to Immortalize the Memory, and above all things to Immortalize the Ministry, of the Father, who is not suffered by reason of Death, to continue with me.

"In the Ministry of our Departed Pastor, there were some Articles of a more frequent and cogent Inculcation, whereof you shall allow me to be this Day, a Remembrancer unto you. Though he Preached over the whole Body of Divinity, in the Amesian method among you,[303] and went over the Epistles to the Seven Churches; The Ten Commandments; And the Lord's Prayer; The Parables of the Builders; And the Sower; And of the Tares; The Second Chapter of the Epistle to the Ephesians; The Eighth Chapter to the Romans; The Seventeenth Chapter of John; The whole Spiritual Armour; The Temptations of our SAVIOUR; The Chain of Graces in the Second Epistle of Peter; And other Portions of the Scriptures; And Occasional Subjects without Number; yet there were all along some Articles, which in the Fulfilling of his Ministry, he pressed with a Peculiar Flame; And I hope, you will apprehend him Speaking to you, in my short Recapitulation of them. It was mentioned as a Fault; Heb. XII. 5. *Ye have forgotten the Exhortation.* O Dear People, on whom his Doctrine dropt as the Rain, and his Speech distill'd as the Dew, as the small Rain on the Tender Herb, and as the Showres upon the Grass; Let not this Fault be what you shall be Charged withal.

"I. Remember how you have Received and Heard, That Sin is an Odious and a Dangerous Evil. Your Pastor began his Ministry here, (which, Does any Living Remember?) with several Sermons, on Lam. V. 16. *Wo is unto us, that we have Sinned;* wherein he Discoursed on, The Woful Effects of Sin. Few now Alive Remember That! But This you may all of you Remember; That the unknown, and the too much Unregarded and Unlamented Evil of Sin, was what his Ministry did exceedingly mind you of. What Pains did he take, to Convince you, That none but Fools make a Mock of Sin; That it is a most Vile thing by Sin to Deny the GOD that is Above; That the Sinner cannot look to go Unpunished. How Vehemently did he, with the *Hammer which breaks the Rocks to Pieces*[304] drive this home upon you, That no Sin is to be Indulged and Harboured, nor so much as a Sinful Thought with Allowance Lodged within you? How often, How often, has he Declared it unto you, *That any one gross, known Sin Lived in, is incompatible to a state of Salvation;* but will be Leak enough to Sink the Soul that persisted in it! What mighty Thundrings did you hear from this Pulpit, as from a flaming Mountain, against those things for which the Wrath of GOD comes on the Children of Disobedience? What warnings did he therefore give against the Particular Sins, by which he saw the Souls of Men Endangered?

"But when the Wrath of GOD was Revealed from Heaven against all Ungodliness and Unrighteousness of Men, in his doing the part of a Reprover, there was especially One Sin, that he singled out for his Frequent Fulminations; That was, the Sin of Drunkenness; Bruitish, and Baneful, and Woful Drunkenness; Intemperance in Drinking; A Slavery to the Bottle. Of this, with what Vehemency did he warn the Tippling Tribe, That at the Last! At the Last! At the Last! it will Bite like a Serpent, and Sting like an Adder! His, *Wo to Drunkards,* has been twice Printed among us.

"Oh, Remember these things, and from the Words of his Lips, which came from the Lips of GOD, Learn to keep yourselves from the Pathes of the Destroyer. Afraid of the Wounds whereof he forewarned you, if you so do, oh! Let none of you go on still in your Trespasses!

"II. Remember how you have Received and Heard, That a Real, and Thorough, and Sound Conversion to GOD, is the ONE THING that is of all the most Needful for you. The Sermons which your Pastor Preached, and which have been more than Twice Printed, on Mat. XVIII. 3. *Except ye be Converted, ye shall not enter into the Kingdom of Heaven;* These were not the only Sermons, in which he pressed upon you the Necessity of Turning and of Living unto GOD. The Alienation from GOD, which our Fall as brought upon us, was a Thing so Grievous unto him, that the Necessity of a Regeneration appeared unto him a Thing that could not be too frequently or too earnestly pleaded for. With what loud calls and peals did he Thunder it over you; That you must have a Good Work of Grace wrought in you, and an Holiness without which no Man shall see the Lord; That you must have the Experience of a New-Birth, or else it had been *Good for you that you had never been Born;*[305] That you must become New-Creatures, or else He that made you will not have Mercy of you, and He that formed you will show you no Favour?

"And though he continually asserted the Humane Impotency, and would have you sensible, That you cannot Convert yourselves; yet he urgently dehorted you from sitting still Profanely, as if you had nothing to do; urgently directed you to make that Cry unto the Glorious One, *Turn thou me and I shall be Turned,*[306] urgently Charged you to make yourselves a New Heart, by seeking unto GOD, that He would bestow a New-Heart upon you.

"But then, like the Angel, that Hastened the Lingerers out Of Sodom, how Zealously, how Terribly, did he call on the Delaying Sinner, *Fly for thy Life!*[307] The Word with him, was, *To Day; To Day! To Day!*—Can you forget the Piercing Sound of it? The uncertain Approaches, and Surprizals of Certain Death, and the Hazardous Madness of Disobliging the Holy SPIRIT, whose Influences your Conversion depends upon; how powerfully for this purpose, were you minded of them!

"Hence, as he had been himself a Pattern of Early Piety, and in the close of his Days, there was no one thing that so much Comforted him, as This; *I gave myself up to GOD in my Youth!* So he was a most fervent Preacher of it. Early Piety, how Mightily, how Ardently, and with how Frequent Excitations, did he Sollicit for it! His Printed Essays upon it, are in your Hands, Children, may your Hearts feel the Efficacy of them. Oh, Remember these Things; And know that you are deaf to Thunder, if you continue in your Unregeneracy.

"III. Remember how you have Received and Heard, That Persons may go very far, and seem very fair, in a Profession of Religion, and after all, be Hypocrites and Castaways. It was with a singular Agony, that your Pastor many Years ago, Preached several Sermons, on Job XXVII. 8. *What is the Hope of the Hypocrite?* But how often, how often, & in how many Sermons, & with what an Unparallel'd Solemnity, did he tell you; That many seem to be Religious, whose Religion is Vain? That many flatter themselves with vain Expectations to be found among the Good whom GOD will do Good unto, who yet after all shall be Led forth with *the Workers of Iniquity?*[308] That many pass through Convictions, and Contritions, and Awakenings, and come to some Reformations, and some Consolations, and for want of closing with a CHRIST in all His Offices, and for keeping some Lust from which they are not willing to be Divorced by Him, and for Him, they find themselves Miserably Deceived at the Last? *A Deceived Heart has turned them aside!*[309] How Pathetically would he Bewayl the Fate of these Poor Self-Deceivers!

"Oh, Remember these things; and let us Beware that we be not found the Sinners in Zion and the Hypocrites thereof! What, what, will be our Portion, if it should be so!

"IV. Remember how you have Received and Heard, That to Pray with all manner of Prayer, is the Best way to all manner of Good. Your Pastor, not only Preached what you have on your Shelves, oh!

may it be also in your Minds!—on Psal. XXXII. 6. *Every one that is Godly will Pray:* But in his Preaching you heard it more than a Thousand Times over from him; That, *Behold, he Prayes!* is the first Note of a Soul Returning to GOD, and capable of Good: That without Prayer there is nothing to be done, and no Good can be look'd for; That Prayer is the Main Engine with which all Good, Purposes are to be carried on. Prayer, Prayer was that which he us'd with an unceasing Assiduity; And he Preach'd it as he us'd it. He saw amazing Answers of Prayer; The Prevalency of Prayer was Demonstrated and Exemplified unto Admiration in what he had himself met withal; And this, also added flame to the Fervent Heat, with which he would have Melted you to run into the like Devotions, and have Prevailed with you to Go and do likewise.

"How Potently have you heard Secret Prayer Commended to you, Demanded from you, as a Thing which it is Impossible any Child of GOD should be a Stranger to? How forcibly, and with what an Arrest upon the Conscience, have you heard Houshold Prayer called for; And with what Flashes of Lightning have you heard that Voice of the Lord uttered among you; *The Fury of GOD Poured out on the Families that call not on His Name!*[310]

"Oh, Remember these Things; and let none of you be the Inexcusable Workers of Iniquity, which call not upon GOD!

"V. Remember how you have Received and Heard, That the Table of the Lord, is to be Seriously and Thoughtfully Prepared for, and not Unworthily Approach'd unto. It was a Grief unto your Pastor, to see so many turn their backs upon the Table of the Lord; so many which openly Procla[i]med, that after all the Means used upon them, they have left the Case of their Souls yet in a Wretched Uncertainty. He pressed the plain Command of our SAVIOUR, *Do This;* and could not see, why we should be so Afraid of Disobeying the Command of coming Suitably, as to shake off all Fear of Disobedience to the Command which bids us to come as well as we can. But yet he strongly urged the Preparation of the Sanctuary in all that came unto the Holy Table there. He did not look on the Supper of the Lord as designed for a Converting Ordinance;[311] He thought, the Bread there belonged unto none but the Children, and the Living. Though he did not judge it necessary, that a Communicant should have a Full Assurance of his being Sincerely Converted, yet it was his Judgment, that he should be one who upon Trial might not have cause to Pronounce himself, an utter Stranger to the Work of GOD; and find that he did not Heartily Consent unto the Baptismal Covenant. How Powerfully did he Preach, on Mat. XXII. 12. *How camest thou in hither, not having a Wedding Garment?* A Process of Repentance, to be first gone through; This he forever insisted on.

"And then he proposed an Actual Preparation, like what should be in People Advertised, That at such a Time GOD would come down unto them. He would say, when it is Propounded on the Lords[-]Day before it, *The next Lords-Day the Holy Supper is to be Administred,* it should be even almost as if it were said, *You shall Dy the next Lords-Day; Prepare to shew forth your Lords Death, in some Respects as if you were to meet with your own.* His own Custome accordingly it was, for Threescore Years together, to spend a whole Day in Secret Interviews with Heaven, and Praying and Fasting, before the Celebration of the Eucharist.

"Oh, Remember these Things; and let none of you Eat and Drink Judgment unto yourselves, by Unworthy Approaches unto the Table of the Lord.

"VI. Remember how you have Received and Heard, When the ETERNITY into which we are all hastening, has been Declared unto you, Displayed before you. What was there, that your Pastor did with a *Countenance like that of an Angel of GOD,*[312] more mind you of, than ETERNITY! Eternity! Eternity! He often told you, The Word ETERNITY, is enough to Break the Heart of any one, that will with any Attention look upon it! He often told you, That if you would spend one quarter of an Hour in thinking on ETERNITY, he doubted not, but it would have an happy Consequence! With what Anticipations of the Last Trumpet was it, that he Preached, on Heb. IX. 27. *After Death the Judgment!* How Solemn was he in it, when, The Judgment of the Great Day; and The Eternal Judgment, was to be spoken of? And how often was it spoken of?

"You saw him Opening the *Bars of the Pit,*[313] and setting before you the Second Death in the most Lively Colours, and bringing up the Damned Spirits from the Place of Torment, into the view of the Living, and showing you the everburning Lake, and the Smoke of the Torment Ascending forever and ever. He removed the Skreen, and gave you a sight of *the Fire that never will be quenched;*[314] the Fire which the Unfruitful Trees are to be thrown into. This he did, that so, knowing the Terror of the Lord, you may be Perswaded into the way of Understanding, and not go down to the Congregation of the Dead.

"You saw Heaven Opened, in the Discoveries which he thence brought unto you, concerning the Worship of GOD, by Myriads of Angels, and the Spirits of the Righteous, with JESUS the Mediator of the New-Covenant at the Head of them, carried on in the True Temple above: Discoveries of the Rest from the Days of Evil, and

Fulness of Joy and Pleasures forevermore, to be enjoy'd in the Blissful Mansions. He drew aside the Veil, and shewed you what is to be seen in the most Holy place; to be seen without Presumption or Profaneness; but with the greatest Advantage for a Progress towards Perfection of Holiness in the Fear of GOD. Thus he Invited you to accompany him in the way to Zion, with your Faces thitherward; He said, *Come, let us join ourselves to the Lord, in a perpetual Covenant; and go to the City of the Living GOD.*[315]

"Oh, Remember these things, Remember and Flee from the Wrath to come: Remember, and Lay Hold on Eternal Life!

"VII. Remember how your have Received and Heard, Concerning a Glorious CHRIST, & the Matchless Glories of the Lord-Redeemer, the Infinite SON of GOD, Incarnate and Enthroned in our JESUS. Your Pastor knew very well, how to Preach, and he did it more than once, on Col. III. 11. *CHRIST IS ALL.* In his Ministry, he made Him so: Yea, Determining to know nothing but a CHRIST, in his Discharging of it. You never saw him so much in his Element as when the Glories of His Precious CHRIST, were to be set before you. The Preaching of CHRIST, was the Grand Thing to which he advised them who would be the Preachers of the Gospel; The Reverse of what he with Grief saw advised by some Celebrated writers, in our Unhappy Days, wherein—*Actum est de Religione CHRISTI apud Anglos.*[316] And he took the Advice for his own Ministry, in a manner well worthy to be Imitated. Remember how clearly you have had, *The Mystery of CHRIST,*[317] explain'd unto you. Remember what you have Heard about the Importance, of Accepting a Glorious CHRIST with all His Benefits, as Offered in the Gospel, to be Preached unto every Creature. And, Remember what you have Heard, about the way of Living on a Glorious CHRIST, in all that you have to Do, and in all that you have to Bear, while you are in this Dying World: and the way of Living to Him, which you were told must be your Study, if you would be able to say, *For me to Dy, shall be my Gain.*[318] And oh! Let the Remembrance of these Things make you Well Established Christians.

"After all this[,] you will not think me to have done, if I should leave it wholly Unmentioned; That though the Ministry which has now left you, did principally insist upon such Indisputable Matters, yet it had now and then in it, very Solemn Admonitions unto you, To keep Inviolate the Religion of the Second Commandment, which brought our Fathers over into this Wilderness, and was the Love of our Espousals, and will be the perpetual Test of our Loyalty to our SAVIOUR: And to keep close unto the Faith and Order of the Gospel, which they that went before us, have left as a most Precious

Legacy unto us. These Charges you have Received and Heard; And they must not be Forgotten with you!

"But,

"I have now done. The Sermon that I have this Day Preached unto you, must be called, *A Sermon to bring to Remembrance*. It will not be an Unuseful Sermon, if they are made Pure Minds, that are stirred up to and by this Remembrance. Verily, more than a little depends upon it!"

One Article more, and the Testimony is Finished!

Article XXXIV.
Dead Abel, yet Speaking.

The PREACHER, who sought out the Acceptable Words we have heard of, was One who wrote as Obscure an Hand perhaps, as his Admired Ramus, of whom Naucellus Complains, That a Stranger would ask a deal of Time to spell out so much as Two or Three Lines of his Writing; or a less worthy to be Honoured Lipsius, of whose Writing Bonciarius makes the very same Complaint: and herein also he was not unlike to Bucer, who wrote an Hand so bad that the Printers could not read it: (and Erasmus's too, it seems, was bad enough:)[319] Yet his Pen may say to the World, *Have not I Written unto thee some Excellent Things?*[320] Which he has dropt for us, as the Prophet his Melota,[321] when he was Ascending to the Heavenly World. Thus does he Leave something behind him, that may be doing of Good upon Earth, after he is gone to Heaven.

Behold, the Catalogue [of Increase's books]!—Without any mention of the Learned and Useful Praefaces, which the Publishers of many Books Obtained from him, as a Beautiful Porch unto them; and which Collected, would make a considerable Volumn.

1669.

The Mystery of Israels Salvation.

1670.

The Life and Death of Mr. Richard Mather.

1673.

Wo to Drunkards.

1974 [1674].

The Day of Trouble near.
Important Truths about Conversion.

1675.

The First Principles of New England.

A Discourse concerning the Subject of Baptism, and Consociation of Churches.
The Wicked Mans Portion.
The Times of Men in the Hands of GOD.

1676.

An History of the War with the Indians. With, an Exhortation to the Inhabitants.

1677.

A Relation of Troubles of N. E. from the Indians, from the Beginning.
An Historical Discourse, on the Prevalency of Prayer.
Renewal of Covenant, the Duty of Decaying and Distressed Churches.

1678.

Pray for the Rising Generation.

1679.

A Call to the Rising Generation.

1680.

The Divine Right of Infant Baptism.
The Great Concernment of a Covenant-people.
Heavens Alarm to the World.

1982.

Diatriba de Signo Filii Hominis.
Practical Truths.
The Church a Subject of Persecution.

1683.

Cometographia. Or, A Discourse concerning Comets.

1684.

Remarkable Providences.
The Doctrine of Divine Providence.

1685.

An Arrow against Profane & Promiscuous Dances.

1686.

The Mystery of CHRIST.
The Greatest of Sinners Exhorted.
A Sermon on the Execution of a Poor Man for Murder.

1687.

A Testimony against Superstitions.

1688.

De Successu Evangelii apud Indos; Epistola.

1689.

The Unlawfulness of using Common-Prayer; And, of Swearing on the Book.

1690.

Several Papers relating to the State of New-England. Besides, A Relation of the State of New-England.

The Revolution Justified.

1693.

The Blessing of Primitive Counsellours.

Cases of Conscience, concerning Witchcraft.

An Essay on the Power of a Pastor for the Administration of Sacraments.

1695.

On the case, whether a man may Marry his Wives own Sister.

Solemn Advice to Young Men.

1696.

Angelographia. A Treatise on Angels.

1697.

A Discourse on Mans not knowing his Time.

The Case of Conscience, concerning the Eating of Blood.

1698.

David Serving his Generation. A Funeral Sermon.

1699.

The Surest Way to the Highest Honours.

A Discourse on Hardness of Heart.

The Folly of Sinning.

1700.

The Order of the Gospel Vindicated.

1701.

The Blessed Hope.

1702.

Remarks on a Sermon of George Keith.

Ichabod: Or, The Glory Departing.

The CHRISTIAN Religion the only True Religion.

The Excellency of a Public Spirit.

1703.

The Duty of Parents to Pray for their Children.

Soul Saving Gospel Truths.

1704.

The Voice of GOD in Stormy Winds.

Practical Truths, to Promote Holiness.

1705.

Meditations on the Glory of CHRIST.

1706.

A Discourse concerning Earthquakes.
A Testimony against Sacriledge.
A Dissertation concerning Right to Sacraments.

1707.

Meditations on Death.
A Disquisition concerning the State of Souls Departed.

1709.

A Dissertation concerning the Future Conversion of the Jews. Confuting Dr. Lightfoot and Mr. Baxter.

1710.

A Discourse concerning Faith and Prayer, for the Kingdom of CHRIST.
A Sermon on, Be very Courageous. At the Artillery-Election.
Awakening Truths Tending to Conversion.

1711.

Meditations on, The Glory of the Heavenly World.
A Discourse concerning the Death of the Righteous.
The Duty of the Children of Godly Parents.

1712.

Burnings Bewayled.
Remarks upon an Answer to a Book against the Common Prayer.
Meditations on Sanctification of the Lords Day.

1713.

A plain Discourse showing who shall, and who shall not enter into Heaven.
The Believers gain by Death. A Funeral Sermon for his Daughter in Law.

1714.

Resignation to the Will of GOD. On the Death of his Consort.

1715.

Jesus CHRIST a Mighty Saviour. And other Subjects.

1716.

A Disquisition concerning Ecclesiastical Councils.
There is a GOD in Heaven.
The Duty and Dignity of Aged Servants of GOD.

1718.

The Duty of Praying for Ministers. A Sermon at the Ordination of his Grandson.

Sermons on the Beatitudes.
Practical Truths plainly delivered;—with an [O]rdination Sermon.

1719.

Five Sermons on several Subjects. One of them on the Authors Birth-Day.

1721.

Advice to Children of Godly Ancestors. A Sermon concluding the Boston-Lectures on Early Piety. Beside several small Sheets to justify and recommend the happy practice of saving Lives, by Encountring the Small-pox in the way of Inoculation.

1722.

A Dying Pastors Legacy.
Elijahs Mantle.

As they noted of such a Writer as Bartholinus.

Libros Authoris quicunque recenset et Annos,
Annos tot poterit, quot numerare Libros.[322]

Revelation XIV. 13.

They Rest from their Labours, and their Works do follow them.

Epitaphium.

Crescentius Matherus.
Magnum RICHARDI, quo gaudebat NOV-ANGLIA
Patre ac Patrono semper Memorando,
Incrementum:
NON-ANGLIAE Indigena,
Ornamentum et Munimentum;
Sed
Patre ac Patria sua Notior;
Quem novit fere tota Gens Christiana;
norunt et Antipodes.
A teneris Annis Veri Bonique Studiosus;
eoq; potitus atq; politus:
Cui in Pueritia nil Praeter aetatem fuit Puerile;
Vir quem nulli unquam aliter
quam ut Virum aspexerunt:
Quem Juvenem Senes admirati,
Quem Senem Juvenes amplexati:
Insigni Gravitate, Comitate, Autoritate preditus:
In cujus Vultu vere Venerabili una sedebant,
Majestas et Amor:
Angeli Facies, et Hominis.
Collegii Harvardini
Annos per Viginti Praeses;
Ecclesiae Bostonensis,
Annos per plusquam ter Viginti Pastor:
Quot Animas Deo lucrifecit?
Quot Modis ac Mediis Orbi benefecit?
Academiae diu Praefuit ac Profuit;
Non tantum Lapides dolavit,
sed et Architectos fabricavit:
In Fidelium Caetibus Ministrum agens,
Minister Verbi, Hoc egit:
Omnesq; semper velut Orientalium Sydus,
duxit ad CHRISTUM;
CHRISTI Amore animatus et inflammatus,
pro CHRISTO Vitam erogavit;

imò et Mortem anhelavit;
CHRISTUM amavit,
Plusquam suos, plusquam sua, plusquam se,
A CHRISTO doctus,
Nil tanquam CHRISTUM discere,
Nil praeter CHRISTUM docere,
voluit:
Sacras SCRIPTURAS
Assidue Legens, Accuraté Scrutans,
Acutissimè Enucleans,
Cordi suo habuit apte inscriptas:
Et cordibus Auditorum Clavos Aureos
reliquit alte infixos:
Cui Mysteria S. S. Scripturarum reconditiora,
Quae Rimari nequaquam licet,
Quae Mirari quam maximé decet,
Credere et Vivere,
Summa semper fuit Religio.
Cui Peccatum, vel Minimum quod sic,
imò vel ipsum illius umbraculum,
Nunquam sine Dolore admissum,
Nunquam sine Odio pervisum;
Summo semper cum zelo percussum.
Erga Pié Ingentes Barnabas;
Erga Impiè degentes Boanerges;
Concionator Eximius
Cujus, Facienda Faciendo praedicantis,
Non Magis in Voce audivimus,
quam in Vita Spectavimus,
potentissimas Conciones:
Fulmina in Sermonibus resonantia
et
Fulgura in Moribus Coruscantia,
Attoniti unà Observavimus.
Fide solà Justificari,
Sperans ac Scribens;
Fidem verò Solitariam
ad ima ipsa Tartara damnans, ac trudens.
Cum Gaudio
in Salutis aeternae Obsignatione Securus;
Cum Tremore
de Salutis propriae Operatione Sollicitus;

Laetabundus Fidelissimum Salvatorem,
Tremebundus cordis perfidias,
contemplatus.
Ecclesiasticae Disciplinae
Verbo Divino Conformatae et Confirmmatae,
acerrimus Vindex;
Noluit leges Divinas Mutari,
aut Aedes nutari:
Cui Ecclesias evertendi vel pervertendi
Conatus nefarios retundere;
Turrisque demoliendae Linguas confundere;
Et in Fide Cultuq; Evangelico
Stabilitas Ecclesias defendere, ac Erigere;
Cura fuit perpetua.
Helluo Librorum
Locupletissimam in mente sua instruxit
Bibliothecam;
Et in ejus Alveario,
E quo oracula produxit melle dulciora,
nullus Otio Dies periit.
Generosus, et feré ad prodigium Liberalis,
Qui nullius rei novit praeter honestam,
Temporis parsimoniam.
In Caeteris Artibus peritus;
In Arte Deo Vivendi petitissimus;
Multijuga Eruditione florentissimus;
In Corona Eruditorum Gemma
quàm nitida! quàm lucida!
In Cathedra Doctorali stella fulgidissima,
Primaeq; Magnitudinis;
Ad Sublimiores et Invisibiles jam
Caelitum sedes,
E Terrestrium Conspectu subducta.
Coram REGIBUS Mortalibus
pro Populo suo variis oppressionibus Vexato,
Orator
Prudens, Fidus, Indefessus,
Et Exorator faelicissimus;
Apud REGEM etiam IMMORTALEM,
Supplicibus votis accedens,
Orationibus,
Et Caelum tundere et misericordiam extorquere Solitus:
Cujus Preces et lacrymae

Tua, O Novanglia, fuerunt Arma,
Et Castra Everterunt Exterorum.
A REGE REGUM
Eundem ad Populum Legatus,
Diu ac Bene in Legatione fungenda
Commoratus et Occupatus,
Ad Caelestia Palatia,
Terrenis Omnibus multo Splendidiora,
jam revocatur.
Quod corpus mortui tegit Monumentum
Exiguam habet Sancti in Terris partem;
et ipsum sanè Morietur.
Per Opera et Merita insignia
sibi Vivus paravit Monumenta,
Quae post mortem, et mortis nescia,
per omnia durabunt Saecula.
Optimo Monumento non indignus,
Nullius Monumenti indigens;
In quo Laudando, Fama
non potest esse Loquax,
nec timet esse Mendax.
Annos habuit, et libros Edidit,
(In quibus, et in PARENTATORE Typis Excuso ac
Emisso, eos et multò plures ad huc Annos habebit).
Octuaginta Quinque.
Cui Nato Dorcestriae, Jun. 21. 1639.
Sibi optabiliora advenere Natalitia,
Bostonae, Aug. 23. 1723.
An Totus Recessit? Non Reliquit—
SAMUELEM.

Epitaph.
Increase Mather.

Great is Mather, progeny of Richard,
in whom New England accustoms its joy.
New England has need to remember his father and our patron as well,
native to New England,
its pride and its bulwark.
More famous than father and country was Mather,
whom Christians, a family, knew,
and whom children of the night knew too.
From tender years zealous in pursuit of

goodness and truth,
master of truth and goodness,
well cultivated,
child only in age when a child,
man of honor only when mature.
Old men admired him when young;
Young men cherished him when old.
Remarkably possessed was he of
gravity,
affability,
and perspicuity.
A visage truly venerable,
A visage angelic and humane,
dignity and love transfixed.
At Harvard College,
he professed for twenty years;
At church of Boston,
he pastored for sixty years.
How many were the souls gained for God?
How many measures of kindness performed for
creatures mundane?
For a long time academics did he prefer and superintend.
Not only did he sculpt students,
but sculptors of students did he make.
A minister among the faithful of the Word,
He led all men to Christ,
as star of the East.
By love of Christ, animated and inflamed.
For love of Christ, exhausted in life
breathed he his last.
Christ
he loved more than
ones beloved,
property and self.
Christ, his teacher,
he wished to teach;
Nothing to teach as much as Christ;
No one to learn of more than Christ.
Reading Sacred Scriptures always,
exploring Sacred Scriptures carefully,
explaining Sacred Scriptures aptly.
Sacred Scriptures he held within his heart.
In the hearts of hearers,
the golden symbols of Sacred Scripture did he deeply fix.
The mysteries of Sacred Scripture recondite,
to uncover never,
to admire ever,

to live ever and ever to believe,
were his religion sublime.
Sin, small or dark,
never without sorrow passed,
never without hatred cast,
ever with zeal struck.
Pious, therefore, his laments for Barnabas;[323]
Impious, therefore, his endurances for Boanerges.[324]
Inventor eximious, proclaimed he what needs be done by doing.
Not less in his voice was heard
than in his life seen.
Thunder in sermons sounded,
And lightening in person rebounded,
And we observing, thunder struck.
Hoping in faith as justification,
By faith alone we are justified, he wrote.
To the depths of hell he damned with joy those without faith.
With the pledge of eternal salvation
to eternal solicitude
confided he those with faith.
Joy with compulsion he took in the Saviour most faithful.
Fear with compulsion he bore when contemplating
perfidies of the soul.
Confirmed was he by divine word in the church.
A most stern judge of laws divine,
Nor did he nod for church to transform laws divine.
Those wicked men who inverted church
and who perverted church,
he ejected.
The tongues of men who tore down the bulwark of the church
he confounded.
Firm in faith and learning,
defended he the church;
The church raised he up in the world.
Devouring books,
a most rich apiary, his mind's library, constructed
orations sweeter than honey; no leisure lost,
therein he produced.
Generous,
liberal,
almost prodigal,
honest,
parsimonious with time.
Learned in other liberal arts,
Learned most in one art,
the art of Godly living.
Of learned men a jewel in their crown;

In learning complex the fullest flower.
How polished!
How bright!
A glimmering star of greatest magnitude
in the professor's chair.
To seats of heaven, sublime and invisible, from earthly sight transported.
His people by various oppressions vexed by mortal kings,
This prudent,
faithful,
tireless,
most facile rhetor with humble progress
approaches the immortal King,
presses heaven,
and mercy wrested he alone.[325]
Prayers and tears for him, O New England.
You were at arms and by your arms
the camps of those not your own you overturned.
From King of Kings to this very people a legate sent.
Legatine, long and well occupied, he lingering performed.
To palatial heavenly abodes from earthly things,
To abodes now more splendid is he recalled.
The monument, which covers the body of holy deceased,
encompasses a small space upon this earth.
It will itself doubtless decease.
Monuments, when living, for self he prepared
through works and distinguished works of merit,
which will endure through all ages
after his death and the forgetfulness which death brings.
The finest monument he deserves;
No monument needs he reserve.
Rumor loquacious cannot be
about one who must have laudes.
Nor need one fear rumor mendacious will be.
He lived to eight[y] and five years
and published books
(which [titles] are in the *Parentator*, which is printed and published,
and through which [titles] he still will live more years by far).[326]
He was born at Dorchester,
June 21, 1639.
The dear birthday wished for came
at Boston, August 23, 1723.
Has he completely returned? He has not left.

Samuel Mather[327]

(Translation by
Anthony C. Florek
St. Edwards University)

Notes to the Introduction

1. Josephine K. Piercy has suggested that the use of a form of character essay in sermons was directly related to the origin of Puritan biographical works: *Studies in Literary Types in Seventeenth Century America* (New Haven: Yale University Press, 1939), pp. 168–75.

2. Kenneth B. Murdock, *Literature and Theology in Colonial New England* (New York: Harper and Row, 1963), p. 117.

3. Peter Gay, *A Loss of Mastery: Puritan Historians in Colonial America* (New York: Vintage, 1968), p. 60. More recently the *Magnalia* has been assessed as a very significant work, the rhetoric and imagery of which figure centrally in the ideation of America: see Sacvan Bercovitch, *The Puritan Origins of the American Self* (New Haven: Yale University Press, 1975).

4. Kenneth B. Murdock, *Increase Mather, the Foremost American Puritan* (Cambridge: Harvard University Press, 1925), p. 97.

5. Ibid., p. 96.

6. Robert Middlekauff, *The Mathers: Three Generations of Puritan Intellectuals, 1596–1728* (New York: Oxford University Press, 1971), pp. 10, 101.

7. On a later Puritan's use of images of the father and the family, see William J. Scheick, *The Writings of Jonathan Edwards: Theme, Motif, and Style* (College Station: Texas A&M University Press, 1975), pp. 40–50. Relatedly, useful insight is given by Cecelia Tichi, who observes that in writing history Puritans expanded spiritual biography to include not only the individual but the entire select social unit: "Spiritual Biography and the 'Lords Remembrancers,'" *William and Mary Quarterly* 28 (January 1971): 64–85.

8. Quotations from *Life and Death* and *Parentator* are cited, with corresponding page numbers, from the editions printed in this volume.

9. In *The Soveraign Efficacy of Divine Providence* (Boston, 1682) Urian Oakes writes: "The Lord is pleased, not through any *defect of power* in Himself but out of *the abundance of his goodness* to communicate causal power and virtue to his Creatures, & to honour them with the Dignity that they may be his Instruments" (p. 6).

10. Puritans distinguished between a pastor, who principally concentrated on ecclesiastical administrative details, and a teacher, who served as an educational and doctrinal leader in the parish. Neither position was higher than the other. See Vergil V. Phelps, "The Pastor and Teacher in New England," *Harvard Theological Review* 4 (July 1911): 388–99.

11. See, for example, John Cotton, *The Way of Life* (London, 1641), pp. 162–65.

12. This concept of civil or federal freedom as opposed to natural freedom is explained in detail by John Winthrop in his famous speech to the general court (3 July 1645). See Perry Miller and Thomas Johnson, eds., *The Puritans: A Sourcebook of Their Writings* (New York: Harper and Row, 1963), 1:206–7.

13. See n. 38 to *Life and Death*.

14. In his undergraduate oration, "The prayse of Eloquence," Michael Wigglesworth noted that it is "ould truth" that "receivs a new habit" through the power

of eloquence, that although truth's "visage" might be "so altered that it may currently pass and be accepted as a novelty," yet "its essence be the same": Samuel E. Morison, *Harvard College in the Seventeenth Century* (Cambridge: Harvard University Press, 1936), 1:180.

15. Murdock, *Increase Mather*, p. 97.

16. The psychological features of this transformation as well as of some of Increase's other experiences described by Cotton can be better understood in the light of William Sargant's *Battle for the Mind* (Baltimore: Penguin, 1961).

17. Perry Miller discusses the Puritan regard for a plain style in *The New England Mind: The Seventeenth Century* (Boston: Beacon Press, 1961), pp. 302–4.

18. In *A Briefe Exposition with Practicall Observations upon the Whole Book of Ecclesiastes* (London, 1654) John Cotton remarked that human wit detracts from the desired simplicity of sermonic style just "as painted glasse windowes darken the light" (p. 269).

19. David Leverenz would probably interpret these characteristics differently. In *The Language of Puritan Feeling: An Exploration in Literature, Psychology, and Social History* (New Brunswick: Rutgers Unviersity Press, 1980) Leverenz speculates that Increase resented his father, disapproved of his accommodating spirit, and after Richard's death sought "covertly to shut his father out" (pp. 97–98).

20. "The Autobiography of Increase Mather," ed. Michael G. Hall, *Proceedings of the American Antiquarian Society* 71 (1962): pt. 2, 289.

21. Ibid.

22. Edmund S. Morgan, *Visible Saints: The History of a Puritan Idea* (Ithaca: Cornell University Press, 1965), p. 131.

23. On Dorchester's resistance to the idea, see Robert G. Pope, *The Half-Way Covenant: Church Membership in Puritan New England* (Princeton: Princeton University Press, 1969), pp. 33–35.

24. Norman Pettit, *The Heart Prepared: Grace and Conversion in Puritan Sacramental Life* (New Haven: Yale University Press, 1966), p. 201; Mason Lowance, *Increase Mather* (New York: Twayne, 1974), p. 156. An earlier date, one much too early, is vaguely intimated by David Levin, who says that soon after 1667 Increase changed his position on the halfway covenant: *Cotton Mather: The Young Life of the Lord's Remembrancer, 1663–1703* (Cambridge: Harvard University Press, 1978), p. 2.

25. That Increase might not have completely revised his position on the halfway covenant by 1670 is a possibility suggested by his edition of Eleazar Mather's *A Serious Exhortation to the Present and Succeeding Generation in New-England* (Cambridge, 1671), though even this work seems to have been modified by Increase.

26. No doubt this is another feature of what in *The Puritan Family: Religion and Domestic Relations in Seventeenth-Century New England* (New York: Harper and Row, 1966) Edmund Morgan has described as Puritan tribalism, a sense of the exclusiveness of the collective Puritan family of saints and their children (pp. 161–86).

27. A challenge to Mather's view that his wife was insane has been raised by Virginia Bernhard, in "Cotton Mather's 'Most Unhappy Wife': Reflections on the Uses of Historical Evidence," *New England Quarterly* 60 (1987): 341–62.

28. Levin, pp. 12, 26, 89–90.

29. Kenneth Silverman, *The Life and Times of Cotton Mather* (New York: Harper & Row, 1984), pp. 27, 29, 42, 49.

30. Kenneth Silverman, ed., *Selected Letters of Cotton Mather* (Baton Rouge: Louisiana State University Press, 1971), p. 376.

31. In "Cotton Mather," in *Major Writers of Early American Literature*, ed. Everett Emerson (Madison: University of Wisconsin Press, 1972), pp. 93–149, Sacvan

Bercovitch makes the observation that Cotton's enormous number of books represents his desire to create an imaginative world different from the one in which he lived.

32. Middlekauff differs from my view of this detail in Cotton's biography; he believes that Cotton criticizes Increase for spending too much time in the study (p. 365).

Notes to *Life and Death*

1. The Latin reads: "The life of a minister is a judgment and an object of attention."

2. Hebrews 13:7, mentioned also on the title page.

3. *A Farewel-Exhortation to the Church and People of Dorchester in New-England* (Cambridge, N.E., 1657).

4. This is a conventional seventeenth-century pun on the heart (will) as the temple of the Holy Spirit.

5. Plutarch was a Greek historian (see n. 19 to *Life and Death*); Diogenes Laertius was a second-century commentator on Greek philosophers; Flavius Philostratus was a third-century Greek Sophist; Eunapius was a fifth-century Greek rhetorician; and Gaius Plinius Caecilius Secundis was a Roman poet and orator. Although wary of the misinformation and the potentiality for harm evident in pagan writings, Puritan divines tended to respect the classics. Increase certainly thought well of them (see *Christ the Fountaine of Life* [London, 1651], p. 145). Increase's son Cotton Mather, would later express a prevalent Puritan view of such authors as Homer and Virgil when he explained that their pagan stories reveal, in a disguise and fable, the history of the Old Testament (see *Manuductio ad Ministerium* [Boston, 1726], pp. 38–42). In article 26, section 11 of *Parentator* Mather explains that at their best, pagan authors were inspired by "Natural Conscience," which means that what is valuable in their works derives from the light of reason, even if that reason, unaided by grace, is ultimately inadequate. For a discussion of various classical allusions in early American writing, see Richard M. Gummere, *The American Colonial Mind and the Classical Tradition* (Cambridge: Harvard University Press, 1963).

6. Dorotheus, *De vita ac morte prophetarum et apostolorum.* There were many editions of this work after 1560.

7. Bishop Epiphanius (ca. 315–403) was an opponent to Origen (see n. 30 to *Parentator*); Isidore of Seville (ca. 570–636) was a bishop who preserved learning; and Prochorus appears in Acts 6:5. Mather also refers to Johannes Schopffius, *Academia Jesu Christi* (1593); Daniel Tossanus, *A Synopsis or Compendium of the Fathers* (London, 1635); and Melchior Adamus, *Decades duae continentes vitas theologorum exterorum principum.* Adamus was a German Protestant divine, and his book saw several editions after 1618.

8. Samuel Clarke, *A Collection of the Lives of Ten Eminent Divines* (London, 1662). Increase owned a copy of this work (see Julius Herbert Tuttle, "The Libraries of the Mathers," *Proceedings of the American Antiquarian Society* 20 [April 1910]: 269–356). Increase also owned Clarke's *A General Martyrologie,* of which there were several editions after 1659.

9. Thomas Brightman (1562–1607); Roger Parker (1564–1614); William Ames (1576–1633); Jeremiah Burrough(e)s (1599–1646); and Thomas Hooker (1586–1647).

10. This slightly inaccurate quotation comes from the odes of Horace: "Many brave men lived before Agamemnon, but all are overwhelmed in unending night, unwept for, unknown, because they lack an inspired poet" (4. 9. 25–28).

11. Flavius Josephus (ca. 37–110); Robertus Bellarminus (1542–1621); Gerolamo

Cardano (1501–76); Franciscus Junius (1545–1602); probably John Collins (1632?–87); probably George Buchanan (1506–82); John Bale (1495–1563); Robert Burton (1577–1640); Joseph Hall (1574–1656); and probably Laurence Bodley (?–1615).

12. These lines, out of sequence and somewhat inaccurate, appear near the end of Horace's prose entries in *Ars poetica:* "He must have done much and suffered much, as a child, who wants to reach the desired goal on the race course." Increase seems to have deliberately avoided Horace's reference to the abstinence from wine and sex that appears in the original source.

13. Samuel Hieron (d. 1618), of Modbury in Devonshire; William Whitaker (1548–95), Master of St. John's, Cambridge; and Richard Vines (1600–1655), of Weddington in Warwickshire.

14. William Perkins (1558–1602) was an English divine of significant influence upon Puritan thinking. He particularly concentrated on the psychology of sin and regeneration. Although Increase owned several of Perkins's works, it is difficult to guess specifically which book he has in mind in this passage.

15. The distinction between mere conviction and true conversion is an important one: see Norman S. Fiering, "Will and Intellect in the New England Mind," *William and Mary Quarterly* 29 (October 1972): 515–58; and William J. Scheick, *The Will and the Word: The Poetry of Edward Taylor* (Athens: University of Georgia Press, 1974).

16. The Greek reads: "With God['s help]."

17. Petrus Ramus (1515?–72) was a sixteenth-century thinker whose principles of logic greatly influenced Puritan divines. In contrast to Aristotle's tripartite syllogism, for instance, Ramus stressed the principle of dichotomy, according to which every idea should be paired with its counterpart. The effect of Ramus's influence is readily apparent in the formal structure of many New England Puritan sermons. On Ramus's thought, see Walter J. Ong, *Ramus, Method, and the Decay of Dialogue: From the Art of Discourse to the Art of Reason* (Cambridge: Harvard University Press, 1958); and Leon Howard, *Essays on Puritans and Puritanism* (Albuquerque: University of New Mexico Press, 1986).

18. Thomas Cartwright (1535–1603) and Arthur Hildersham (also Hildersam) (1563–1632) were both influential Puritan divines. Increase owned several volumes of their works. Sherwood has eluded identification, in spite of the fact that his name appears in Increase's library (Tuttle, "Libraries," p. 285). I have identified this work as *An Answer to a Sermon Preached the 17 of April . . . 1608, by G. D.* (London?, 1609), but curiously the *British Museum Catalogue* makes no mention of Sherwood in regard to this work and lists it under the name of George Downame.

Something of the controversy over funeral sermons, especially their tendency to flatter the dead falsely and thereby misguide the living, is noted in the Preface to James Fitch's *Peace the End of the Perfect and Uprigh[t]* (Boston, 1672). See also Scheick, "Tombless Virtue and Hidden Text: New England Puritan Funeral Elegies," in *Puritan Poets and Poetics,* ed. Peter White (University Park: Pennsylvania State University Press, 1985), pp. 286–302.

19. Increase refers to Plutarch's *Vita parallelae,* specifically to the accounts of Publius Valerius and Furius Camillus. This work was well known (chiefly in the Thomas North translation) and well admired by Puritan divines in general. Cotton Mather, for example, expressed his appreciation of the work in *Magnalia Christi Americana,* ed. Kenneth B. Murdock (Cambridge: Harvard University Press, 1977), p. 96.

20. This quotation is from book 3, chap. 10 of *De rerum inventoribus* by Polydorus Vergilius (ca. 1470–1555): "Hence the custom of praising the dead, which we today observe."

21. The quotation reads: "See *The Magdeburg Centuries*, book 4, chap. 6." This work was the first Protestant universal history of the church written by several writers who defended the Reformation. Increase owned five volumes.

22. This description derives from Revelation 1:16.

23. This passage by Marcus Fabius Quintilianus (ca. 35–?) reads: "No one is able to achieve great fame and contentedness at the same time."

24. Thomas Cartwright (see n. 18 to *Life and Death*), Roger Parker (see n. 9 to *Life and Death*), Paul Baynes (d. 1617), and William Ames (see n. 9 to *Life and Death*) were influential early Puritan spokesmen and theologians. Increase owned several of their works.

25. William Prynne (1600–1669) wrote *A Briefe Survay and Censure of Mr. Cozens His Couzening Devotions* (London, 1628) in response to *A Collection of Private Devotions: In the Practice of the Ancient Church Called the Houres of Prayer* (London, 1627) by John Cozen, Bishop of Durham.

26. The Greek reads: "With great ostentation."

27. The Greek reads: "Nothing sound."

28. The Latin reads: "A wise man foresees." The source might be Aelius Donatus.

29. Probably martyred minister John Bradford (1510?–55), who wrote several epistles, such as can be found appended to Clement Cotton's *The Mirror of Martyrs* (London 1615) and Miles Coverdale's *Certain Most Godly, Fruitful, and Comfortable Letters of Such True Saints and Martyrs of God* (London 1564). I was unable to identify the exact work cited by Increase.

30. John Brinsley, *The True Watch, and Rule of Life, or a Direction for the Examination of Our Spiritual Estate* (London, 1614); Thomas Cartwright, *Commentarii Succincti & Dilucidi in Proverbia Salomonis* (London, 1617), which saw several editions, one of which Increase owned.

31. Franciscus Junius (1545–1602) was a French Huguenot, whose works include *The Revelation of Saint John the Apostle and Evangelist, with a Briefe and Learned Commentarie, Written by Franc. Junius* (London, 1594) and *The Bible, That Is, the Holy Scripture, etc. (With the Annotations of Fr. Junius upon the Revelation of S. John)* (London, 1599), both of which saw several editions.

32. John Cotton (1584–1652) and Thomas Hooker (see n. 9 to *Life and Death*) were major first-generation New England ministers.

33. See Acts 20:36–38.

34. Brentius might be Johann Brentz, author of several commentaries on Scripture.

35. Jonathan Mitchell (1624–68), coauthor with Richard Mather of *A Defence of the Answer and Arguments of the Synod Met at Boston in the Year 1662* (Cambridge, N. E., 1664), was a crucial influence on Increase's eventual endorsement of the halfway covenant. He succeeded Thomas Shepard (1605–49) at Cambridge, Massachusetts.

36. John Avery (d. 1635). Another description of this hurricane appears in William Bradford's *Of Plymouth Plantation*, ed. Samuel Eliot Morison (New York: Knopf, 1952), pp. 279–80.

37. Edmund S. Morgan speculates that John Warham's emigration, with a number of Dorchester families, to Windsor, Connecticut, might have been stimulated, at least in part, by the fact that the ecclesiastical practice concerning church membership was less exclusive in Connecticut than it was in Massachusetts. Warham apparently believed that the visible church consisted of the godly as well as the ungodly (*Visible Saints: The History of a Puritan Idea* [Ithaca: Cornell University Press, 1967], pp. 107–8).

38. Responding to Dorchester's wish to gather a church, neighboring ministers

(Thomas Shepard among them) visited the town in 1636 in order to examine the applicants. Although these ministers declined to give their permission because of insufficient evidence of true conversion in several of the applicants, they did give their assent later in the same year: see B. R. Burg, *Richard Mather of Dorchester* (Lexington: University Press of Kentucky, 1976), pp. 32–37. Whether or not Richard Mather subsequently became more conservative, to a significant degree, in his view of the prerequisites for church membership is not as easily ascertained as some scholars have suggested. That his church, on the other hand, did become increasingly acute in its view of membership is certain.

39. The Latin reads: "To have prayed well is to have studied well." Compare "Many times I have learned more from one prayer than I might have learned from much reading and speculation" (*A Simple Way to Pray [1535], in Luther's Works* [Philadelphia: Fortress Press, 1968], 43:198).

40. John Norton (1606–63), successor of John Cotton at the First Church in Boston, was an adamant foe of Antinomianism and an important member of the Synod of 1637.

41. For Asaph, a Levite in charge of the liturgical music used in the public worship in Jerusalem, see 2 Chronicles 29:30; for Heman, see 1 Chronicles 6:33.

42. Girolamo Zanchius, an Italian Calvinist theologian, wrote many books, several of which served as texts at Harvard: see Samuel E. Morison, *Harvard College in the Seventeenth Century* (Cambridge: Harvard University Press, 1936). Increase owned at least the volume entitled *De divinatione.*

43. The Latin reads: "A good diet is more effective than any Hippocrates" (i.e., a doctor).

44. The Latin reads: "We have prospered in synods and now we shall die in them."

45. The fifth proposition reads: "Church-members who were admitted in minority, understanding the Doctrine of faith, and publickly professing their assent thereto; not scandalous in life, and solemnly owning the Covenant before the Church, wherein they give up themselves and their Children to the Lord, and subject themselves to the Government of Christ in the Church, their Children are to be Baptized" (*The Creeds and Platforms of Congregationalism,* ed. Williston Walker [Boston: Pilgrim Press, 1960], p. 328).

46. Ambrose of Milan (340–97); Gorgonia (d. 375). The next name Increase gives probably refers to Conrad Gesner, a sixteenth-century scholar, well known for his editions of the classics. Philip Melanchthon (1497–1560), a colleague of Luther, was famous for his scholarship; Increase owned at least one volume of his works. The other divine mentioned is possibly Hugh Sanford, whose *De Descensu Domini Nostri Jesu Christi ad Inferos Libri Quatuor* (1611) was in Increase's library.

47. Thomas Goodwin (1600–1680), *Patience and Its Perfect Work* (London, 1666). Another edition was published the following year; Increase owned a copy of this work.

48. Austin is a shorthand term, frequently used by Puritan authors, referring to St. Augustine (354–430).

49. Gregory of Nazianzen (330?–90?); Gregory of Nyssa (332–98); Basil the Great (ca. 330–79); and Hilary of Poitiers (ca. 300–367).

50. Richard Mather's *Catechisme, or, the Grounds and Principles of Christian Religion, Set Forth by Way of Question and Answer* (London, 1650). A shorter version is said to have been printed in New England, but no extant copy has been located.

51. Most likely Increase is referring to John Dod (1549?–1645), an acquaintance of William Whitaker (see n. 13 to *Life and Death.*) Increase owned a copy of *A Treatise or Exposition upon the Ten Commandments,* a very popular book by John Dod and

Robert Cleaver that saw numerous editions after 1603. Cotton is identified in n. 32 to *Life and Death.*

52. The followers of Henry Barrow (ca. 1550–93) and Robert Browne (1550–1633) radically dissented from the Anglican church. They felt that internal reform was too slow and so they separated from the church in order to form independent congregations.

53. Richard Mather's *A Modest & Brotherly Answer to Mr. Charles Herle, His Book, against the Independency of Churches* (London, 1644); *A Reply to Mr. Rutherford, or, a Defence of the Answer to Reverend Mr. Herles Booke against the Independency of Churches* (London, 1647).

54. This work is known only by Increase's reference to it here.

55. The Greek reads: "I communicate new things commonly and common things in a new way."

56. The Latin proverb reads: "The function of art is to conceal art." Horace is the general source of this idea for the Renaissance; compare Ovid *Metamorphoses* 10., 252: "Ars adeo latet arte sua."

57. *Gellibrand* is the correct spelling of the name, but precisely who Increase means is not clear.

58. Richard Mather's *Church-Goverment and Church-Covenant Discussed, in an Answer of the Elders of the Severall Churches in New-England to Two and Thirty Questions, Sent over to Them by Divers Ministers in England, to Declare Their Judgments Therein* (London, 1643).

59. John Cotton, *The Way of the Congregational Churches Cleared* (London, 1648). This work refuted Robert Baillie, *A Dissuasive from the Errours of Our Time* (London, 1645). The other work cited by Increase is Cotton's *The Bloudy Tenet, Washed, and Made White in the Bloud of the Lambe* (London, 1647), an answer to Roger Williams's *The Bloudy Tenent of Persecution* (London, 1644).

60. This particular epistle by Nathaniel Mather (1632–97) appears in *A Disputation concerning Church-Members and Their Children, in Answer to XXI Questions* (London, 1659).

61. Ralph Partridge (d. 1658), of Duxbury, worked with Richard Mather and John Cotton in preparing a model of church government for the consideration of the Cambridge Synod.

62. Jerome (ca. 347–420) revised the Latin New Testament, translated the Old Testament into Latin, and wrote biblical commentaries. Philo Judaeus (30B.C.–A.D.50) wrote a commentary on Holy Writ.

63. Several of these sermons form a part of Richard Mather's treatise on justification entitled *The Summe of Certain Sermons upon Genes: 15.6* (Cambridge, N.E., 1652).

Notes to *Parentator*

1. John Owen (1616–83) was an English Puritan who supported Parliament during the English Civil War, who became Oliver Cromwell's chaplain to Ireland and Scotland, and who was deposed after the restoration of King Charles II. He was offered the presidency of Harvard, but he declined. The Mather libraries contained several of his books, and he is mentioned elsewhere in Mather's book.

2. Antoninus is Marcus Aurelius (121–80), best known for his Stoic philosophy and a work of contemplations.

3. This is a quotation from Deuteronomy 33:9.

4. Cotton Mather is speaking of the Protestant idea of a continuing Reformation, as Christianity (he believed) became increasingly purified from the influence of the Roman Catholic Church.

5. This is a quotation from Genesis 30:8.

6. Robert Woodrow (1679–1734) was a Scottish minister and ecclesiastical historian. William Jameson (ca. 1689–1720) was a Presbyterian historian at the University of Glasgow. The Mathers owned at least two of Jameson's books.

7. This quotation is from Numbers 5:13.

8. John Wycliffe (ca. 1330–84) was an English religious reformer.

9. The quotation is from Revelations 21:15.

10. On the Nethinims see chaps. 2 to 8 of Ezra and chaps. 3 to 11 of Nehemiah.

11. Probably Mather refers to David Willison, an Edinburgh printer and publisher.

12. The Latin by Dutch Calvinist Gisbertus Voetius (1589–1671) reads: "They have even tried to persuade many outstanding men that the ministers of the Church we have are not legitimate."

13. Joachim Hildebrande, Lewis Seckendorf, Balthasar Bebelius, and John Adam Osiande(r). Osiande(r)'s *Dissertatio de Jubliaeo Ebraeorum Christianorum Academicorum* (1690) was owned by the Mathers.

14. The Latin reads: "Pontiffs and hierarches in England."

15. The Arian heresy occurred in the fourth century and argued that Christ was not the same as God the Father. Jerome (see n. 62 to *Life and Death*) was a church father who had studied under Gregory of Nazianzen (see n. 49 to *Life and Death*) and who sometimes disagreed with Augustine (see n. 48 to *Life and Death*).

16. Mather is associating the Roman Catholic church with the Tower of Babel (Genesis, chap. 11).

17. Cotton is referring to Psalms 74:20 and Lamentations 3:6.

18. Zachary Boyd, David Calderwood, Samuel Rutherford, David Dickson, and James Durham. The Mathers owned a copy of the third edition of Durham's *Law Unsealed* (1676) and many books published by Rutherford during the 1640s and 1650s.

19. *Peag* is the word for strung beads or shells that some native Americans used for money.

20. *Ultima Thule* refers to the region on ancient maps that indicates the farthest point of known exploration.

21. The quotation is from Isaiah 49:20.

22. Mather might be referring to a specific person or persons who have eluded me. He might also be playing on the Scottish word *Clydigh*, which means talk or discourse (but which—contrary to Mather's intention to flatter—can mean particularly strange or inarticulate language). He certainly means the river Clyde.

23. A Teraphim was a room in the homes of some ancient Hebrews in which were kept images of ancestors. These deified departed ancestors were called Manes, who were consulted to predict the future. See Judges 17:5.

24. The Latin from a work by minor Roman historian and biographer Flavius Vopiscus Syracusius reads: "There is no one who does not lie about something."

25. Harry Stephen did not turn up in my searches, not even in the *British Museum Catalogue*.

26. Peter Heylyn (1600–1662) was a theologian and historian who defended William Laud, the Archbishop of Canterbury (see n. 209 to *Parentator*).

27. Richard Baxter (1615–91), an English nonconformist and chaplain in Oliver Cromwell's army (1645–47), wrote many books that influenced Puritan thought.

28. The quotation is from Isaiah 15:12.

29. The word should read *sanbenitoed*, and it means made to appear as a heretic.

30. Origines Adamantius (185?–254?) was a self-castrated Christian scholar and philosopher who wrote about eight hundred books, many of which influenced the Puritans in major ways. He is also mentioned later in Mather's book. Montanus of Arduban was a prophet and founder of a Christian sect.

31. Martin Luther (1483–1546) and John Calvin (1509–64) were the two chief founders of the Protestant Reformation. See also n. 39 to *Life and Death*.

32. *Athenae Oxonienses* is probably a taxonomic identification of an owl. Unfortunately, the expression does not occur in Cotton's *The Christian Philosopher* (1721), where one might reasonably hope to find it. *Athenae* refers to the goddess Athena, who made use of the owl, and whose name was really Anatha (Athena spelled backwards, some claim), from which we get the word *anathema*. This gives the owl a certain sinister context.

33. *Skorakizes* means excoriates.

34. Bishop Gilbert Burnet (1643–1715) wrote *History of My Own Time*.

35. Quintas Fabius Pictor was a minor Roman historian who is classified by scholars among the Annalists. Philimus did not surface in my search for his identity.

36. Paulus Jovius (1483–1552) was an Italian bishop and historian, whose *Historiarum temporis* (1552) was owned by the Mathers. John Basilovitz is Joannicus (or János) Basilovits (754–846), a Near Eastern monk.

37. The Latin by historian Jacobus Thuanus (1553–1617) reads: "When one writes for esteem and in hate, and has a venal pen, all are almost persuaded." Thuanus is also mentioned elsewhere in Mather's book.

38. Antoine Varillas (1624–96) was a French historian, and Florimond de Raemond (ca. 1540–1601) was a church historian.

39. Lucian (ca. 125–?), author of *Verae historiae* (critiquing the superstitions of his time), was a Greek satirist.

40. More literally than Mather's translation, the Latin reads: "All for opportunity and nothing for truth."

41. This is a difficult passage. Is Mather referring to Johannes Meister Eckhart (ca. 1260–1327), a German mystic, and Jeremy Collier (1650?–1726?), author of an ecclesiastical history of Britain and opponent to theater productions?

42. Cyrus II (the Great) was a king of Persia (559–529 B.C.), who was friendly with the Jews; he is mentioned in the Bible, especially in the Book of Ezra.

43. The Latin reads: "In the faith of true history."

44. Flavius Josephus (see n. 11 to *Life and Death*) was a Jewish historian who was eventually granted Roman citizenship and then wrote partially reliable accounts of the Jews. Livy is Titus Livius (59 B.C.–A.D. 17), a writer of highly stylized histories.

45. The quotation is from the fifth verse of the Third Epistle of John.

46. Cotton is probably referring to Joseph Pitton de Tournefort (1656–1708), who wrote a number of books on botany, herbalism, and medicine. The quotation apparently derives from a dedicatory statement in one of these books.

47. Mather refers to *Magnalia Christi Americana* (1702), which he discusses in the next paragraph.

48. The Latin by Pliny reads: "Truth suffices when things are done honestly." Pliny the younger (62–ca. 114) was known for his oratorical ability and his letters.

49. Mather's imagery refers to an altar (cf. Exodus, chap. 27).

50. Gauis Sullustius Crispus (86–34 B.C.) was a Roman historian interested in literary form. His work was known by John Milton (1608–74), the great English poet whose work was known in colonial New England. See, for example, George F. Sensabaugh, *Milton in Early America* (Princeton: Princeton University Press, 1964).

51. A buckler is a shield, or (metaphorically) a defense.

52. Vincent Alsop, about whom very little is known, was a minister, contemporary with Cotton Mather. His comment is reported somewhat differently in a letter of July, 1720, which appears in *Selected Letters of Cotton Mather*, ed. Kenneth Silverman (Baton Rouge: Louisiana State University Press, 1971), p. 313.

53. The Latin reads: "Although of a modest spirit, he expressed the maledictions of an unbridled adversary."

54. John Oldmixon (1673–1742) was a poet, playwright, biographer, and historian. Cotton had good reason to be angry over the comments about his *Magnalia* in Oldmixon's *The British Empire in America* (London, 1708) because the book saw more than one edition and was translated into at least two other languages.

55. *Stercoreous* is a rare form of the word *stercoraceous*, meaning "fecal."

56. Proverbs 26:4 reads: "Answer not a fool according to his folly, lest thou also be like unto them." In applying this advice, Mather then says in Latin, "Be silent; you have given me a deadly plague."

57. Cotton Mather, *The Right Way to Shake Off a Viper* (1720). This book saw two impressions in the same year.

58. *Allatrations* are barkings.

59. Palaephatus was a Greek author who interpreted the Greek myths.

60. Robert Beverly (1673–1722) is the author of *The History and Present State of Virginia* (1705), a successful book reprinted many times, which attracted colonists.

61. Josephus, Franciscus Junius, Gerolamo Cardano, and Joseph Hall are identified in n. 11 to *Life and Death*. Thomas Goodwin and Austin are identified, respectively, in n. 47 and 48 to *Life and Death*. John Owen, Richard Baxter, and Jacobus Thuanus are identified, respectively, in n. 1, n. 27, and n. 37 to *Parentator*. The second edition of Joseph Hall's *Resolution of Cases of Conscience* (1650) was in the Mather library. And a late edition of Heir Cardanus's *De Vitalitate ex adversus capienda* (1724) was also in the Mather library.

62. Matthew Henry (1662–1714) was a strong supporter of Cotton Mather, especially with his publications.

63. Gregory Nazianzen, also mentioned in article 11 of Mather's book, is identified in n. 49 to *Life and Death*.

64. The apparent quotation echoes chap. 12 of Revelation.

65. See n. 10 to *Life and Death*.

66. Monica was the mother of St. Augustine (see n. 48 to *Life and Death*), who was greatly influenced by her life in his return to Christianity.

67. *Lemuel* means "by God" and is a name applied to Solomon.
68. The quotation is from Proverbs 22:29.
69. The quotation is from 1 Corinthians 2:9.
70. The quotation is from Daniel 12:3.
71. The quotation is from Luke 5:26.
72. Dr. Henry More (1614–87), who is quoted later in article 17 of Mather's biography, is the author of several books, including *Epigrammata* (1638).
73. On John Norton n. 40 to *Life and Death*.
74. The quotation is from Ephesians 4:17.
75. On William Perkins see n. 14 to *Life and Death*.
76. Rabshakeh is an Old Testament Assyrian figure, in chap. 18 of 2 Kings and chap. 36 of Isaiah, who shouted in Hebrew that King Hezekiah was deceiving his own people with a false reliance on God.
77. This apparent quotation rephrases the imagery of Ezekiel 11:19, 36:26. The image of the stony heart, which also appears in Homer's *The Odyssey*, is in Puritan discourse a cliché for the sinful soul that requires breaking by grace. It can, however, be used in special ways; see William J. Scheick, "Standing in the Gap: Urian Oakes's Elegy on Thomas Shepard," *Early American Literature* 9 (1975): 301–6.
78. Thomas Hooker (see n. 9 to *Life and Death*), a leading Puritan figure, authored such books as *The Poor Doubting Christian Drawne unto Christ* (1629, 1684) and *Survey of the Summe of Church Discipline* (1648), both in the Mather library.
79. The quotation is from Psalms 38:4.
80. The quotation is from Esther 4:16.
81. The quotation is from John 6:37.
82. The quotation is from Mark 2:17.
83. Menasseh was a King of Judah (see 2 Kings) whose reign saw the rise of idolatry before he later instituted reforms.
84. Jonathan Mitchell is identified in n. 35 to *Life and Death* and is mentioned elsewhere in Mather's book.
85. Nicodemus helped Joseph bury Jesus (John 3:1–21) and is the author of a gospel in *Pseudographia*.
86. Origen is identified in n. 30 to *Parentator*.
87. Josiah Woodward (dates unknown) is the author of *Five Warnings to a Careless World*, another book in the Mather library.
88. The quotation is from Psalms 23:4 and appears again in article 32 of Mather's book.
89. *Stagyrite* refers to Aristotle, who was born in Stagira and who was an authority on discourse.
90. The Puritans preferred the methods of Petrus Ramus (see n. 17 to *Life and Death*) to those of Aristotle.
91. The Latin by Mitchell reads: "He goes on, I say, O most eruditely."
92. The quotation from Saint Augustine reads: "He will not be a good cleric who was not a good student in solitude," like a monk.
93. The quotation is from Mark 7:33.
94. *Praecisian* means someone punctilious in the observation of form or method.
95. On this friendship see chaps. 19 and 20 of 1 Samuel.
96. Henry Cromwell (1628–74) was the fourth son of Oliver Cromwell and was the ruler of Ireland during the Protectorate.
97. The quotation is from Revelation 1:16.
98. John Cotton is identified in n. 32 to *Life and Death*.

99. Cotton Mather, *Maternal Consolations. An Essay on the Consolation of God Whereof a Man Whom His Mother Comforteth* (1714).
100. Cotton Mather's tribute to Nathaniel, *Early Piety Exemplified*, first appeared in 1690 and then saw three editions during the next century.
101. The titles of these works by Samuel Mather (1674–1733) are: *Discourse Concerning the Necessity of Believing the Doctrine of the Holy Trinity* (1719): *Discourse Concerning the Godhead of the Holy Ghost* (1719); and *Vindication of the Holy Bible* (1723). They were published in London.
102. The Danite hero is Sampson, and the reference to his encounter with a lion occurs in chap. 14 of Judges.
103. The story of this storm appears in Luke 8 :22–25.
104. *Colaphizations* means buffets.
105. Martin Fotherby (1549?–1619) published *Atheomastix* (1622) to attack atheists.
106. The quotation is from Psalms 34 :6.
107. Increase's book is titled, *A Discourse Concerning the Existence . . . of God* (1716).
108. The apparent quotation echoes 2 Corinthians 8 :9.
109. The Latin by Increase reads: "O, I have lost the better part of God."
110. *Manes* refers to the beneficent spirits of departed ancestors. See n. 23 to *Parentator.*
111. Hugo Grotius (1583–1645) was a Dutch historian, at least two of whose books were in the Mather library. Grotius's *De Veritate* is mentioned in article 30 of Mather's book.
112. Cato is Marcus Porcius (234–149 B.C.), best known for his oratorical skills and his Latin histories of Rome.
113. Cotton alludes to Jean Baptiste Moliere's play, *Le Tartuffe* (1664), a study of a hypocritical cleric.
114. To a Puritan, the New Covenant refers to the Covenant of Grace, whereby through the death of Christ saving grace is extended to a select few chosen for salvation by God, through His will only and for His own reasons. The Covenant of Grace, which is a gift divinely given to certain individuals (no human works can earn it), replaces the Old Covenant, the Covenant of Works, which was in effect in Eden and which allowed humanity to maintain its state of bliss through its works conforming to divine rules.
115. *Afflation* means characterized by a miraculous communication of supernatural knowledge.
116. Epicurus (341–270 B.C.) was a Greek philosopher whose ideas were reviewed in Lucretius's *De rerum natura.*
117. *Desertious,* usually spelled *desertuous,* means to be like a desert; *aridities* means to be withered, or characterized by dryness, barrenness.
118. *Chymaerical* means imaginary.
119. Charles Chauncy (ca. 1592–1672) published *Anti-Synodalia Americana* in 1662. Mather probably also refers to John Allyn (dates unknown), Secretary of Connecticut and author of a defense of his colony in 1694.
120. The Latin reads: "Truth [is] better than a female companion."
121. The Mathers owned several books by John Davenport (1597–1670), whose *Another Essay for Investigation of Truth* appeared in 1663.
122. The Latin reads: "If Pergamum were able to be defended on the right, they also would have defended by this."
123. John Higginson (1616–1708) was a strong defender of New-England Puritan

orthodoxy. The word *Ansiberers* is most unusual, and the sense of Higginson's remark seems to be that Richard Mather was a perfect example of how one should conduct an argument among kin.

124. Theodore Beza (1519–1605) was a French defender of reformist theologian John Calvin (see n. 31 to *Parentator*), and his *In Epistolam D. Pavli ad Galatas Notae* (1578) was owned by the Mathers. Beza is again mentioned in article 26 of Mather's book.

125. Austin is Augustine (see n. 48 to *Life and Death*), and his interesting *Retractions,* composed late in life, reviews and revises his earlier arguments. Robertus Bellarminus (see n. 11 to *Life and Death*) was an Italian Jesuit, two of whose other books, published in 1618 and 1627, were owned by the Mathers.

126. Martin Luther is identified in n. 39 to *Life and Death* and n. 31 to *Parentator.* Martin Bucer (1491–1551), also mentioned in article 34 of Mather's book, tried to reconcile Protestant views of the Lord's Supper. (Although Luther never used the term, Lutherans believe in *consubstantiation*—the idea that during the celebration of the Lord's Supper the reality of Christ does not, through *transubstantiation,* replace the bread and wine, but, as it were, exists in apposition to them.) Huldreich Zwingli (1484–1531) was a Swiss Protestant reformer who desacrilized the Lord's Supper. Antipaedo baptism refers to the beliefs of Baptists that infant baptism is ineffectual: see William G. McLoughlin, *New England Dissent, 1630–1833: The Baptists and the Separation of Church and State* (Cambridge: Harvard University Press, 1971).

127. John Robinson was the author of *A Justification of Separation from the Church of England* (1610).

128. The Light of Africa is Augustine (see n. 48 to *Life and Death*). The Antenicene Fathers are those patristic writers of the early church before the Council of Nicaea (see n. 140 to *Parentator*).

129. The Donatists comprised a schismatic sect in the ancient church that was given to extremism and violence, and that was refuted by Augustine.

130. Jean LeClerc (1657–1736) was an Arminian theologian.

131. Austin is St. Augustine (n. 48 to *Life and Death*); Bonifacius is St. Boniface (675–755), who united the churches in Germany; and Vincentius (?–440) is the author of *Commonitorium,* a major influence in the establishment of orthodox Christian beliefs.

132. *Infandous* means unspeakable.

133. Flavius Cresconius, also known as Coripus, was a sixth-century poet and historian.

134. The Latin from Augustine reads: "Not every son of the church ought to entertain a hope of attaining this office."

135. The Latin Maxim reads: "Men through erring are almost taught."

136. Is Mather refers to Martin V (1368–1431), a pope who successfully resolved divisions within his church (referring favorably to a Pope would be rather unusual for a Puritan), or to Francis Martin (1652–1722), a minister who wrote a book defending the reign of William of Orange (see n. 198 to *Parentator*). *Ithacian Spirit* might refer to the divisivness and dissipation that characterized Ithaca at the time of Odysseus's return from his voyages, to which troubles he put an end, as did Martin V, to problems in the church during his reign.

137. John Davenport is identified in n. 121 to *Parentator;* Mr. Greenhil is the nonconformist William Greenhill (1591–1671); and Mr. Hook is William Hooke (1601–78).

138. Increase's *The Mystery of Israel's Salvation* appeared in 1669.

139. *Protevangelium* is a primitive gospel, and it specifically refers to an apocryphal gospel attributed to St. James the Lesser.

140. The Nicene Council convened in 325 and defended the divinity of Jesus Christ.

141. Quintus Septimus Florens Tertullien (ca. 155–ca. 222) was a Carthaginian theologian. The title of his book translates: *The Hope of the Faithful.*

142. *Romish Beast* refers to the Roman Catholic church.

143. The Latin of Mather's title translates: *Diatribe on the Meaning of the Son of Man and Concerning the Second Coming of the Messiah.*

144. See n. 47 to *Life and Death.*

145. Epaphroditus appears in Phillipians 2:25.

146. Hypocondriac affection is an ailment of the liver, gallbladder, and spleen, which were considered to be the seat of melancholic "vapours." Cotton is saying that Increase was very melancholy.

147. Ephialtes are nightmares.

148. The quotation is from Hebrews 11:34.

149. See Isaiah 38:3 for the tears of King Hezekiah, and Genesis 37:35 for weeping Jacob.

150. Increase Mather, *Some Important Truths about Conversion, Delivered in Sundry Sermons* (1674; republished 1684).

151. Urian Oakes (ca. 1631–81), briefly president of Harvard, was known for his erudition and wit. He is mentioned again in article 19 of Mather's book, where he is likened to Pampilus, who might be Leontius Pamphilus, author of *Apologia seu recriminatia* (1604).

152. The quotation is from Matthew 3:7.

153. King Philip (Philip Metacomet, king of the Wampanoag tribe) waged war with the settlers during 1675–76, and the fighting came within twenty miles of Boston.

154. The Latin reads: "To storm heaven and extricate mercy."

155. The quotation is from Hosea 12:4.

156. The Latin by Calvin reads: "Never will prayers irritate."

157. Increase's *An Historical Discourse* appeared in 1677.

158. Jehu is an Old Testament prophet who predicted the fall of King Baasha of Israel; his comment appears in 2 Kings 9:25.

159. John Amos Comenius (1592–1670) influenced the Bohemian Brethren, a Czech religious reform group.

160. Cyprian (ca. 200–258), a Bishop of Carthage, preached that salvation exists only within the bounds of the visible church. Cyprian's Latin reads: "We are flogged in order that we might merit."

161. The quotation is from Jeremiah 5:26.

162. The quotation is from The Acts 14:22.

163. The *Vaudois* are Waldensians, followers of twelfth-century Peter Waldo who eventually allied themselves to the Protestant reformers.

164. The quotation is from Proverbs 13:34.

165. Thomas Cobbet (1608–85), also praised by Increase, defended infant baptism.

166. The quotation is from Isaiah 58:1.

167. The identity of Wolferdus Senguerdius has not surfaced, but the *British Museum Catalogue* shows that a second edition of his *Philosophia Naturalis* appeared in 1685.

168. Probably Mather means John Eliot (1604–90).

169. *Factor* means representative or seller.

170. Jephthah, an Israelite judge who defeated the Ammonites, is mentioned throughout Deuteronomy.

171. Naboth's comment appears in I Kings 21 :3. He was killed by Queen Jezebel because he refused to sell his vineyard (inherited from his father) to King Ahab.

172. The Latin reads: "With no man contradicting."

173. *Johnsonized* is a very unusual word and probably refers to Francis Johnson (1562–1618), a nonconformist who preached separation from the Church of England. Hence the word would mean to make one a radical or extremist.

174. Edward Randolph (1632–1703), and his many troubles with the colonists, are discussed in Michael G. Hall's *Edward Randolph and the American Colonies, 1676–1703,* (Chapel Hill: University of North Carolina Press, 1960).

175. To be *Ahabitic* is to follow the example of the evil King Ahab, a subject of 1 Kings and 2 Kings. Cf. n. 171 to *Parentator.*

176. Mather might mean Sir Philip Sidney (1554–86), the great English poet, also regarded by Puritan poet Anne Bradstreet. Precisely who Cornish is remains uncertain, although a Henry Cornish was tried in 1685 for conspiring against the life of the English King. Mather's other reference is most likely to Thomas Rosewell (1630–92), a nonconformist minister.

177. *Aestuation* means a feverish disturbance.

178. Sir Roger Strange (1616–1704) published *Observators* in 1681.

179. The apparent quotation echoes several passages in Scripture, typically Pslams 22 :7 and Mark 5 :40.

180. *Myrmidon* means someone of a warlike race.

181. *Immanities* means monstrous cruelties.

182. William Guthrie (1620–65) died young, and his *Christian's Great Interest* appeared posthumously in 1701.

183. Edmond Andros (1637–1714) was caught up in the same political troubles as was Edward Randolph (n. 174 to *Parentator*).

184. The Latin by (probably) Roger de Wendover (?–1236), author of *Flores Historiarum,* reads: "Courts are entrusted to unjust judges, laws to the lawless, peace to the quarrelsome, justice to bad jurors."

185. *Phaetontic Praecipitation* is probably redundant in its meaning. The first word means to set the world on fire like Phaeton; the second word means to move violently in a headlong direction.

186. Cotton probably means Charles Morton (1627–98), who was invited by Increase to become the pastor of Charlestown and the president of Harvard. However, the Mather library contained a book by Thomas Morton (not the author of *The New English Canaan*) entitled *De Pace Evangelicos procuranda Sententiae* (1638).

187. The quotation is from Isaiah 14 :19.

188. *Idumaeam* means a prophecy of the coming of judgment, like that delivered to the Idumean people in Isaiah 34 :5–6.

189. In the late sixteenth century the Huguenots opposed royal absolutism in France because of persecution for their religious beliefs.

190. The Latin reads: "Beyond the concern of theology."

191. *Cheated* means deceived.

192. The Latin reads: "Why might I hear words rather than see deeds?"

193. The Goggle-Ey'd Monster (or round-eyed monster) is the cyclops as described in Homer's Odyssey.

194. The quotation is from Mark 16 :18.

195. A Staff of Laurel refers to bay laurel, which is a powerful antiseptic. In Classical mythology laurel, associated with the god Apollo, stands for triumph, knowledge, and success; and in Christian symbolism (adapting this image, even as it adapted the image of Apollo to represent Christ) laurel came specifically to refer to heavenly bliss.

196. Henry Neville Payne (1672–1700) was a political conspirator.
197. Is Mather referring to the fourth-century (B.C.) Greek painter Apelles?
198. The Prince of Orange (1650–1702) became King William III (1689–1702). He married his cousin Mary (1662–94), who was the Protestant daughter of King James II and who became Queen Mary II. Their accession to the head of the English realm, filling the Puritans with so much hope, is known as the Glorious Revolution.
199. See Genesis, chap. 22.
200. The quotation is from Psalms 124:6–7.
201. See chap. 8 of Daniel.
202. Mather is using the title of Virgil's *Aeneid* to mean epics.
203. The Latin reads: "The prudence of the old church."
204. Theodosius (346–95) was a Christianized Roman emperor.
205. A secretary, Gnaeus Flavius, in 304 B.C., made public certain regulations defining what causes could be pleaded.
206. *Prorogued* means prolonged.
207. Sisyphaen labor refers to the underworld punishment of sly Sisyphus, who was condemned to push a stone up a steep hill, only always to see it roll back and to have to start over again.
208. The apparent quotation is a paraphrase of Matthew 9:37 or Luke 10:2.
209. *Land* is a misprint. Mather means William Laud (1573–1645), the Archbishop of Canterbury who persecuted the Puritans and thereby encouraged many of them to migrate to the colonies.
210. William Phips (1651–95), also mentioned in article 27, fascinated Cotton, who might have seen him as an example of self-fathering, of unsuppressed desire and of freedom of the sort he wished for himself: see Robert Breitwieser, *Cotton Mather and Benjamin Franklin: The Price of Representative Personality* (Cambridge: Cambridge University Press, 1985).
211. The Latin reads: "Words covered in gold forebode a golden omen."
212. The Latin reads: "He says New York."
213. A *high-flyer* is a high-handed critic.
214. The apparent quotation echoes many scriptural passages, of which Luke 2:10 is typical.
215. *More Wonders of the Invisible World* (1700) was written by Robert Calef (ca. 1647–1719) and existed in the Mather library, although the Mathers detested the book.
216. *Ignis fatuus* is light that sometimes appears at night over marshy ground, and it metaphorically means a deception.
217. On Brentius see n. 34 to *Life and Death.* At least four works, including an introduction to logic, by Pierre du Moulin (1568–1658) were owned by the Mathers, whose library also contained a copy of *Conciorvm in Isaiam Prophetam* (1610) by Abrahamus Scultetus as well as at least nine books (published in Holland from the 1620s through the 1640s) by French Calvinist André Rivet (1572–1651). Calvin and Beza are identified in n. 124 to *Parentator.*
218. John Selden (1584–1654) was an English historian.
219. The Latin reads: "The last farewell."
220. The Latin reads: "Heaven is whatever a learned hand has built."
221. The quotation is from Psalms 11:6.
222. The Latin reads: "[Known] by a single trespass." This quotation is drawn from line 65 of the first book of *The Aeneid* by Virgil (Publius Vergilius Maro, 70–19 B.C.): "From a single crime know the nation." (See n. 201 to *Parentator.*)
223. *Fleering* means grinning scornfully.
224. Increase Mather, *Cases of Conscience Concerning Evil Spirits Personating*

Men, Witchcraft, Infallible Proofs of Guilt in Such as Are Accused with That Crime (1692). This book was enlarged and republished in 1693.

225. The Latin reads: "Godly without acrimony." Richard of Abkond did not surface in my search for his identity. It is unlikely that Mather meant Richard of St. Victor (ca. 1110–73), the Scottish or English born theologian in the Augustinian tradition.

226. Francis Hutchinson (1660–1739) was a bishop and the author of *Historical Essay Concerning Witchcraft* (1718).

227. *Hudibras* is a ludicrous figure of Puritan persuasion who made his first appearance in Samuel Butler's satirical poem *Hudibras* (1663–78).

228. The Latin from St. Jerome (n. 62 to *Life and Death*) reads: "No person is able more strongly to point the finger at ignorance than you yourself while you write."

229. The Latin reads: "Temporary Head [President]."

230. Thomas Hollis (1659–1731), also mentioned in article 32 of Mather's book, was a London benefactor of Harvard College.

231. The Latin reads: "As is traditionally done academically in England in theology, the power resides in us through the authority of the most glorious governor and the Massachusetts legislature to confer academic degrees. In the most fair reign of William and Mary, the certificate given to us by them is conferred on Increase Mather (also because this illustrious Doctor Increase Mather is a president of Harvard College of New England who must be respected). He published as many books as possible in Latin as he did in English. The books unlock literature of every kind and in many forms. Mather is most learned not only in language and the liberal arts, but he has also demonstrated his versatility in Holy Scripture and theology. He is also a man who is extraordinary in zeal and merit. He is commended not only in the American churches, but also in the European churches. Therefore we judge the said Increase Mather worthy of the doctoral chair. By the authority commissioned to us we name him Doctor of Sacred Scripture and Theology, and we give notice of this. In testimony of this we afix the academic seal on this document. We write our names here in assignation. This was done at Cambridge in New England on the seventh of November in the year of our Lord, seventeen hundred and ninety-two" (translated by Anthony C. Florek).

232. On Titus, the Greek Christian associate of Paul and leader of the church in Corinth, see 2 Corinthians. George of Anhalt was a sixteenth-century German prince, later George III. Antoiné Sadeel (ca. 1534–91), also known as La Roche de Chandieu, was a sixteenth-century Swiss theologian. Johnnnes Alasco is the Polish Protestant reformer John Laski (1499–1560).

233. The quotation is from 2 Corinthians 4:5.

234. Marcus Tullius Cicero (106–43 B.C.) was a Roman orator moved by the death of Julius Caesar to come out of retirement. Lucius Annaeus Seneca (ca. 3 B.C.–A.D. 65) was the most famous Roman writer after Cicero. Epictetus (ca. 50–ca. 138) was a stoic philosopher whose indifference to external things and whose belief in the brotherhood of humanity appealed to the Puritans. Plutarch, some of whose works the Mathers owned, is identified in n. 19 to *Life and Death*.

235. The Latin reads: "The name of Christ is not there."

236. These verses describe the conversion of St. Paul.

237. *Manuduction* means introduction.

238. The quotation is from John 16:14.

239. Isaac Watts (1674–1748) was a liberal Calvinist.

240. Richard Sibbes (1577–1635) was a divine of significant influence upon the Puritans. The Mathers owned at least seven of his books published during the 1630s. On Thomas Goodwin, n. 47 to *Life and Death*.

241. Mather alludes to chap. 25 of Matthew.
242. Eusebius of Caesarea (ca. 263–ca. 340), a Christian apologist and historian, is considered to be a second-generation Origen (see n. 30 to *Parentator*).
243. The Latin by Thomas à Kempis (1380–1471) reads: "Never do I find rest except in a book or in a study."
244. The quotation is from Acts 10:31.
245. The Latin reads: "The ancients offered the tenth of whatsoever they produced to their own gods."
246. The quotation is from Genesis 28:22.
247. The Latin reads: "Do not give the tenth you pledged; give more."
248. Conservative Puritan doctrine, defended also by Jonathan Edwards (1703–58), held that faith alone (and faith was an unearned, gratuitous gift of God) justifies one's deeds, that good works possess no intrinsic virtue of any sort that might earn justification. The Mathers supported this orthodox view against the Arminians.
249. The quotation is from 1 Timothy 3:2.
250. For an idea of the sort of social behavior Mather objects to here, see George Etheredge (1635–91), *The Man of Mode, or Sir Fopling Flutter* (1676).
251. The Latin reads: "Twice in revision before a single time as a speech."
252. Henry Wotten (1568–1639) was an English poet and diplomat.
253. Nathaniel Ward (ca. 1578–1652) of Ipswich, Massachusetts, wrote *The Simple Cobler of Aggawam in America* (1647). The Latin abbreviations mean: "Sobriety, Justice, Piety, Joy."
254. The Latin reads: "Present to me any man with a great name, and I will tell you what he has missed in life."
255. The reference is to chap. 17 of 1 Samuel.
256. *Illapses* means gliding into something, including spiritual states of mind.
257. The quotation is from Psalms 119:51.
258. The quotation from the Dutch author and editor of Latin poetry Daniel Heinsius (1580–1655) reads: "Through some desire or other (I know not what) all, who have some virtue, aspire to the highest of these things. They have excelled, [and] we are drawn [to them]."
259. Mather alludes to the green olive tree in Jeremiah 11:16. A *Proseucha* is a place set aside for prayer. The Latin reads: "Sluggish old age does not weaken the springs [sources of influence] of the soul; it transforms their vigor."
260. *Rabby* means Rabbi, although who he means here remains unclear. The Latin reads: "An old man is called wise even if he has a few days left."
261. The quotation is from Proverbs 16:31.
262. The posthumous publication of *A Discourse on the Two Covenants* by William Strong (?–1654) occurred in 1678.
263. *Awful* means awe-inspiring.
264. The Besom of Destruction is a broomlike agent that sweeps something away. The image derives from Isaiah 14:23 and appears again at the end of article 32 in Mather's book.
265. The Latin by Cicero (see n. 234 to the *Parentator*) reads: "Discernment and reason and deliberation."
266. The Latin by Greek scholar George of Trebizond (ca. 1396–1486) reads: "I cannot blame old age for anything."
267. Mather might mean M. Livius Drusus, a Roman tribune murdered in 91 B.C. The Latin reads: "Old age has been better to me than youth itself."
268. Calvin's Latin reads: "One must hold that an outstanding part of old age, which is good, consists in a conscience and a soul that are good, serene, and tranquil."

269. The Greek word (pronounced EUGERIA) means "a green [good] old age."
270. See chap. 25 of Genesis.
271. The Latin, by Diogenes Laertius (see n. 5 to *Life and Death*) appears in his *Lives of Eminent Philosophers* 4:47 and reads: "O how a long old age is filled with continual and great maladies."
272. *Deliquium* means a failure of the affections.
273. John Higginson (1616–1708) and William Stoughton (1631–1701), the latter, a chief justice during the witch trials of 1692. *Elijah's Mantle* (1722), not to be confused with John Barnard's funeral sermon of the same name (1724), is a collection of sermons by several hands.
274. The Latin reads: "In perpetual memory of the thing."
275. The apparent quotation echoes Deuteronomy 29:23.
276. The Latin reads: "He drew the lot of an easy end, and always wished for such."
277. *Hickets* are hiccups.
278. *Obnubilation* means darkened or obscured as if by a cloud.
279. *Obtenebrations* means overshadowings.
280. The quotation is from John 12:26.
281. The image is from Ecclesiastes 12:6.
282. A *polypus* is a polyp.
283. The Latin reads: "Your spirit bristles to have remembered and flees from the affliction."
284. William Dummer (1679–1761) was commander in chief and lieutenant governor of Massachusetts with whom Cotton had considerable dealings. Well known today for his unusual diary, Samuel Sewall (1652–1730) was an important political figure in his time.
285. Thomas Foxcroft (1697–1769) was minister of the First Church of Boston.
286. Jehojada was a long-lived Old-Testament Israelite priest who saved a young prince from his murderous grandmother (see 1 Kings and 2 Kings).
287. Callimachus (?–ca. 240 B.C.) was a Greek scholar and poet who authored *Pinakes.*
288. See Isaiah 13:12.
289. Joseph Sewall (1688–1769), Thomas Prince (1687–1758), John Webb (1687–1750), William Cooper (1694–1743), and Thomas Foxcroft (see n. 285 to *Parentator*).
290. The quotation is from 2 John 4.
291. The scattered quotation is from 1 Peter 1:24, which is cited fully a little later in this article.
292. Sixteenth-century theologian Rabbi Hadarsan is also known as Siméon ha-Darsan or as Simon Darschan.
293. The Latin reads: "Easily the prince of all theologians and of all philosophers through the whole of New England, wherever it broadly spreads." The title of Increase's book translates: *Christ Descended into Hell.*
294. Luther's Latin reads: "Who teaches most simply."
295. On Arthur Hildersham see n. 18 to *Life and Death.*
296. *Tonitruous* means full of thunder.
297. Guillaume Farel (1489–1565) was a French reformer. The Latin reads: "No person fulminated more courageously."
298. The Latin reads: "To say by heart what has been written."
299. Joannes Carolus Rosenbergus's book *Rhodologia* (1631) is a study of roses.
300. The Latin reads: "There is nothing human on earth that must not be buried; / The soul departs from here; the earth swallows up the rest."
301. The quotation is from 1 Peter 1:25.

302. The Latin reads: "Stop speaking blasphemies; my father is immortal."

303. The Amesian method means after the manner of William Ames (see n. 24 to *Life and Death*), which (given Ames's *Technometria*) means Ramistic (see n. 17 to *Life and Death*).

304. The quotation is from Jeremiah 23:29.

305. The quotation is from John 26:24.

306. The quotation is from Jeremiah 31:18.

307. The allusion is to Genesis 19:17.

308. The quotation is from Job 31:3.

309. The quotation is from Isaiah 44:20.

310. The quotation is from Jeremiah 10:25.

311. Mather refers to a drawn out argument between the Mathers and Solomon Stoddard (1643–1729), who took the unorthodox position that the Lord's Supper was not to be restricted to the visible saints because it could actually convert a partaker and make him or her a visible saint. See Thomas M. and Virginia L Davis, eds., *Edward Taylor vs. Solomon Stoddard: The Nature of the Lord's Supper* (Boston: G. K. Hall, 1981) and Philip F. Gura, "Solomon Stoddard's Irreverent Way," *Early American Literature* 21 (1986): 29–42.

312 The quotation is from Judges 13:6.

313. The quotation is from Job 17:16.

314. See chap. 9 of Mark.

315. The quotation is from Jeremiah 50:5.

316. The Latin reads: "The end in the religion of Christ among the English."

317. Increase's *The Mystery of Christ Opened and Applyed* appeared in 1686.

318. The quotation is from Phillipians 1:21.

319. Petrus Ramus (see n. 17 to *Life and Death*); Johannes Nauclerus (author of *Chronica* [1544]); Martin Bucer (see n. 126 to *Parentator);* Desiderius Erasmus (1461?–1536); and Justus Lipsius (1547–1606).

320. The quotation is from Proverbs 22:20.

321. The prophet is Isaiah, and his Melota was a garment made of skins.

322. Possibly Bartelomaeus Angelic, thirteenth-century author of *De proprietatebus rerum,* a very popular and influential work in Tudor and Elizabethan England. But Mather might mean Paul Bartelomaeus, author of *De Ratione Quantitatis Syllabariae* (1578). The Latin reads: "Whoever writes books in clusters will be able to count his numbers of books as he counts the numbers of his years."

323. Barnabas is a disciple mentioned in Acts. He was instrumental in introducing Paul to the leaders of the Christian church in Jerusalem and Antioch.

324. *Boanerges* means loud ministers preaching like sons of thunder.

325. These lines repeat a quotation cited in *Parentator;* see footnote 154 of Notes to *Parentator.*

326. In seeking a second edition of *Parentator,* to be published in Scotland, Mather says in a letter (28 January 1726) to Robert Woodrow: "If the *Parentator* should be reprinted with you, let the last line of the Epitaphium be left out" (Silverman, *Selected Letters,* p. 410). The line does indeed mar the poem, and given its reiteration of a thematic interest in books in *Parentator* (as remarked in my introduction), possibly it is Cotton's own addition to his brother's poem. This would explain his strange, unexplained request to delete it.

327. This Samuel Mather (1674–1733) is Cotton's brother in England. He is mentioned in articles 5 and 31 of Cotton's book.